COMPLEMENTARY

<u>**Moral Capitalism and the Essential Economy**</u> is currently a part of both undergraduate and graduate classes. This is occurring in an Arts and Sciences curriculum and that of Business Administration. Whether you are personally interested or, alternatively, interested in calling anothers attention to the work please know that

<u>WAGNER BOOK LLC</u>

publishes this title with the pledge of keeping it in print for no less than ten years and providing prompt delivery.

MORAL
CAPITALISM

MORAL
CAPITALISM

AND THE
ESSENTIAL ECONOMY

AS MANAGED BY THE WORKABLE MARKET

WALTER C. WAGNER

Alexander Herron Distinguished Professor of Economics

UNIVERSITY OF THE PACIFIC

Foreword by

William C. Frederick

Professor Emeritus, Katz Graduate School of Business

UNIVERSITY OF PITTSBURGH

 **WAGNER**BOOK

Published by Wagner Book

Wagner Book L.L.C.
PO Box 4005
Stockton, CA 95204
(800) 290-7785
www.moral-capitalism.com

Cataloging-in-Publication Data

Wagner, Walter C., 1917–2004.
   Moral capitalism and the essential economy : as managed
by the workable market / Walter C. Wagner ; foreword by
William C. Frederick.
      p.   cm.
   Includes bibliographical references and index.
   1. Capitalism.   2. Economic policy.   I. Title.
II. Frederick, William Crittenden, 1925–

HB501 W34 2006
330.122 – dc22   2006920902

First Edition
Printed in the United States of America
ISBN-13 978-0-9776834-6-8
ISBN 0-9776834-6-X

10   9   8   7   6   5   4   3   2   1

Contents

To My Students
Who Made College Teaching
More Rewarding Than Making Money

Foreword

Within the brief compass of ten chapters filled with eloquent, flowing, inspiring language only rarely seen, economist Walter Wagner urges his readers to wake up to the realities, the opportunities, and the risks found in today's global economy. His central concern—his life's quest, as he calls it—is to find a moral economic order sufficient for the times in which we live and for a future bearing down upon us at warp speed. Known to his colleagues and students as "Mike," he sums up here a lifetime of thinking and teaching. And what a teacher he was! Inspiring, stimulating, humorous, down-to-earth, combative, challenging—he once demanded of a stubbornly resistant prospective student, "I *dare* you to enroll in my class!"—Mike Wagner influenced generations of young college students and not just a few of his professional colleagues. No one was ever indifferent to Wagner's views; he wouldn't allow it because he wanted you to think about important questions whether you agreed with him or not. It is that insistent quality of honest intellectual pursuit that you will find in these pages which constitute Mike Wagner's final testament, his last chance to get you to think through the moral issues that confront and confound all economies today. What a grand way to go, still inspiring, still challenging, still questing!

As one of those students enormously influenced by Wagner, I can scarcely be neutral about his views, but I can tell you a few things that may encourage you to read deeply for his central message. Anyone—public citizen, student, or professional economist—can find something here that is worthwhile and lasting, particularly the persistent need to identify the moral core that drives all economic enterprise.

With an historical brilliance, Wagner roots his concept of economics in Adam Smith's theory of moral sentiments, linking it to modernist notions of a moral sense that drives human behavior to seek out mutually adaptive ways of living together. Unlike many contemporary critics, he does not reject but builds upon the best that can be found in free market theory. His own unique contribution to that continuing debate is his concept of the Essential Economy driven by the Workable Market, which turns out to be a blend of Smith and Darwin, of market institutions and continuous change, of progress towards betterment amid the perils of world upheaval, and of a human nature uniting economic need and moral sentiment.

Peppered throughout are tantalizing ideas and phrases, each one a moral brick in his larger economic edifice: "the morality of mutual adaptation," "futurity morality," the "insights, oversights, and illusions" of any brand of economic thinking, snapshots of a looming future: "most likely scenario," "worst scenario," "most necessary scenario," "ethical pragmatism," and an "Apollo project for humanitarian economics."

Wagner does not shy away from controversy, and some of what he says may upset some readers. He defends the core of market economics, saying only that it is incomplete, not intellectually bankrupt. He builds a case for the use of coercive power in economic affairs, he derives values from technology and scientific method, he takes shots at the sybaritic and pathological consumption practices of the wealthy, he builds a Godlike function into economic research, he favors triage rationing of pure research, he laments a public ideology that worships an automatic market mechanism based upon false ideas of economic rationality.

In the end, though, emerges a magnificent view of humanity's economic prospects, if only we sensibly blend our most basic impulses of moral order and pragmatic sense making. One hears an echo in Wagner's philosophy of that most famous phrase penned by Charles Darwin on the final page of his own masterwork: "There is a grandeur in this view of life [that] from so simple a beginning endless forms most beautiful and wonderful have been, and are being evolved." Wagner's quest and his compelling message, driven onward by the spirit of Adam Smith, exhibit an expansive grandeur of their own. It is, as he says, "our best bet" for global economic prosperity and a humane world.

A NOTE ABOUT WALTER WAGNER'S LIFE

Less than a year after completing this book, Mike Wagner passed away at his home in Stockton, California, where he had been professor of economics at the University of the Pacific since 1962. Growing up on the Connecticut shoreline following World War I and during the Great Depression, he early on learned economics the hard way working in his family's grocery store. Formal economics education began at the University of North Carolina and was almost immediately put to the test as an Army administrator of supplies at Supreme Headquarters for the Allied invasion of Europe in World War II. Trained for that job at Harvard Business School, he subsequently studied economics at the University of Texas where he received a PhD in economics and anthropology. From faculty positions at Drake University, the University of Kansas City, and the University of the Pacific he also taught in programs for corporate executives, labor unions, government agencies, trade associations, and after retirement to Elderhostel audiences. He and his sociologist wife, Pat Wagner, who also taught at the University of the Pacific, were great admirers of William Shakespeare's dramas which brought them yearly to the Oregon Shakespeare Festival. A polished, rounded, open-minded scholar, Mike Wagner lived as he taught: upbeat, optimistic, a believer that things could always be made better if only we use our heads and hearts.

William C. Frederick
Professor Emeritus,
Katz Graduate School of Business
University of Pittsburgh
author, *Values, Naure, and Culture in the American Corporation*

1

The Quest

A society without a sense of proper purpose, in a world moving at its present pace, is destined to lose its way. Most of us cherish the wonders of modern progress, but many cringe at the disruptions and the vacuous values of modern life. Analysts and commentators throughout the world fear life is drastically wrong for the vast majority of people on our planet. The twenty-first century promises worse. When pondered as a totality of related conditions, the problems do suggest crises brewing. The entire global community confronts an era of dramatic, costly and dangerous metamorphoses: environmental, technological, scientific, social, political, and economic. The theoretical and moral beliefs that are relied upon to guide practical policies may well be inadequate for the challenge.

A primary focus of this inquiry is to confront this global quandary by describing how nature's laws, human nature, economic institutions, and science-technology interact over time and what the implications are for humanity. That done, I develop an appropriate *monitoring morality*. This is essential for providing criteria by which economies and governments can be judged for the goodness or badness, the success or failure, of their systems.

Advanced economies are powerful mechanisms for enhancing our well-being or for servicing our gross compulsions and appetites. Our free competitive market ideology provides principles that both direct

1

and misdirect us. Freedom permits creativity but often lacks responsibility for its consequences. Democracies with quasi-workable market economies are confused over values and purpose. We must find worthy objectives and effective methods of organizing dynamic economies or pay the price of expanding global conflict and tragedy coexisting with affluence. The times call for a practical philosophy to provide moral guidance for economic progress, efficiency, and justice in this age of escalating transformation.

In the long run, technological and social changes, subtle over decades but substantial over centuries, can be readily recognized and generally accepted by the populace. Less readily discernible or generally accepted are the philosophical and moral transformations needed to accompany these changes. We can observe this technical-social change and the culture lag of moral philosophy by reflecting on the eighteenth century Enlightenment. During that era, innovations in agricultural, manufacturing and transportation technology gave rise to a vast expansion of trade, commercial markets, and commercial classes. The rising importance of the commercial classes resulted in freer trade, demise of the power of the guilds and merchants' rigid rules of trade, and early experiments in democracy that transformed power from the landed aristocracy and the crown to a broader segment of society. The moral indignation associated with these transformations was dangerous and costly, causing violent bloody revolutions.

Near the end of the eighteenth century, the distinguished moral philosopher and "father of economics," Adam Smith, provided the Enlightenment and Western civilization with a theoretical and moral model to explain the nature of wealth, the means of its creation, and its justification.

The pre-Renaissance world had believed that the sun traveled around the earth. The evidence was as clear as the light of day. Yet it was an illusion. Similarly, in the world before Smith, merchants believed that just as money was the source of individual wealth precious metal money was the source of the wealth of nations (the doctrine is referred to as *mercantilism*). The evidence seemed as good as money in the bank. Adam Smith didn't believe the sun went around the earth, in spite of what he saw every day. Nor did he believe that money income was the source of the wealth of nations, in spite of what he saw about him every day.

So in 1776 Smith published his now famous *Wealth of Nations* to prove the fallacy of the mercantilist's money illusion. He saw labor, not money, as the true cause: the productive force that created that wealth. He established the field of economics as an application of his moral philosophy, founded upon the observation that Natural Laws are automatically beneficent. For Smith, Nature was the most effective organizer of labor for the economic well-being of humanity. Humanity's economic well-being, he concluded, is maximized when the functioning of the market is left to the self-interests of individuals, constrained by competition, and governed by Natural Laws of supply and demand. This view he held with modest and unheralded exceptions (that now turn out to be of profound importance).

Smith's *Wealth of Nations* is a practical moral statement as well as a brilliant technical analysis. His theory of competitive market economics still stands today as the touchstone moral philosophy that validates market managed economies of the Western world. But my agenda in introducing Smith's ideas is not to explore them per se; rather, it is to use them as an elegant historical introduction into the dominant moral philosophy of present day economics. Starting from this established moral foundation and theory, I initiate an inquiry into how economics can contribute to our understanding of the nature and causes of the well-being of humanity, provide guidance to progress, and calculate the costs of change. Competitive economic theory purports to provide the standard model and "first approximation" of economic reality. That theory is the source of serious oversights and illusions that must be confronted as we seek a more encompassing moral philosophy to guide us in clarifying the nature and causes of economic progress.

FAST FORWARD TWO HUNDRED YEARS

To acknowledge that things go wrong in economies is to imply the existence of tests by which to judge the good from which the wrong has deviated. Indeed, we face a moral dilemma. Is a free market competitive price system the proper model by which to judge an economy? Or are there other moral criteria by which a market economy should be judged? To date, no well-articulated ethical benchmark of economic effectiveness exists to assess the current global economy with its international industries and corporations that change the world at such a turbulent pace. How do we judge better policies from detrimental practices? We confront the need to construct appropriate philosophy and procedure by which to judge economies.

This work starts philosophically where Smith did, with nature. However, it has significant advantages over Smith's distinguished contributions. First, it profits from Smith's insights coupled with those of his peers of the Enlightenment. Further, it has over two hundred years of historical perspective of "the great transformation" of industrialism, capitalism, individualism, and the "free market." In addition, we have those two-hundred-plus years of accumulated observations of nature and warnings from ecology. We also have subsequent major developments in the social sciences, as well as extensive philosophical exploration to help us.

Anthropologists have observed that humans have evolved cultural survival mechanisms that supplement our biological survival mechanisms. By means of genetic traits, coupled with culture traits, humans have transformed their economic niche in nature to their own advantage. Culture trait innovations profoundly affect the human species, sometimes for better, sometimes for worse. Discerning economic better from worse is a compelling moral matter. Among significant developments in the social sciences has been the transformation of Smith's economics into a sophisticated analytical and public policy tool of profound importance. But economic models, including the fundamental competitive one, are acknowledged to be limited abstractions from the whole of nature and human interaction. Economic models are insufficient beacons unto themselves for constructing the larger perspectives necessary to identify and select moral economic imperatives.

Economics, as practiced, has become a very technical discipline. Its practitioners measure and predict change in economic variables such as production, distribution, consumption, growth, and stability. Technical economics, as a technical science, provides technical data much in the same way as chemistry informs medicine. But chemists do not prescribe the medication we take. In a similar way technical economics does not determine what wealth is or should be. Nor does it determine morally proper production, distribution, consumption, growth, or progress. The technical can, even must, provide data and project consequences of policies. But even here, accuracy and meaning are dependent upon the validity and reliability of theory and the appropriateness of the philosophy which designates the more relevant from the less, the good consequences from the bad. Is the dollar cost of education a more relevant variable than data on the flow of human consequences from that education? Should AIDS treatment (in Africa, for instance) be determined by the ability of carriers to pay their own way, or by the ability of humanity to stop the epidemic? Economics can try to calculate whether it costs less in dollars to stop the epidemic than it will cost (in dollar terms) if it is not stopped. This is helpful, but it does not weigh the suffering and anguish nor tell us who should help or how assistance should be provided.

Economics, for the short run, must clarify the particulars of policies so that we may get on with the nitty-gritty of day-to-day provisioning. For the long run, economic philosophy must identify principles and practices that allow us to morally determine purposeful directions for public policies. Practically, we have no alternative but to start where we are. But where are we? Are market economies and their business enterprises automatically and naturally as magnificently beneficent as their staunch supporters claim? Or are economies and enterprises as disastrous, or even evil, as severe critics contend? There is widespread belief that economists are confused, irresponsible, perhaps immoral, for supporting selfish interests and evaluating humanitarian needs in cold cash, bottom-line profits, while lacking concern for moral consequences; money efficiency above humane effectiveness. But there is also, among the compassionately concerned, a frequent oversight and failure to consider the need for any economic system to address the issue of scarcity and the usefulness of effective economizing. A practical moral philosophy of economics must confront the scarcity issues.

If an economic philosophy is to provide a basis for decisions, it needs to expose current illusions and fill in the oversights of market theory with superior insights that provide effective ethical guidance for economic growth and change. Western thought has been in process of transformation from the medieval view of socio-economic organization as Divine design to that of a beneficent Natural order composed of natural laws and rights, and toward the current slowly developing acknowledgment that economies exist as part of an evolutionary process in which humans evolve the rules and rights of their cultures day by day in an ongoing process of change. In this evolutionary mode, it would be well to define and seek to solve problems as a mutual effort to adapt with each other in cooperation with nature and its natural laws. Increasingly, incrementally, humanity recognizes and accepts the daunting burden of taking charge of its own fate. The degree of human failure and success is up to us as a species and to our understanding of nature and how to adapt through its natural laws.

RESPONSIBILITY OF THE WESTERN WORLD

The market economy and the central economic theory that explains and legitimizes it are precariously inadequate to meet the economic problems and the dangerous consequences that threaten us in the twenty-first century. However, both the market and certain aspects of the theory are essential instruments that will help guide us as we encounter the thickets ahead. The effectiveness of that guidance depends upon an economic philosophy that will provide proper moral purpose with which to confront the future.

A moral philosophy requires that we think about economies as if we humans should be and are responsible for the quality of the wealth of nations. We should not think about the wealth of nations as if it comes into being by leaving fate in charge (free private enterprise governed best by automatic natural economic laws of supply and demand). If humanity shuns responsibility, can we blame fate if we find it fickle? We must be cautious that we do not urge the world to assume that natural economic laws know best how to provide human well-being.

We of the West provide a model (competitive markets and democratic governance) that we recommend to nations of the world for restructuring their own economies and political processes. Further, our international judgments and expectations of the non-Western world are shaped by theories and ideologies derived from the Enlightenment and legitimated in our constitutions. Recognizing the importance of our image, theories, public philosophy, ideology, and industrial-military power places a heavy responsibility on us to be intensely aware of the dangers of our illusions (that our success is a product of a competitive market controlled by beneficent natural laws) and oversights (neglect of our history of technological evolution) while taking pride in our insights (education for the masses, "free" speech within limits). Expounding the virtues of the "free market" on the basis of our perceived economic experience seriously warps reality. The ideology of such a market overlooks the causes and importance of our technological head start, method of open inquiry, role of public dialogue, good fortune of natural resources, attitudes of trust, and laws limiting the excesses of "competitive" markets. The competitive market ideology can severely mislead ourselves and others, as we will see.

Individuals in a market managed economy tend to believe that theirs is the best ever for managing human well-being. This has truth in the same sense that the human body is the best ever for human well-being. But humans can and do get sick, even die. We critique lifestyles, diets, lack of exercise, smoking, and the like, not to criticize the body nature has wrought. We do so to understand the human organism, to escape tragedies, and to improve individual lives. In a similar manner, and when exploring market failures, I do not condemn our spectacular economic body but rather view it as medical and scientific research would, seeking to enhance that same human well-being. We seek a healthy economic body which I will refer to as the "Essential Economy."

Competitive theory has perpetuated the illusion that the market is designed by natural laws that are automatically beneficent. This assumption has captured our attention and inhibited (not stopped) economic theory, philosophy, and practice. The assumption has inhibited timely and adequate inquiry into improving the design and functioning of the market system. Supply and demand are not natural laws whose consequences cannot be modified, nor are they morally beyond human discretion. Supply and demand reflect social forces shaped by cultural history through folkways, mores, customs, rules, law, and technology. All make up a kind of changing "social contract" that causes the market economy to function as it does.

With these insights in mind, I focus on issues raised by the economic ideology of Western democracies, especially the United States. Nowhere in American culture do we have a consolidated analytic framework or vocabulary appropriate to the time, conditions, and pace of change with which we and the other nations of the globe struggle. We in the West conduct a public dialogue on issues confronting our democracies, but we do not possess a common language with which to think creatively about a moral philosophy of economics for this changing world. We speak in terms of "justice, equity, fairness, freedom, cooperation, contribution, value added, fair exchange, supply and demand price," and so forth. The meanings of these terms are not nearly as clear to the populace as the individual feelings we experience upon hearing or using them.

Competitive economic theory abstracts its perception of the positive contributions of human nature in the concept of "economic man." "He" is self-interested and rationally motivated. Being so, he meets the social demands as they are registered in the market. In doing so, he economizes scarce means and maximizes the satisfaction of his chosen ends. In doing these things he is self-reliant. In being self-reliant, self-interested, and rational he is economically and morally responsible. This perspective provides a limited but legitimately useful view of ethical behavior for the individual frame of reference in the present context. However, it overlooks that which is necessary for a moral philosophy of economic *systems*. The language of our ideology covertly depicts the world from an individualistic perspective. It is largely inadequate for the problems of systems and the tasks ahead. We must critique the economy by means of an expanded vocabulary and thereby explore newly perceived variables in the system as they impact on humanity.

It seems reasonable to assert, in light of contemporary knowledge, that a moral philosophy can be formulated from the natural laws through which we humans have evolved and by which we live, our own inherent natures included. Hence a philosophy of economics, inescapably, must be founded in the nature of humanity and its relations with the natural environment. Therefore, a proposed philosophy is to be constructed from the inherent qualities of human natures.

However, care should be taken that we do not assume that because something is inherent in our biology it is therefore morally necessary or right. Nature has endowed humanity with potentials that lead to economic betterment as well as potentials that lead to problems, agony, and even human evil.

Fortunately, in our human natures, there are qualities through which public purpose rationality is formulated. Individuals are not exclusively individualistic and self-interested. They are also participants whose empathy creates concerns for others and thus for the society. It has been argued that we have a "*moral sense.*" On this, a morality of mutual adaptation can be built. However, we do not at the same time possess inherent knowledge of what the right ways are. Further, we have inherent qualities that generate cultural dynamism that changes our world and regularly raises new questions of right and wrong: the invention of technology and of social instruments is the way we continuously reconstruct our changing niche in nature and confront the resultant challenges. It appears that humans may not have evolved with genes (or culture traits) that prepared us well to adapt to the present-day rate of change. Human nature has conditioned us to invent but not for the present pace and complexities of modern life.

I seek to identify, from the process of our evolution, the natural sources of moral beneficence, debasement, stagnation, and the positive contributions of human nature from which to construct an increasingly moral economic system.

DEPENDENCE UPON APPROPRIATE KNOWLEDGE

Inherent human qualities (curiosity, creativity) coupled with cumulative science-technology, create a profound dynamism in cultural innovations. This dynamic inescapably involves humanity in a process of continuous experimentation. The consequences for human transactions among ourselves and with the environment are knowable only through the generation and accumulation of increasingly reliable knowledge. Otherwise, we cannot know what we should do, what the consequences are, or how to reform our practices. Therefore, I argue that the ultimate objective in determining the nature of wealth and its creation and utilization is the experience-based generation of human understanding, not the *automatic* functioning of natural laws.

Mine is a quest to comprehend how economies go right, how they go wrong, and how to figure out what policies to follow. I write in the spirit of "the nature and causes of the wealth of nations," "the best of times; the worst of times," "progress and poverty," and with an optimist's reluctant apprehensions. I emphasize construction of what it should mean for an economy to become a more moral system. I refer to the philosophy of this dynamic process as the "morality of mutual adaptation."

Morality here has a practical meaning. It means a search for that which will improve the well-being of our fellow humans. It involves a distinction between more appropriate and less appropriate practices, between workable humanitarian modes and detrimental paths. It recognizes that however good a principle or practice is, it can be pushed (applied) to the point that its consequences become pathological. The term "moral" throughout this work should not be confused with the use of moral as an absolute command derived from outside the range of human experience and intelligence.

Regrettably there are not enough of the world's goods and services for all to have all they might want or need. The meaning of morality in an economic context necessarily relates to the nature and causes of the wealth of humanity under conditions of scarcity. Managing economic scarcity has unique moral implications. Some people may be surfeited while others have insufficient means to survive adequately or contribute effectively. Resolving this scarcity matter must be sought, as conventional theory has emphasized.

Since one focus of this work is on progress, I use morality not to determine eternal right and wrong, good and bad for all time, but what is "righter" and "wronger," better and worse over time. Good medical care changes over time. The care that should be provided, the moral objective for medical care, is determined by the advancement of medical knowledge. However, the moral right to medical care is determined by more than medical know-how alone. It is conditioned by scarcity, other needs, and the general level of societal affluence.

A philosophy of economic progress requires more than technical economic analysis. It calls for a theoretical locus of morality. I find that locus of morality in the evolution of human natures and their needs, the contribution of technology and science in formulating standards of those human needs, the environmental context within which humanity evolved (and upon which it depends), and an ecological mode of social organization.

Such a philosophy of economics can and should provide public policy guidance for societies dedicated to doing what is morally better. It makes its moral case on naturalistic grounds which are not dependent on sacred sanctions. Its concern is with the well-being of humanity as a collective of individuals for the sake of all individuals. As far as this deliberation ventures, its integrity prevails whether the evolutionary process is explained as the design of The Deity or a process about which we mortals will probe so long as we shall survive.

The issues discussed are dealt with primarily at the level of philosophy, to a lesser degree at the level of theory, and to a still lesser degree at the level of pragmatic strategy. I do not present a moral resolution to each economic problem. But if philosophy is to justify itself, it must provide guidance for conceptualizing the principles by which to mitigate matters of long-term human importance. Seeking the nature and causes of the wealth of nations fits this expectation. Philosophical economics becomes both a moral philosophy and a theory of what wealth might better be, how it is better created, distributed, consumed, and transformed.

This exploration of economics is a challenging quest. It is not a modest effort. It is a quest for practical idealism in a world of relativism in conflict with absolutes. It is a quest for firm foundations in a world of change. It is a quest for direction in a world of dramatic change. It is a quest for reconciliation in a global village of diversity. It is a quest for justice in a world suffering the pangs of scarcity in the shadow of affluence.

2

Adam Smith's Footprints

ECONOMIC THOUGHT AS A MORAL COMPASS

Historically, economics has assumed the task of explaining why societies are as prosperous or as destitute as they appear to be. This is a moral matter in desperate need of resolution. I shall seek to discover a way to lessen the economic hardships and likelihood of tragedies that threaten much of humanity. I do so by reviewing key ideas that earlier economists have held, searching for a moral philosophy of economics to guide their world. Scanning the history of economic thought alerts us to the frailty of ideas people have striven to live by. Economics, as with other fields of thought, is haunted by illusions and oversights.

Economies change and theories essential to understanding what is happening struggle to catch up. For a sense of the struggle visualize tiny micro-organisms smaller than a mite. They are born, reproduce, and die in a life span of seconds. One must wonder whether they could ever discover daylight and darkness. In many ways, humans are like those tiny creatures, seeking over eons to put together the puzzle of our own well-being. We can think of the puzzle pieces as economic ideas. No picture of a completed puzzle exists for guidance. We do not know what pieces are missing, misshaped, or misleading. Complicating our task further, the absent picture, the missing reality, is not itself fixed but ever changing, more like a video than a snapshot. Further confounding the whole, we are not altogether sure what economics and economies are, what their essential components may be. Economic illusions linger as ghosts in our intellectual closets, some resident there since medieval times and well beyond (a just price). Here I seek to discover a moral economic compass by verifying insights (the role of price in rationing scarce means), identifying oversights (technology's role in values formation). and nullifying illusions (just price) handed down from the past.

THE SMITHIAN HERITAGE

Most Americans today live and work in an economic system heavily dependent upon the ideas of a once obscure but now famous Scottish philosopher who died 200 years ago. He was not an economist, for the discipline hadn't been invented then. His name was Adam Smith. He taught *moral philosophy* to students at Edinburgh University. It is not at all surprising that Smith's insights still have an intense appeal to so many today. His ideas still provide, both covertly and overtly, a major philosophical basis for Western economic ideology. They appear to justify laissez-faire markets free of government control. They support free private enterprise ideology. Smith's major ideas permit a generalized condemnation of virtually all government regulations of the economy. They uphold those who insist on an inalienable right of consumer sovereignty. They buttress the argument with the presumed justice of earning a fair day's pay for a fair day's work coupled with a sense of the consumers' right to keep and spend that income as they wish, without being deprived of their rights by taxes.

This philosophy, as evolved from Adam Smith's ideas, provides further rationale for a belief that a free market is a just arbiter of how income is distributed among rich and poor alike, and for the indignation over public policy that redistributes incomes by an "entitlement" process. All interference with the automatically beneficent market system is viewed as unjust, unproductive, inefficient, antimotivating, demoralizing, and playing God. These intellectual roots from Smith are responsible for many of today's ideological commitments. They are largely unquestioned givens. They are the stuff that we believing creatures use as truths, just as medieval and mercantilist views once were accepted as true. Smith's emphasis on the competitive market with supply and demand prices automatically providing a just, effective and free economic order reflects his philosophical stance that nature knows best. This view has diverted attention from individual and government responsibilities in shaping human destiny.

One might conclude that Smith had demonstrated government's lack of a constructive role in economies. In many ways that is so. And yet it is not entirely the case. He had an additional perspective, one that is generally overlooked. "According to the system of natural liberty, the sovereign has only three duties to attend to... ." They are the defense of country, the administration of justice, and that of "erecting and maintaining certain public works and certain public institutions, which it can never be for the interest of any individual, or small number of individuals, to erect and maintain; because the profit could never repay the expense to any individual or small number of individuals, though it may frequently do much more than repay it to a great society." These he considered "plain and intelligible common understandings." Clearly, Smith was not an absolutist exclusively committed to laissez-faire capitalism. When profits could not be made from a service needed by society, it is appropriate for government to step in, either directly or by subsidy.

We are challenged to renew Smith's quest for a philosophical economics by seeking "plain and intelligible common understandings" of today's complex and dynamic world of change. Smith was a man of his times. Although an academic philosopher, he was remarkably insightful in viewing the practical dimensions of his world. In forging a new economic theory, he rejected old, unworkable ideas from the past while incorporating the latest insights from science. We can appreciate Smith's contributions to modern thought best by reviewing the ideas he rejected and the ones he embraced. We have been enlightened by his contributions to the Enlightenment.

MEDIEVAL JUST PRICE

The medieval idea of the just price has played a major role in historical efforts to understand the puzzle of economic justice and well-being. Scholars reflecting on that period regularly tell us that medieval society was a synthesis of the sacred and secular realms. It was the all-knowing God's social order structured in a hierarchy of ranked status, with Him at its apex followed by the Pope, Cardinals, Bishops, Priests, Monks, and Nuns. The hierarchy of the Church served God and administered to the souls of men. The parallel secular status hierarchy of the feudal manorial system was arranged with the King at the top, followed by Nobles, Lords of the Manor, Sons, Bailiffs, Serfs, Wives, and Daughters. As merchants and artisans emerged they became "free" citizens (in developing towns). No longer were they bound by strictures of feudal manorialism. Yet artisans too were ranked in their proper place in the evolving system of guilds, arrayed in a hierarchy of master craftsman, journeyman, and apprentice.

The puzzling question then, as it is now, was what explained and justified the existing social order? Medieval theology answered that the social order was part of a divinely perfect plan under the continuing intervention and control of God. Could this have been a foreshadowing of the later notion of a perfectly competitive natural order but ruled by market competition instead of Divine power?

The cornerstone of medieval economic thought was the "just price," not an analysis of resources, technology, and human skills. The just price was the amount the medieval guild artisans could charge, which would provide them with an income that could purchase a standard of living appropriate to the station in life into which it was believed God had placed them. Thus, the price of goods entered Western thought as a theological principle reflecting one's social standing and personal worth in God's hierarchy. Price was not seen as a means of appraising the worth of a good for consumption. It was not yet a mechanism used to balance scarce supplies with effective demand, as today's theory sees it. The medieval economic system rationed its scarce goods and services by means of *status rights*. Theology provided the philosophy, the theory, and the legitimation.

However, medieval society was not static. A new world order was developing. With trade came expansion and the use of cash facilitating exchange. The number of merchants, artisans, and traders continued to grow. They emerged as an expanding commercial class socially inferior but some richer than their noble betters.

That wearing away of the status foundations of a social order generated the social changes of the Renaissance where consciousness surreptitiously transformed other-worldliness to earthliness. Beliefs began to shift from sacred causation to the secular, from emphasis on Divine Law as the primary causation of human conditions to Natural Law as that primary governing power. With this came a shift from hereditary rights of ascribed status toward status achieved by deeds. These belief transformations were in no way total, only modified. Yet that degree of difference in thinking allowed major social changes, without wiping clean the content of traditional social beliefs.

NEW TECHNOLOGY, NEW HORIZONS

We humans seldom change our ideas on a whim. Medieval mindset and prevailing attitudes were not relinquished without cause. Faithfulness to hallowed beliefs did not, by spontaneous generation, give rise to cravings for democracy, capitalism, or civil liberties. It was changing conditions, with new options, that tempted people to change their practices and seek explanatory theories that legitimized those practices. The underlying dynamics of change came from cumulative technological inventions and scientific discoveries which both contributed to and were products of the Renaissance.

For instance, medieval farming was transformed by the horseshoe, horse collar, waterwheel, windmill, yoke for oxen, wheelbarrow, and deep plough with wheel, inventions which multiplied available energy. For a perspective on the economic and social importance of these ordinary items, consider that no Egyptian, Greek, or Roman ever saw a wheelbarrow. Athens, in all its glory, numbered one slave for every two free men, but with the technology of horseshoe and collar, one horse could equal, in physical effort, the work of ten slaves.

The transformation in land transport caused by the horse harness was accompanied by a technological revolution in transport on the high seas. Mediterranean shipbuilders copied the fixed rudder from China and borrowed the deep keel from Norsemen who ventured into their waters. The introduction of Arabic numerals and invention of the zero made shipbuilding and navigation more reliable for those ships when at sea. Astronomy improved as ground lenses were developed and the telescope was invented. The magnetic compass was introduced resulting in further advancement of reliability of navigation. As a result of these many improvements, previously unimagined land and water transport possibilities blossomed. The early stages of globalization were apparent even in these earlier times.

Options expanded for commerce. Exchanges increased. The use of money and credit spread, creating a growing need for keeping and improving accounting records. As a result, commercial instruments which are taken for granted today were devised: double-entry bookkeeping, promissory notes, early public banks, partnerships, joint-stock companies, stock exchanges, and shared-risk insurance. The main elements of today's market management of the economy were emerging.

One of the most significant inventions of the millennium was Gutenberg's printing press, around 1440 to 1460. Printing would become a force generating the secularization and democratization of knowledge. Books found their way into the hands of the curious. As with inventions generally, they were a result of combining previously accumulated knowledge and technologies. The phonetic alphabet provided the printing press with a limited number of letters that could be combined in a virtually limitless number of combinations, capable of expressing and preserving a limitless number of ideas. Ink could preserve the letters on paper. The seal of ancient times (an identifying mark on a clay tablet or hot wax inscribed but a single time) had become a printing block. Each letter inscribed on its own block was cloned as often as needed. Movable type was invented. When arrayed in the permutations and combinations of written language, placed in an adapted wine press, supplied with ink, and pressed on paper, this combination of inventions produced that first famous book, the Gutenberg Bible. The curiosity genie was out of the bottle.

Books quickly became relatively inexpensive and widespread. Within sixty years of the invention of the printing press, nineteen new universities were cultivating the life of the mind in Germany, France, and Spain. The Church of Rome's monopoly in supplying ideas that justified the existing social order was now at risk. Previously, the answers were available only verbally through priestly teaching and exhortation, but the Church could no longer completely control what might be thought, written, published and read by interested and curious individuals. The social foundations of the medieval economy were almost imperceptibly being undermined by technologies and attitudes unknown to earlier times and places. Rank, hierarchy, churchly power, and landed privilege were in for an earth shattering transformation.

MERCANTILISM: A NEW PHILOSOPHY, A NEW POLITICAL ECONOMY

The interlocking of technology and trade created by these inventions revolutionized the Western world's political structure. It generated interdependence among an expanding range of diverse people. It allowed a slow pulling together of feudal manors, separate kingdoms and principalities, and developing cities into what eventually became national states, such as Italy, Spain, France, and England. This political transformation was not a peaceful one. It was facilitated by the introduction of new weaponry such as the expanded application of gunpowder.

What economies might become was yet to be determined, as is true of the global economy today. Thinkers must invent explanations of what was happening as well as theories and philosophies with which to prescribe appropriate practices to be followed. With hindsight, the following is what the emerging ideas looked like.

During the period from 1492 to 1776, the pattern of ideas and policies that evolved and prevailed is now known as mercantilism. It was a pattern focused on strengthening the power of the nation state and its crown. Mercantilist theorists perceived that national power was built on wealth. Wealth came from the accumulation of money; it seemed obvious. It was seen in the marketplace every day. People who accumulated money were wealthy. Precious metals, like gold and silver, served well for money. To be wealthy a nation, like an individual, must accumulate these metals. Policies were designed for the crown to build up its stores of precious metals. By the early sixteenth century, Cortez's mission was to steal gold from the Aztecs in the name of Spain. England's Walter Raleigh and Francis Drake did their best, in turn, to steal that treasure from Spain for the English crown.

Colorful as these episodes may appear in retrospect, piracy was a minor practice compared with an entirely new economic theory unknown to medievalists. This was the central mercantilist theory and policy of pursuing a favorable balance of trade. A favorable balance of trade policy seemed to make sense, if a nation's getting rich by getting gold makes it wealthy. The national state must establish colonies to produce raw materials like timber, cotton, furs, spices, iron ore, and of course, tea, which were sold and shipped to the Mother Country. There they were processed into finished products for resale abroad at a profit paid in precious metals. This trade was conducted in gold and silver, so that the Mother Country and the crown's treasury could accumulate precious metals, the money that made the state wealthy.

Triumphant at the beginning of the sixteenth century, mercantilism as an economic system faltered by the end of the eighteenth. The American colonists' Declaration of Independence may be summarized as a refusal to countenance England's insistence upon practicing mercantilist policies that placed the colonies at such an economic disadvantage. In that same year, Adam Smith published his *Wealth of Nations*, a remarkably bold theoretical-philosophical challenge to mercantilist economic theory and practice.

Smith's scholarly treatise confirmed what others knew by common sense. Not all nations could be net exporters. The accumulation of precious metals resulted in inflation at home, which meant money supply was increasing faster than the increase of goods. Inflation made the Mother Country's goods more expensive at home and abroad. This constrained sales both at home and in export markets.

Further, the mercantilist policies set conflict ablaze: nation states fought other nation states as they competed for colonies, raw materials, and markets. Conflict also broke out between colonies and Mother states over royal restrictions. A rising new class of manufacturers and merchants grew more and more eager for freedom from mercantilist constraints. Merchants clashed with the clergy's morality and the king's policies. Mercantilist-induced wars over colonies required money to pay for materials and men. In search of money, the crown taxed its rising commercial class at home and in its colonies. This "taxation without representation" created increased agitation for representative government.

In England, by 1750, shadows of the coming Industrial Revolution were already spreading. Peasants were pushed from the land they had traditionally relied upon for home and food, in favor of sheep to produce more wool for newly rising textile factories. New factories initiated a dramatic rise of an industrial working class. Largely overworked and mistreated, the working classes and displaced peasants began to form a discontented mass. They were mobilized by growing expectations for greater participation in the fruits of industrial progress, such as the luxury of woolen socks.

As 1776 approached, the eighteenth century faced these conundrums with traditional explanatory insights, oversights, and illusions. Theology, as it had for centuries, offered the explanation of Divine design being thwarted by free will and tempted into the sin of avarice. Mercantilist illusions of money as the source of wealth were increasingly suspect. Other profound ideas were entering the arena of explanations. The curtain was about to rise on the Edinburgh philosopher, Adam Smith.

SCIENTIFIC REVOLUTION

But for Smith to make his case, some additional pieces of the puzzle had to be already in place. They were drawn from a Scientific Revolution in the making. When assembled into a single picture, they delivered a revolutionary message that remains resonant today. The Scientific Revolution's most compelling contribution to humanity was its refinement of a way of thinking, discovering, and verifying increasingly reliable knowledge; in short, its epistemology. The scientific method, as a mode of thought, has had widespread impact on rational thought. Its importance to the major themes of this analysis will be introduced again and again as we struggle more directly with matters of philosophical and theoretical concern.

Our immediate concern, however, is with the bit by bit, mundane modifications in knowledge and technology that had world-changing significance; new sources of physical power and attendant increases in productivity. A mosaic of ideas slowly emerged over the centuries. It ground through the world of Western thought with a glacial pace and force. The emergence of this pattern was piecemeal in character and cross-cultural in scope. Nonetheless, if the time, the locale, and the content are focused enough, the outcome may well be called the Scientific Revolution. The impact of this revolution on the evolution of economic ideas was truly and massively transformative.

Let us begin with Nicholas Copernicus (1473–1543). He transformed the Egyptian astronomer Ptolemy's second century earth-centered view of the universe. Since Copernicus, we puzzle posers have increasingly recognized the illusion that the sun goes around the earth. We now comprehend the idea that the sun is the center of the solar system and the earth is one of its planets. The question Copernicus left us with was what propels the planets in their paths? There was no adequate theory of motion to explain the movements. Previously, the view of an object's normal condition was that it lies in a state of rest. If it were to move, it had to be pulled or pushed. To this day, it is still difficult to comprehend that this view is another illusion.

Galileo Galilei (1564–1642) discovered the answer to how planets move. Proceeding with the scientific study of astronomy in ingenious ways he altered the entire approach to motion. He experimented with how things actually moved on the earth by rolling balls down inclined planes and across flat surfaces and observing the results. He discovered that rolling balls tended to roll endlessly on a smooth level surface. They also would roll up an inclined plane as far as they came down from another. The same was true of pendulum swings: up as far as they came down, endlessly equal, the pendulum of the clock would keep swinging perpetually, except for the drag of friction. Galileo concluded that once in motion an object would move forever, if not stopped. Thus planets in motion need not be either pulled or pushed. Once in motion they continue in motion. But if so, why do the earth and other planets not fly off into outer space? How do they maintain regular paths around the sun?

Isaac Newton (1642–1727) discovered the answer. He studied Galileo's terrestrial mechanics of motion and was aware of William Gilbert's findings from fooling with magnets from the early 1600s, in which it was demonstrated that force operates across space. That fact was observable, and Newton postulated magnetism in the stuff of the earth; it draws things to itself. Thus was the Law of Gravity made explicit. Flying planets are held by gravity from careening off into space. But why then, does gravity not pull all the planets into the sun?

Christiaan Huygens (1629–1695) identified centrifugal force. A stone tied to a string and swung around one's head demonstrates it. That being the case, said Newton, gravity acts as the string, and the planets, following the law of motion, twirl like the stone, around the sun in natural paths. Isaac Newton had fitted bits of insights into the puzzle of ideas and filled some gaps in the jigsaw of universal existence. The solar system is governed by natural laws that function automatically in an "eternal" equilibrium. It was here that Adam Smith hitched his star to the work of scientists who had discovered natural laws. If the heavenly bodies were governed by natural laws, could the same be true of commerce and trade?

THE AGE OF REASON AND THE ENLIGHTENMENT: NATURAL LAWS GOVERN

One spin-off of the Scientific Revolution was the structure of thought that could be built upon the foundations of the new principles from science. There were natural laws that governed the universe. Smith and his contemporaries began to wonder if they must apply to the social world, as well as to the physical universe. Natural laws functioned automatically. Rather than creating chaos, they brought the orderliness of balanced forces, which later generations of economists would label as "equilibrium." We can see these natural science principles that explained the solar system being applied to understand economic activities.

Mercantilist regulations were severe in France. The prevailing theory asserted that the source of wealth was a favorable balance of trade, bringing an accumulation of bullion to the crown. However, a French physician trained in the natural sciences sought an alternative explanation to the mercantilist theory illusion that money (bullion) was the source of wealth. He was Francois Quesnay (1694–1774). His views were arguably the first systematic vision of an economy governed by natural laws. It is nature, he said, not bullion, that is the real source of national wealth and power; wealth comes from cultivating the soil. Land cultivators are the true culture heroes, the farmers who produce the crops, for they tap the net product from nature and account for the increase in real wealth. All other groups were, in Quesnay's own word, "sterile." Count among them the landed aristocracy, who own but do not themselves till, and merchants and manufacturers, who only transform nature's wealth into the multitude of familiar products.

Quesnay envisioned a cosmic harmony in an agricultural economy, that harmony being a natural order of Deistic design, untouched or controlled from the time of its inception, not even by an intervening God. This design is discovered by *Reason*, a natural process such as that employed by Copernicus, Galileo, and Newton in their pursuit of physical laws. The exercise of Reason, Quesnay believed, would also lead to discovery of the beneficial natural laws making an agricultural economy productive. The sovereign could then require that these natural laws be obeyed as laws of the realm.

After the sovereign enunciated these natural laws as positive laws of the realm, Quesnay believed the crown, like the Deistic watchmaker God, could step back. No mercantilist meddling with God's natural design, natural laws will set natural prices, natural justice and nature's well-being will prevail. The inefficiency of mercantilism, which interferes with man's greatest advantage, his net product from agriculture, would be eliminated.

Quesnay and Enlightenment thinkers sought to discover and to explain the political and economic order in the manner of natural science that discovered and explained a physical order governed by natural laws. They saw themselves as using their natural reason to discover God's natural social design, one operable through the same kinds of laws that must be employed in any effort to alter existing social conditions. Only thus, they believed, could the conflicting chaos of mercantilism be corrected. These ideas had come to focus by 1776.

The Enlightenment offered democracy as a form of social order, with its doctrine of natural rights, commitment to the power of human reason, and the view that property rights result from the application of human labor. This became a justification for the American colonists' increasing desire to overthrow the English yoke of mercantilism. Not only were we colonists in the right in breaking away, but it was our moral obligation to God. One hears this in the *Declaration of Independence*, in such phrases as ". . . all men are created equal; endowed by their CREATOR with . . . inalienable rights; . . . life, liberty, and the pursuit of happiness; . . . when a long train of abuses evinces a design to reduce them . . . it is their right, it is their duty to throw off such government. . . ."

ENTER, ADAM SMITH

Of the great thinkers of the Enlightenment Adam Smith (1723–1790), Scottish moral philosopher, stands tall among the rest. Smith founded the discipline of economics as we know it, building it upon three powerful and closely linked intellectual pillars that moved Enlightenment thinkers. One was Isaac Newton's physics. The second was the view that natural laws applied to human social organization, as well as to the physical world. The third was the search for a moral philosophy emerging from the rational quality in human nature. In Smith's view, Newton's physics possessed the greatest insights ever contributed to philosophy. An automatic, mechanistic planetary system provided a vivid illustration of the harmoniously ordered system of natural laws in equilibrium. Smith was convinced that all nature functioned in the same way. He wrote a book about it, saying in a final paragraph that Newton's system "... has advanced to ... the most universal empire that was ever established in philosophy ... the discovery of an immense chain of the most important and sublime truths ... the reality of which we have daily experience." Thus, to explain events such as the nature and causes of the wealth of nations, one should look to these natural laws for they were created by a watchmaker God who designed the universe including humankind's place in it. As Smith explained, "The happiness of mankind ... seems to have been the original purpose intended by the Author of nature ... intended to promote happiness and to guard against misery."

With Newton having provided the basic theory and the Divine having provided the natural laws intended to promote happiness, how do these laws contribute to fulfillment of the design? Smith's answer was that God's design for humanity's well-being is acted out by human nature; that is, by peoples' sentiments, passions, or instincts.

Since all is foreordained to occur as designed in the pattern of God's harmonious natural laws, how do human sentiments achieve their proper moral purpose and end? They do so "... by acting according to the dictates of our moral faculties ... By acting otherwise ... we seem to obstruct ... the scheme which the Author of nature has established for the happiness and perfection of the world. ..." These observations provided the foundation for Smith's moral philosophy, one where Nature knows best, even better than human reason. From this moral philosophy, Smith developed the theory that dominates Western economic policy today.

Concluding that God's design is manifest through human sentiments and passions, Smith focused on the sentiment of self-interest,
or self-love. On the surface, this sentiment appears to be selfish and
contrary to public interests; but Smith believed its actual effect was
precisely the opposite. How then can self-interest, through a chain of
truths, bring automatic beneficence? Smith tells us that public virtue
or well-being arises not only out of benevolent intent but out of privately focused sentiments. All sentiments ultimately bring harmony.
They do so in spite of appearances to the contrary. By following inherent human sentiments we are naturally rewarded (with success and
love) and thereby motivated to pursue the morally right path.

The revolutionary reach of this Scotsman's ideas can scarcely be
grasped, even now. Natural laws, inborn natural sentiments, even
natural interests in one's own personal desires—these were to be
the ways mankind could achieve happiness and be blessed by God at
the same time. That is what he meant, and he said it in a book that
is now a classic in the English language. In it, he provided a master-
fully persuasive statement of a moral philosophy of economics: that
nature's laws know best, perform best through private interests, and
that through those interests public virtue is achieved. The book is, of
course, *An Inquiry Into The Nature and Causes of The Wealth of Nations*,
published in the year of the American Declaration of Independence,
1776. The intellectual climate of Deistically designed natural laws,
coupled with hostility to practices of mercantilism, were in no small
measure responsible for both Smith's *Wealth of Nations* and America's
Declaration of Independence and faith in democracy.

INSIGHTS, OVERSIGHTS, ILLUSIONS

What did Smith seek to demonstrate? He first dispensed with two
popular ideas about wealth creation. Money, or bullion, was not the
source of wealth as mercantilists believed. And the cultivation of

agricultural land was not the source of net addition to a nation's wealth. Instead, Smith argued that labor was the source of the wealth of nations. He opens his great work with that assertion: "The annual labour of every nation is the fund which originally supplies it with the necessaries and conveniences of life which it annually consumes, and which consist always either in the immediate produce of that labour, or in what is purchased with that produce from other nations."

An important point must be made at this crucial juncture, even at the cost of temporarily digressing from Smith's magnificent line of argument. Here we see the problem that new theories constantly face. "Every insight is an oversight" and often there are illusions. The mercantilists' focus on precious metals (money) as the source of wealth was an illusion. Quesnay's insight into agriculture's contribution to net output "oversighted" (overlooked) labor's contribution and much more. Smith's insight into labor's contribution to the wealth of nations slighted the contribution of more than a million years of humankind's accumulated knowledge and technology. His labor insight both captivated and stultified his insights.

Smith saw labor as the sole productive factor. He did not deny the existence of technology but minimized its relevance: "(T)he invention of . . . machines . . . [is a means] by which labour is so much facilitated and abridged. . . ." As a consequence he observed the emerging Industrial Revolution as arising from commercial motives, and thereby failed to develop a theory and philosophy which recognized the role of technology in shaping the nature of wealth, the causes of wealth, and the fundamental processes of progress through capital formation and cumulative innovations. Commerce in labor's products, not cumulative knowledge of technology, became Smith's truncated perspective of the cause of wealth accumulation. For him "The merchants and artificers . . . in pursuit of their own peddler principle of turning a penny where a penny was to be got . . . have been the cause . . . of the improvement and cultivation of the country."

This oversight—his failure to include the impact of technology among the nature and causes of the wealth of nations—has had repercussions to this day for the development of economic philosophy. A contrast may be made with patronage of the arts. Such patrons are never confused with the process of sculpting and the finished sculptures, nor with the composers' compositions and performing of music, or the painters and paintings of the Sistine Chapel. Without patrons, much of the great art might never have been produced. Even so, we have no difficulty distinguishing the history and production of art from its sponsorship. Art has not experienced the theoretical tragedy of becoming a second-class analytical category.

Not so, however, with industrial technology whose "patrons" (the owners, investors, businessmen) appear over and over again, in theory, to be credited with responsibility for the nature and cause of the wealth of nations. A result is that the monetary power of patrons is confused in public ideology. That monetary power is imputed to be the source of productive power, rather than the technological innovations themselves. Monetary illusion lingers. The patrons of technology are perceived as having extraordinary productive power, as distinct from their necessary entrepreneurial and managerial skills.

Technology's productive power must be made analytically distinct from these other factors. It is functionally distinguishable even if, at any given time, it appears to be inseparable from the others. Thus a possible theory and philosophy of the co-evolution of technology and humans, as a necessary cause of the well-being of people, did not appear in Smith's explanation of a nation's wealth. Technology was not denied. Rather, it became a victim of intellectual apartheid. The founder of economic theory, from his opening sentence, inadvertently committed the contributions of productive knowledge and technology to second-class citizenship by his oversight. This neglect of cumulative knowledge-technology and emphasis on labor set the foundation for Karl Marx's labor theory of value that appeared to explain capitalist exploitation. Smith's oversight of technology allowed Marx to provide a justification for proletarian revolutions that have rocked the globe.

That oversight is (should be) an alarming lesson for today's theoreticians. Their insights, oversights and illusions have consequences for the mass of humanity. During Smith's lifetime, the factory system was rapidly displacing cottage handicraft and the artisans' labor in the guilds. Smith, himself, composed a classic vision of the efficiency of newly rising factories in his famous illustration of the division of labor in a pin factory. But he neglected the economic and social importance of technology. So too, Karl Marx later noted the development of the "forces of production" but still considered human labor the sole contributor to wealth. In each instance brilliant insights also resulted in oversights because of the author's particular focus, and this has had continuing ramifications in explaining economics to this day.

SERVING CONSUMERS, FINDING FAIR PRICES

What is the moral purpose of a productive economy; for what moral purpose did labor create wealth? Adam Smith's answer was simple and straightforward. It was not to serve medieval status rights, nor to prepare the individual for an afterlife which both sacred and secular powers had taught in the past to be true. It was not to serve the crown's quest for gold and silver as the source of national power, which mercantilist policy pursued. It was not to serve the landed gentry who, according to Smith, "like all other men, love to reap where they never sowed." Nor was its purpose to serve the interests of the rising industrial and commercial profit seeking entrepreneurs. Rather, "Consumption is the sole end and purpose of all production; and the interest of the producer ought to be attended to, only so far as it may be necessary for promoting that of the consumer."

How was labor to be most effective in producing for this more

democratic purpose of consumption? Smith's answer was specialization of labor as he illustrated in his eloquent pin factory example.
Here, as in all things, Smith believed that nature knows best. Nature
functioning through innate human sentiments brings about specialization of labor. "This division of labour . . . is not . . . the effect of
any human wisdom . . . It is the consequence of a certain propensity
in human nature . . . to truck, barter, and exchange one thing for
another." So, market exchange was itself an outcome of nature—
human nature.

Mankind, indeed, has had long standing division of labor founded in
social mores and based on age, gender and traditional ascribed status.
And here again Smith overlooked advances in technology as the cause
of this new division of labor. Rather, he saw natural laws as the direct
cause. Whatever the source of exchanging one thing for another,
complicated issues arise for moral philosophy, theoretical economics,
and economic practice. For example, how *will* the exchange fairly
occur? And even more complicated for philosophical economics, how
should exchanges justly occur? Is there a morally proper measure of
quid pro quo in exchanges, and if so, how is such a measure correctly
established? Thus, the philosophical question of how to determine a
fair exchange value (just price?) is inevitably raised when division of
labor results in "truck, barter, and exchange."

Smith may have stumbled over these issues, but he did not dodge
them. Thus, given a natural order of division of labor and the penchant to truck, barter, and exchange (to which, for Smith, man seems
naturally to have added the reasoned invention of metal money), on
what terms did Smith believe goods should be exchanged? That is, how
does Smith's view of the natural order solve the medieval question
of a just price, or the contemporary question of where prices ought
properly be set? What is the proper value of goods?

The answers to these questions and the resolution of this puzzle would be neither easy nor clear. As I intend to confront our modern sense of justice in the marketplace, it seems necessary to explore the emergence of value theory in economics. Smith argued for two kinds of exchangeable value, or price: **real** and **natural**.

REAL VALUE AND PRICE

There is, he said, a **real** value, which can be said to be the just exchange price for all goods at all times and places (whether among Londoners or between Londoners and Eskimos). If it "costs twice the labor to kill a beaver which it does to kill a deer, one beaver should naturally exchange for . . . two deer." This was his labor theory of value. That is, the more labor, the more value. On the one hand, for Smith, this theory was an unquestioned Natural truth. On the other hand, he recognized what has later been called "the skilled labor problem," that is, the difficulty of establishing a common denominator among all kinds of labor skills. He noted that different kinds of labor endure different degrees of hardship, require different ingenuity or dexterity, and require different lengths of time necessary to learn different skills. Briefly stated, he encountered the problem of differential skills and how a particular quantity or quality of labor should, or could, determine a real exchange value, or price. At this point in Smith's analysis, he has not demonstrated why the given exchange of labor inputs, or price, is either technically correct, morally just, or even practical. For all we know he may be talking sheer gibberish.

Smith's reasoning leaves an unresolved technical and moral economic issue. Should the real value (or price) in exchange be determined by the labor involved in producing the commodities? Or should the real value of a good be determined by its value to consumers? Smith's entire intent was to demonstrate what it is that nature knows is best so that it could be followed and the shackles of mercantilism identified and abandoned.

NATURAL VALUE AND PRICE

Smith "resolves" the dilemma with his concept of **natural** price, which is the exchange price determined naturally in the market. **Natural** price is a Newtonian-like natural equilibrium price. Previously Smith had written of equilibrium as a general insight, praising its identification by Newton as "advancement to the most universal empire ever established in philosophy." Smith now applied this Newtonian mechanistic insight to explain how nature's laws know best the role of price, and how prices are properly formed naturally. "When the price of any commodity is neither more nor less than what is sufficient to pay . . . rent . . . wages . . . and profits . . . their natural rates, the commodity is then sold for what may be called its natural price. . . ."

To this point Smith has left us not knowing the moral meaning or practical significance of price. If he does not supply an answer to this philosophical question, it is difficult to see how any public policy relating to price could be defended or condemned. He might have simply taken the position that because nature knows best, and nature's natural laws do best, then that which exists must therefore be right.

However, in effect Smith argued that nature provides a total cost of production standard: fair exchange, no robbery. Commodities are worth in exchange what they cost to produce and bring to market. We know that worth by seeing what costs consumers are willing to cover by the price they are willing to pay. Here Smith has discovered (invented?) the natural law of supply and demand. By this means, he made the case that nature knows best how to provide exchange measures, values or prices that are efficient and fair with freedom for all individuals in all economies.

How, then, does the price arrive at this ideal natural condition? Here he set the concept of supply and demand price into the puzzle. "The market price of every particular commodity is regulated by the proportion between the quantity which is actually brought to market [i.e., the supply], and the demand of those who are willing to pay the natural price. . . . [This demand] is different from the absolute demand. A very poor man may be said in some sense to have a demand for a coach and six . . . but his demand is not an effectual demand. . . ." I feel it necessary to note that neither would the working poor man's demand for proper food, clothing, housing, training, and medical care be an "effectual demand," if these are beyond his financial means.

While not confronting these issues of human needs Smith provided economic theory with the basic ideas of supply and demand establishing prices naturally. All is harmony as nature works its wonders within the marketplace. "The natural price, . . . is, as it were, the central price, to which the prices of all commodities are continually gravitating. . . ." Thus, Smith tracked Newton's natural truths in enunciating the idea of supply and demand. The point to which supply and demand prices are continually gravitating is a nature-induced equilibrium. It is where supplies of all commodities equal the effectual demands for all commodities; where natural laws bring practicality and morality to an embrace. The cosmology which explained planetary order for Newton now appears to explain a naturally just and effective economic order.

Mercantilist policies granting royal monopolies, Smith maintained, created a price pattern which "is upon every occasion the highest which can be got. The natural price, or the price of free competition, on the contrary, is the lowest which can be taken, not upon every occasion indeed, but for any considerable time together." Smith concluded that mankind should abandon mercantilist constraints. Give the Deity's natural laws their unrestrained authority. Reap the rewards of Nature's cosmic wisdom. Natural supply and demand prices will be set automatically by unfettered competition. Prices so set will cover total costs of production and the profits that motivate entrepreneurs. Further, such equilibrium prices achieve the moral purpose of an economy, provisioning consumers at prices set by beneficent nature.

This would be achieved with freedom for all. "The natural price, or the price of free competition . . . would be the case where there was perfect liberty."

Smith saw the motivating power behind this entire process to be self-interest. "It is not from the benevolence of the butcher, the brewer, or the baker, that we expect our dinner, but from the regard to their own interest." While eulogizing the self-interest role of the entrepreneur Smith neither trusted nor endorsed the moral propriety of a proprietor's self-interest. "People of the same trade seldom meet together, even for merriment . . . but the conversation ends in a conspiracy against the public, or some contrivance to raise prices."

Monitoring these tendencies to excessive self-interests, and maintaining a harmony of freedom, fairness, and the purpose of serving the consumer revealed another natural force. It was *competition*. Competition, for Smith, was a natural truth similar to the physical truth of gravity. Its natural effectiveness thus far in history had been impeded by lingering ancient customs. The economy, Smith claimed, must be allowed freedom from mercantilist and royal regulations in order that it could be governed by natural laws. Its driving mainspring is natural self-interest. It is kept in harmonious balance by competition. The competitive economy benefits consumers by efficiently allocating labor and capital. Every individual "intends only his own gain, and he is in this, as in many other cases, led by an invisible hand to promote an end which was no part of his intention." To Smith, benevolent Nature will out. "[T]he obvious and simple system of natural liberty establishes itself of its own accord."

CAPITAL AS ECONOMIC CATALYST

One of the ironies of economic history is that the system of free market economies called "capitalism" was actually named by Karl Marx who used the term as a contemptuous rejection of the whole system that he believed exploited workers. In modern economic theory, capital is thought to be a key element responsible for economic growth. Accumulating large quantities of capital is perceived to be both desirable and essential for economic prosperity. But what is capital?

Smith introduced us to the concept of capital formation and its contribution to economic growth (what we now call growth in gross domestic product). He properly pointed out that building up capital requires saving. But he neglected the fundamental moral matter of economic *progress*. Smith set us on an important route to human betterment, but in the process his fruitful insights overlook important causes of improving the wealth of nations. He explained how labor becomes more productive through capital formation.

Smith builds upon his theory that labor is the sole source of the wealth of all nations, including those that are industrializing. He begins with the principle that labor can be used for two qualitatively different purposes. One is wasteful, the other productive. Where labor does not produce an exchangeable product, such labor is unproductive. Where labor produces goods and services that can be exchanged for other products, it is productive. "Thus the labour of a manufacturer adds, generally, to the value of the materials which he works upon. . . . The labour of a menial servant, on the contrary, adds to the value of nothing. . . . A man grows rich by employing a multitude of manufacturers: he grows poor, by maintaining a multitude of menial servants."

Yes, but how is capital created? Smith had earlier asserted labor to be the sole source of wealth creation. Labor then must create capital. But it is a common view that the rich, by saving and investing money create capital. Could money be the source of capital creation? That view was inconceivable to Smith. After all, money as a source of wealth creation was a mercantilist illusion, which he roundly rejected. Money facilitated exchange; it did not produce value or wealth. Money was only a catalyst in an economy based upon the division of labor and accompanying exchanges.

How then was capital created if not by money and not by technological invention? Capital was increased by the action of still another moral sentiment. "Parsimony," Smith said, "and not industry, is the immediate cause of the increase of capital. Industry, indeed, provides the subject which parsimony accumulates. But whatever industry might acquire, if parsimony did not save and store up, the capital would never be the greater." Thus *savings* enter economic theory and the theory of capital formation. Smith seems to have had a very fuzzy vision of what "capital" was and if it differed from "industry." And this confusion likely reflects his oversight of the nature, invention, and evolution of technology. The reason for this neglect is very possibly because he thought in the Newtonian equilibrium ethos and prior to the Darwinian evolutionary intellectual ethos.

For Smith and his ideological followers technological advancement over the history of mankind is accepted as a qualitative given, overlooking the role of cumulative innovations of technology in explaining causes of improving the wealth of nations. Smith's view was limited to simply accumulating more of the same quality of technology. Thus he was explaining the immediate cause of the quantitative increase of capital (industry, technology). Parsimony brings savings; and acquisitiveness directs saved funds to investment in currently extant equipment for increased profits.

Whence savings for Smith? Laborers cannot save because any increase in their income will be used to improve the family's standard of living. This will result in more children surviving. Thus, income that might be saved is used sustaining increases in population. Landlords, who reap where they have not sown, don't save because they live luxuriously and squander on servants who are unproductive labor. Saving is accomplished through parsimonious use of profits earned by the emerging business class. They invest their savings "nearly in the same time" as they are accumulated, and thus direct labor to the productive purpose of capital formation which facilitates the division, and hence productivity, of labor.

There is danger of an illusion here. It is the mercantilist money illusion again: Because it is money that is saved and invested, it is therefore money that creates capital. Smith was not caught in that illusion. Saving and investing money shifted labor from unproductive use to productive use. Thus labor, mediated through parsimony, profits, and acquisitiveness, creates capital which facilitates labors' expanding contribution to the wealth of nations. All of this occurs automatically with liberty for all.

CONCLUSIONS

The discipline of economics has arisen in the Western world out of both moral philosophizing and natural science as they flourished in the Enlightenment. Adam Smith, as a moral philosopher, focused these leading ideas of the eighteenth century on the nature and causes of the wealth of nations. In doing so he established the discipline of economics as a moral enterprise. His ideas have emerged over the past 200 years as a central quality of both the science of economics and the public philosophy sustaining our dominant economic ideology. These ideas have contributed substantially to the well-being of the Western world. They are powerful forces contributing to both our capacity to progress and our incapacity to adequately adapt to changing needs of the modern world. This complexity arises out of the inescapable condition that thinking involves appropriate insights, costly oversights and illusions. We turn next to economic theory's insights, oversights and illusions that we may be better prepared to construct a moral economic philosophy for coping with humanity's promising and threatening future.

3

Insights, Oversights, and Illusions

If in the long run we are the makers of our own fate, in the short run we are the captives of the ideas we have created.   —Friedrich A. Hayek

The broad quest of this book is the well-being of humanity. The focus is on the contribution of economics to that well-being. That quest, with that focus, has led us into economic theorizing and philosophizing. In seeking to reconstruct a combined theory and philosophy of economics, it is essential to confront the problems of theory construction itself. And as social theory involves humans it is inescapable that we must confront human nature and do so in the context of social organization and the natural laws that condition all we may confront and achieve. Traditional economic theory provides insights into these matters as we have seen. That theory also neglects and even overlooks (oversights) imperative conditions upon which human well-being is dependent. And further complicating our thinking are illusions of which we have become victims. This chapter explores these conundrums in preparation for further reconstruction of a moral philosophy of economics.

Rethinking economics is difficult because its insights are hampered by both oversights and illusions. When we focus our thinking on price, or laws of supply and demand, or self-interest, we rivet our attention on limited aspects of social systems without analyzing causal forces outside the range of that chosen vision. On the other hand, we abstract in order to create understandable models and because we do not know all the variables impacting the phenomena we are concerned about (determination of prices for example). Further complicating understanding are illusions we accept as truths (money makes a nation wealthy; full employment is normal; depressions are deviations from automatic equilibrium). We have no idea how many and what kinds of illusions impede our capacity to think our way to better lives for humanity. The difficulties are inherent in the process of thinking and theorizing, not only in the social sciences but in all of life. "God invented time so everything wouldn't happen all at once." (Graffiti.) Scientists invented disciplines because they couldn't think about everything all at once.

ABSTRACTIONS AND OVERSIGHTS

Theory formation inescapably involves abstracting that which seems most relevant to explain particular phenomena. It is largely a result of such "necessary" abstracting that we encounter "unanticipated consequences of purposive action." Every abstracted insight has oversights. Abstracting may be a far more significant source of theory inadequacies than are illusions. Whatever turns out to be relevant, though by abstracting has been left out, is the oversight which limits the effectiveness of the theory to explain the phenomena which it set out to understand. We just don't know or understand all the forces at work and hence we often do not know reliably what will happen if we act, or what will happen if we fail to act. Not acting may be more costly than occasional errors from action. That can be so because we can learn by actively experimenting.

On the other hand, if we question all things at once, we face explanatory chaos. It is theory that gives a sense of order and provides guideposts to action and policy. We can't think of and relate to everything all at once. We invent ideas and abstract some from all others possible. Abstracting is accepted as essential but not as an absolute eternal understanding of the world within which we confront the challenges of endlessly adapting.

Some abstracted insights may distort reality considerably. Historical records suggest that Western market economies have been (compared to all other economies) largely responsible for shaping the nature and causes of the wealth of nations. Do the abstracted insights of competitive market theory explain the success of Western market managed economies? Can there be some explanatory truth in the theory, while it still distorts our understanding of causality? Can the wealth of nations be primarily the result of overlooked forces such as the cumulative dynamics of knowledge-technology?

More than an act of will is required to escape the illusions deeply implanted in our psyche by competitive market theory and its ideology. They seem to explain how our economy efficiently economizes scarce means among competing ends. They seem to show how the market is just in rewarding the worthy for their contributions. Are the abstractions of competitive price theory adequate to explain either economic efficiency, well-being, or justice? U.S. courts, legislators, fundamentalist economists, public economic ideologies, and influential opinion molders seem to think so. Conservative spokesman Robert Bork puts it this way: "Consumer welfare refers to the most efficient distribution and employment of society's resources so that total output, as consumers value it, is maximized. It is a standard concept in economics and is not pro-business. . . . The Supreme Court now takes the position that consumer welfare is the goal of antitrust. . . ." (and the goal of antitrust is to enforce free competition).

Our business here is not to engage in belief bashing. Rather, it is to seek understanding of how so convincing a theory of an automatic market economy can have fallen so short in the past and may continue to be a dangerously inadequate guide to public policy for the future. It is wise, useful, and a quality of science to be skeptical and question the beliefs by which we live. It is dangerous, even foolhardy, to reject our beliefs without reasonable promise of more reliable alternatives. Certainly Adam Smith and John Maynard Keynes provided alternatives to the ideas they questioned. Moderate skepticism serves a useful, even essential, function in the understanding process.

Competitive economic theory and its intimately related ideological beliefs are powerful and justly persuasive ideas that have, compared to other ideologies, served us well. To paraphrase Winston Churchill's wry comment, competitive theory explains the worst possible economy except for all the rest. But our economic ideology and supporting theory must, for humanity's future well-being, continuously face a re-inquiry into the nature and causes of the wealth of nations and humanity.

Several large categories of forces are slighted in competitive theory's explanation of Western economic success. One is a theory and philosophy of technology; another is the fortuitous juxtaposition of natural resources with technology; and a third is the constructive role played by the public infrastructure of Western democracies in making a faltering market structure increasingly effective.

This awareness of economic theory's deficiencies carries with it an obligation to provide a more adequate and more reliable explanation of the causes of the remarkable successes of Western market-managed economies. To construct this fuller explanation of Western economic success, I approach the subject from multiple perspectives and begin by drawing on insights and perspectives not available to the discipline's founders. Needed now is a Darwinian perception of how an economy evolves by adaptation through continuous innovations, some of which fail while others survive and transform the nature of the economy.

Modern industrial economies, in this light, are organized in a cobweb of mutually interdependent organic linkages of people, resources, and technology. Even consumption, especially, must be viewed as a link in the production process. Viewed in this perspective, mutual dependencies are not simply self-centered reciprocal contribute-receive transactions but rather a mutually supporting web of relationships. Farmers produce food, food fuels workers who make steel used in automobiles, automobiles then carry students and teachers to class, where education transmits knowledge of more effective farming practices. All these and more technical permutations and combinations formulate the essential foundations of productive economies.

MULTIDIMENSIONAL HUMAN NATURE

Adam Smith spoke squarely to the character and role of human nature in social organization. He inquired into multiple human sentiments or "instincts" and their interrelatedness. These are discussed in his *The Theory of Moral Sentiments* in initially rather complex contexts. Some are corrupting sentiments. Some are correcting predilections. Some are foundations to a moral order. Some give rise to practical provisioning. Together they paint a picture of a human nature gravitating naturally to fulfilling a Deistically designed order. In the *Wealth of Nations*, Smith applies this moral philosophy that Nature knows best and functions through natural laws. Human nature itself, Smith argues, is an aspect of nature's laws. Out of these many sentiments, Smith abstracted self-interest as the dominant passion driving the economies he so keenly observed. For Smith, self-interest, virtually alone, gives rise to the natural laws of economic markets and the nature and causes of the wealth of nations. Smith's single abstracted human sentiment, once seen as immoral selfishness, is turned into an explanation of how free markets come naturally into being, if only man's mercantilist meddling rules are removed to free God's natural order. Virtually the entire subsequent mainstream history of economic thought is structured upon that central building block.

Out of Smith's utopian image, modern competitive price theory constructs a vision of a whole economy that has been abstracted from a virtual single facet of human biology. The real world is wrong wherever it manifests itself in contradiction to the abstracted ideal built upon this single powerful force, which market competition alone (derived from self-interest) should morally monitor.

An essential step in rethinking moral concerns in economics has been to question society's virtual obsession with the abstract self-interested individual. Human nature's richness and diversity reveals much about the neglected qualities of conventional economic thought. Sentiments of workmanship, curiosity, empathy, loyalty, security, and even altruism are some overlooked predilections needed in understanding both a moral and scientific basis for judging the essential elements of economies.

What then, are the relevant qualities of human nature that contribute to a moral view of economies? Inherent inclinations in human nature have been variously named and vaguely identified over time. "Instincts" is, perhaps, the most commonly recognized term identifying these hardwired responses of complex organisms. There is a growing consensus that there are inherent gene-driven inclinations nudging humans to respond in various ways. Identifying, with precision, the power or compulsiveness of the nudging, the specific quality of response, and the specific genes or gene patterns involved will challenge researchers for some time to come. The uniqueness of this genetic imprinting on each individual will surprise few parents who have reared multiple children. Evolutionary psychology, the genome project, anthropology, sociobiology, ethnology, and other contemporary research should provide us with more and more insights into this matter over time.

It is impressive to see how insightful Adam Smith was without the help of these subsequent disciplines. However, an important point must be made. Smith perceived human sentiments as the creation and implementation of the Deity's design. We now perceive these predispositions from a Darwinian, evolutionary perspective. They exist as the result of an evolutionary, natural selection process. Grasping the principles and implications of that process is essential to construct an appropriate moral system for a philosophy of economics which must confront an emerging world of change.

An essential contribution to understanding moral action comes from anthropology's identification of the *culture* concept. Over our evolutionary span of becoming human, there has been a co-evolution of biological inclinations with "invented" culture traits both of which were survival selective of each other by virtue of their combined survival fitness advantage. In the evolution from pre-human proto-man (some 2 million years ago) to modern *Homo sapiens*, the inventing of tangible tools, for example, was both a product of, and a selecting factor in, the emergence of today's genetically shaped mankind.

As proto-humans became human, they became increasingly social animals, engaging in collective action with physical, social and psychological needs and predilections. We evolved a parental bent, sense of altruism, dominance and submission responses, inclinations to give, take and imitate. We have a natural curiosity, tool-symbol manipulating-inventing talent, and a workmanship bent. In this evolution of proto-man to human, the biological and instrumental developments acted in conjunction, like gravity, that drew individuals together. Both the biological and cultural are powerful bonding forces.

Proto-humans' big-jawed, fighting, food-grubbing mouth mutated and became a more refined organ only as early tools were invented, which could be used to defend and to assist in converting finds in the environment to food. These conjoined developments then combined with other random genetic mutations and cultural inventions.

If together they enhanced survival, they were thereby perpetuated as a modified form of proto-man with adaptive advantage over other forms. Thus one evolutionary step from the past followed another without a preordained destination.

Mutations resulting in forelimbs' greater digital dexterity, possibly already flexible from adaptation to swinging in trees, coupled with mutations resulting in more erect posture, freed the paws-become-hands that grasped clubs and stones, usable for defense, hunting, grinding and general food accessibility. In turn, this front paw's increased dexterity, when combined with more erect posture mutations, made possible better use and improvement of tools that better defended, fed, and contributed to survival. The result was even less dependence on a large fighting food-grubbing mouth, which allowed other important inventions such as proto-words, and other random mutations to evolve.

The development of primitive words most likely accompanied mutations that resulted in a larger brain and a smaller more delicate mouth, jaw, and tongue within a small head. This allowed the bigger, better brain and small head to pass through the birth canal without damage to mother or child. These developments made possible more delicate vocalization giving rise to articulate sounds as symbols of increased specificity communicating more specialized meanings. Sound-symbol communication emerged into language, reinforced bonding, and enhanced thinking. All these promoted careful caregiving to helpless offspring who depended upon an increasing amount of time and attention to reach physical maturity and to learn cultural means of survival security.

Those who talk together, make and use tools together, better bond together. Increased "compassion," "empathy," and "sympathy" (that is, moral sentiments) improved care of pregnant females and fostered greater care of more helpless infants. This contributes to more successful births and improved survival of offspring, hence more secure survival of the species by better bonding.

This scenario, applying the same principles, could be stated in many different patterns, each of which helps explain how we are the way we are. Once we have a sense of how random mutations were survival-selected by the environment and see how "inventing" survival advantage instruments modifies the selecting environment, then we recognize the process of co-evolution of culture and biology from proto-man to modern man. Once we grasp this pattern of evolution we see how modified biological qualities selected these inherent technological talents and social inclinations which contributed a survival advantage for the emerging species. Now we can deduce how other "random" changes in inherent inclinations might further improve bonding, integration, and survival of the species.

Fortunately for humanity, the evolutionary mechanism has provided us the bonding compulsion to get along with each other, not because nature held a preferential bias for humanity over other species, but by genetic chance and survival selection. Thus we have become socio-cultural persons born into and reared in a culture which prescribed values and norms of behavior for recurring contexts. In general, these bonding drives encompass the empathetic qualities of Adam Smith's "impartial spectators."

CONFLICT AND BONDING

Tragically, all was and is not smooth sailing. Why on earth would seemingly sane societies that normally seem to prefer security of health, home, family, retirement, and so forth, choose speedy sports cars, roller coasters, parachute and bungi-cord jumping, and other dangerous and frightening thrills? Why a tendency to deceive or lie, or a tendency to brutality? Why are there good and bad dispositions in virtually everyone? More generally, why the seemingly contrasting qualities in human nature?

Diverse forms of life evolved under constraints of scarcity giving rise to conflict among and within individual species. For evolving humans, survival under conditions of scarcity has given rise to inclinations to protect scarce options, fight to preserve advantages, dominate, be submissive, make peace offerings, perhaps compromise, or inherently follow a tit-for-tat strategy of reciprocal punishment, reward or exchange. Certainly there are conflict-responding tendencies inherent in our humanness. These propensities, too, had adaptive survival advantages in the evolutionary process.

We evolved as all species did. We reproduced and survived. The evolution of genetic impulses was not fine tuned within or among individuals *for* the good of humanity. So far as we know, no purpose was involved. We did not evolve *to* live the good life, a purposeful life, or a meaningful life. We didn't evolve *to* do anything. The evolution of genetically driven impulses was not designed for a teleological purpose of creating a meaningful and fulfilling life for all humanity for all time. We evolved with impulses that resulted in species self-perpetuation (until other natural forces, or our own natural dispositions, do us in).

Instincts or sentiments are not here *for* anything. They *do* things (bring babies into being for example). There are not instincts *for* survival; they are instincts that result in survival. I don't knock it. We are the result. We evolved with no warranty promising a bed of roses. We're here as we are because of the way we evolved. Over ninety percent of the species that have evolved on this planet have failed to adapt and consequently died out. All earlier "human" species except *Homo sapiens* suffered a similar ending. It can be the fate of humanity if we indiscriminately transgress natural laws in order to be "free." We are not free to ignore natural laws. We must learn to live within them by better understanding and using them for our own continuing survival and fulfillment. It will not be as easy as being "free."

There is illusory evidence for the nature-knows-best-be-free inter-pretation. Nature has provided mankind with the physical capacities, psychological and social sentiments, language and tool talents, and general moral sense that have resulted in our survival to date. Human survival adaptations, as with other species, have been so "ingenious" as to make them appear to be the product of an all-knowing designer. But a closer look suggests that human success has not been as elegant as the human species has wished.

Humanity's history has been spectacular but tarnished with self-inflicted tragedies. The nature-knows-best world is indifferent to how or which species suffer, agonize, survive, perish, or prosper. Nature alone evolved no overriding or specific concern for the wealth of nations or welfare of humanity. Symbiotic and competitive survival is raw nature's only test of fitness. Long-run security or the edifying quality of our survival is no one's concern or responsibility other than ours.

RULES ARE OVERLOOKED IN THE CONCEPT
OF NATURAL ECONOMIC LAWS

Anthropology has demonstrated that all cultures develop their own unique patterns of rules that give social structure of sufficient order to sustain their survival. Human-invented rules (folkways, mores, social contract) have evolved with the evolution of humanness and are sur-vival-adaptive instruments of the human species. These rules are the customs that societies' individuals habitually observe. We learn what is expected of us, even if we don't ask or know why.

Habit and customized rules are necessary and irreplaceable, though modifiable. Habit is a naturally evolved mechanism of human biology that contributes necessary efficiency in organizing individual behavior. But habit and custom can impede adaptation in a changing world. In advanced cultures, customs are formalized in legal structures. Custom and law provide the rules by which social systems are structured and sustained. Mankind lives by rules. They are indispensable in making the economy work. Some, however, are detrimental. They often give priority to privilege over progress toward human betterment.

ORDER THROUGH RULE OF LAW

The issue for the moral philosophy of economics being developed here is not whether governments should stay out of the economy or get in. They do not have the option to stay out. The issue is what philosophy and theory we possess to distinguish good government rules from bad ones. To be justifiable, the rules must provide a kind of constitution for directing fairly flexible, quasi-autonomous, and discretionary management of a dynamic economy.

Western monetized market economies are systems of culture-generated rules. Among the more basic rules essential to the "free competitive market" are those rules providing private property rights. These are rules regarding how we may and may not act toward each other in dealing with nature, material culture and "intellectual property." The rules also apply to our own bodies and have provided a bulwark against slavery and other forms of unacceptable power imposed upon individuals. It is private property rules that economic fundamentalists fight so hard to preserve. However, under conditions of change, property rights are vulnerable, because some of the rules defining the rights become obsolete. Rules governing property rights of horse and buggy transportation become unworkable with the emergence of eighteen wheelers and twenty to a hundred miles an hour cruise control settings.

In market managed economies, private property rules are social instruments by which the technology and factors of production of the economy are managed under pluralism, rather than under rigid tradition, feudal customs, or monolithic planning. Because market managed economies feature notable dynamism, organizing rules are constantly threatened by change. Property rules protect owners' rights to demand a reciprocal payment for contributions of owned real capital, land, technology, and knowledge. The cry for freedom (in this context) is a cry to allow property holders to use their power in their own immediately perceived best interests. The ideology and theory of the competitive market create the illusion that freedom in the use of property is the cause of the wealth of nations and thus is in the long-run interest of humanity. Certainly an important insight but also a serious oversight.

When effective, rules contribute to the well-being of a society and hence to the wealth of nations. There is an important illusion that arises here and distorts understanding of how economies are organized and function. The more effective the rules are, the less conspicuous they are. When effective they tend to be taken for granted. This allows a covert assumption that natural laws (not man-made rules) are automatically doing their beneficent thing. Actually, that which is working is not natural laws of supply and demand, but the technical use of productive resources along with the rules that design the market by which that economy is managed. Supply and demand functions within these social rules.

Rules that do not work garner deservedly derisive attention. This we saw in Adam Smith's criticism of mercantilism. But the outcry of extreme economic fundamentalism is not to improve the rules, but to eliminate them. This demand is based on the illusionary assumption that there are self organizing natural laws that are operating to benefit humanity. From this perspective, all rules could be assumed detrimental and should be eliminated. But of course, for economic fundamentalists, private property is not a pattern of man-made rules but nature's natural right. The economic fundamentalists who want a return to the presumed rightful natural laws of the free market are in

essence, saying: "Allow us the natural right to exercise our free will."
This contradicts the reasons for rules granting and protecting private
property rights in the first place. Witness the looting that breaks out
when social order breaks down. Private property is man-made to help
organize the economy and should be designed in the interest of the
populace, not as sacred or natural rights of the property holders.

RULES, WILL, AND RATIONALITY

Human will is environmentally, biologically, psychologically, culturally, and sociologically conditioned. It exhibits a range within which
human discretionary rationality (and irrationality) function. This
rationality is central to finding and directing our way in the present
and into the future. Regrettably, public ideology lacks insights and language adequate to deal with the subtleties of such rationality. Yet, it is
this rationality that provides the means of formulating a moral philosophy, of seeking economic justice, and clarifying economic "freedom"
in a world of changing political, economic and social power.

Two important and rather distinct forms of rationality guide our
discretionary thinking and choosing. Private purpose rationality promotes self-interests. Public purpose rationality promotes the social
rules of the social structure that will direct the world in which we
must live, adapt and enrich the individual lives of humanity over
time.

Private Purpose Rationality

Competitive theory views markets as operating efficiently because
they are populated by a rational species. The concept of the "rational
economic person" has become a central abstraction built into the
theory of the competitive market. The quality of rationality emerges
logically out of the self-interest abstraction. Rational behavior is
action that maximizes self-interests under existing circumstances.

Individuals inherently driven by self-interest exhibit economic rationality when they compute their economic decisions so as to maximize their independent, self-reliant interests. Maximizing one's own gain is both the character and objective of the private purpose, rational thought of private property owners. This is the meaning of private purpose rationality.

In our rational private purpose mode, we are said to be necessarily amoral, or ethically neutral, regarding the possible social consequences that follow inadvertently from our actions. Adam Smith made it explicit that other peoples' welfare was no part of the shopkeeper's intent. This kind of rationality is capable of pushing decisions to the dramatically immoral by cutting corners, pandering to human weaknesses (capacities for dangerous addictions), favoring tawdry preferences over more edifying lifestyles, or pursuing private political interests through "pork barrel" legislation.

Yet some express the view that the only responsible decision for a business person is to minimize money costs and maximize money gains (thus maximizing profits) because this economizes scarce means most efficiently and maximizes consumer satisfaction. All other decisions, it is argued, interfere with freedom and result in economic inefficiency and are therefore irresponsible. This view has some merit but only if the rules impose costs-profit constraints in ways that make the Essential Economy increasingly effective.

As an abstraction, self-interest rationality is not illogical. As a motive to economizing efficiency it has much to offer; as a guideline for economic growth it is limited; as a basis for rationally contemplating economic effectiveness and progress it becomes more limited; and as a means of rationally pursuing a moral philosophy of economics its contribution is modest. As an exclusive model for guiding much human behavior it is grotesque.

However, private purpose rationality in unique circumstances is a profound contribution of competitive theory. There certainly is truth in the position that individuals have unique needs, and the monetized market provides a mechanism by which these individually specific needs may be communicated and satisfied if one has the ability to obtain sufficient income. Of course gaining income also depends on the distribution of genes, property, and social conditioning. And all depends upon the capacity of the Essential Economy to deliver the goods. Nevertheless, self-interest rationality, within a market allowing elbow room for discretion, is well suited to provide creative innovations by individuals under pluralism. These are insights that a philosophy of economics will want to recognize as highly relevant, but they are insufficient by themselves. As an insight explaining the nature of human rationality conducive to the causes of the wealth of nations, self-interest is indeed a compelling hypothesis, yet it overlooks other forms of rationality. Other forms of rationality contributing to the well-being of humanity are, for example, the pursuit of reliable knowledge through science and the logic of rule-making for a market devoted to managing for public purpose.

Thus the theory of private purpose rationality, in the modern world, overlooks as much as it explains. It assumes that economic agents have perfect knowledge. But individuals possess no natural supply of economically coded genes or self-interested rationality to behave instinctively as the theory infers they will. Consumers seldom have the aptitude, time, or resources to gain the information necessary for adequate, let alone perfect, knowledge to understand the quality, reliability, and competitive worth of what they buy and consume. Certainly individuals do not regularly calculate the social consequences flowing from what they buy and how they consume. In fact rational maximizing is not the individual's most fundamental mode of behavior. Instead, habit and custom make most such decisions workably effective or defective for the individual. Western market economies are, to an astonishing degree, dependent on habit and trust. Because commercial products are substantially trustworthy in spite of constant, petty commercial fudging (and not infrequent dangerous deception), consumers survive relying on trust and plain human decency, not on market rationality alone.

As Adam Smith recognized, private purpose, self-interest rationality is a powerful social force. But it is grossly inadequate as the exclusive method of identifying economic practices most conducive to the wealth of nations or the well-being of humanity.

Public Purpose Rationality

Individuals, however, are vulnerable. They need help of a sort that falls outside competitive theory's abstraction of perfect knowledge and perfect competition as adequate moral monitors. In an effective democracy, individuals get a surprising degree of governmental help, in spite of contrary ideology. Consumers, whether or not they are aware of it, depend on legally instituted rules, such as those supplied by food and drug monitoring, public health supervision of food handling, building codes and inspectors, public transportation supervision, and on endlessly. By establishing increasingly reliable norms for most legitimate commercial activities, we free ourselves from being disastrously misled, and we are empowered to obtain the goods and services modestly appropriate to our needs and means. The public rules protecting consumer choices are, when at their best, products of public purpose rational discretion. To the extent these rules help, protect, and even coerce individuals in their exercise of self-interest rationality, that benevolence is a product of public purpose rationality.

Private purpose and public purpose rationality have a common instrumental logic. That is, both involve the logical functioning of instruments and the consequences of how they are used. It is a techno-logic, matter-of-fact cause-and-effect calculation of acts and consequences. To act morally in terms of private purpose rationality requires calculating cause- and-effect consequences for one's personal benefit within existing rules. To act morally, in terms of public purpose rationality, requires calculating cause and effect consequences of introducing innovations into the social system.

This latter rationality is imposed by humanity upon itself for we cannot escape the necessity of formulating a reasonably effective economic system. This requires public purpose rationality applied by rational citizens deciding what kind of a society they would, or better, should like to live in and bequeath to posterity. What kind of technology should constitute a basic factor of the economy? What kind of rules should shape the market? Should there be a market for human slaves? A market for transplantable human organs to the highest bidder? A market for prostitution? A market for all the currently legal and illegal drugs? Is the best business the one that out-competes its rivals by polluting, allowing dangerous working conditions, demanding long work weeks, providing no fringe benefits, hiring child labor, or innovating new and enticing products with inadequately examined consequences?

In short, public purpose rationality is the same form of logic but far more complex than private purpose interest alone. Certainly, the two rationalities are very similar in terms of instrumental consequentialist logic, yet they have quite different ways of calculating consequences. Public purpose rationality is not adequately clarified simply by contrasting it with the inadequacies of private purpose rationality. In the remainder of this book I shall develop a fuller meaning and method of public purpose rationality and its implementation.

PUBLIC PURPOSE, MORALITY, AND NATURE

As may be recalled, Adam Smith's moral philosophy applied to the economy was that nature knows best. But citizens' public purpose rationality may know better than nature. If only nature did know best. If only rational economic man could lead us aright. How comfortable these illusions. How simple to be a responsible citizen. Just acquiesce to our self-interested cravings. But the nature-knows-best world is indifferent to which species survive, to the nature and causes of the wealth of nations, to how well we live, or how long we survive. Nature can go on without us and never yearn for us.

There is a qualification to these observations. Nature, indifferently, provided man with the physical capacities, psychological sentiments, social proclivities, language and tool developing qualities, and crude moral sentiments that have resulted in the species' survival to date. In spite of these wondrous qualities our history is tragically strewn with hardships, pain, sorrow, anguish, and even self-inflicted disasters from doing what comes naturally (such as a quest of dominance, self-interest or ideational conflict). Because of, and in spite of, our human natures, we have made it thus far.

However, past survival is not proof of a right course to take into the future. None of this analysis argues in support of another Platonic perfect system of thought or grand alternative economic system. All new grand alternatives will have similar theorizing limitations. Marx never laid out a very definitive picture of a communist society. Whatever Marx intended communism to be, it was never actually tried by "communist" societies.

Inescapably, we humans evaluate. We make value judgments about what is better and what is worse. Because we are a unique species that looks backward, forward, and sideways at others, we cannot escape comparisons. Because we are inherently empathetic, we cannot escape having feelings about what we observe. Because we inherently seek to explain what we observe, we transform these insights into hypotheses, preferences and rejections. We evolve moral systems of should and should not. An economy encompasses such a value pattern, with commitments of life-and-death importance. How do we, therefore, construct a philosophy that will enhance the prospects of enriching human well-being and reducing its tragedies? The focus here has been on finding fundamental building blocks from which a moral philosophy of economic efficiency, effectiveness and justice may be structured.

There is no moral philosophy "out there," as an independent entity, awaiting discovery like a pot of gold at the end of the rainbow. A moral philosophy must be formulated from the natural laws through which we humans have emerged and by which we must live, our own natural natures included. To do this we eventually shift the focus of our moral thinking from the individual to the primary social modes by which individuals are organized and guided. Before that, however, we take a fuller look at our ideology and public philosophy.

4

Free Market Theory,
Touchstone of Ideology:
Praise and a Critique

The way the economic world works is profoundly influenced by the way people think. Belief systems guide us in deciding what is right and wrong. What we believe to be right and wrong, and why, is our ideology or public philosophy. A generally accepted ideology is a necessary social adhesive. In Western market economies, the theory that stands behind the public philosophy and supports the ideology of capitalism is Adam Smith's free market competitive economic theory. Competitive theory is the touchstone of our economic ideology. The better the moral philosophy behind the theory, which supports the public ideology, the better the prospects of successfully coping with an uncertain future.

Competitive free market economic theory derived from Adam Smith is the major Western source of critiquing and justifying economic practices around the globe. Difficult as the task of economic analysis is in a changing technological, political and sociological world of many dancing variables, our lives would be badly demeaned without the discipline's contributions. These contributions, however, are insufficient, tragically, dangerously so.

This chapter tells some of the story of the Smithian tradition as it exists today: the central ideas, its strong public appeal, its shortcomings and failures, the illusions it fosters.

THE THRUST OF FREE MARKET THEORY TODAY

Adam Smith's economic thought remains fundamental to how we think about economics. His basic theory has undergone two centuries of meticulous refinement. The heart and soul of that economic thinking is competitive price theory. It is the theory of how competitive market economies function most efficiently in producing, distributing, and consuming scarce goods, and how, in the process, they grow most effectively—all in response to consumers' demands in the market.

Competitive-theory-based economics is universally required as a theoretical foundation of every business school curriculum in the United States. In its most fundamentalist interpretation, it forms the foundation to our public economic ideology of laissez-faire capitalism. Without it there is no supportive, sophisticated, comprehensive theory and philosophy of industrial capitalism. I refer to this competitive theory as "fundamentalist theory."

SCARCITY: WHERE IT ALL BEGINS

Refinements of Adam Smith's ideas in the last two centuries have made explicit the implications of his somewhat inchoate discussion of scarcity. That insight into scarcity has been one of the central contributions of economics to human understanding. It is a major fulcrum around which all economic ideas of the present must be structured.

In economics, scarcity is defined as the availability of means for fulfilling wants that are limited. Means are limited relative to the magnitude of wants. The frequency or infrequency of the existence of something is not alone what makes means scarce. The degree of scarcity is determined by the frequency of availability *relative* to the extent of desires. If there were only ten rotten apples in the world and no one wanted them, they would not be economically scarce. However, if there were a million hard, glassy stone-like items in that world and a desire existed for ten billion of them, those million diamonds could be very scarce indeed, even if the world could get by without any of them.

Significant here is not the arithmetic but the deeper meaning that scarcity has for the moral implications of economizing. Human wants of the world's population are virtually without limit relative to the means of meeting them. Availability of arable land, fresh water, space for waste disposal, appropriate technology, reliable knowledge, medical facilities, skills, diligence, and managerial know-how are desperately scarce when laid against the needs and desires for all of them. Simply stated, humanity does not have the means to produce enough goods and services to satisfy all the desires the world population craves. This is scarcity and it necessitates rationing. Economizing is rationing with the goal of optimizing resulting satisfactions. Put another way, economizing is minimizing costs in the process of maximizing the fulfillment of human desires.

To explain maximizing where there is scarcity, fundamentalist economic theory employs a model of a competitive market which automatically sets prices and organizes efficient production, distribution, and consumption. This competitive model also provides the Western world's dominant philosophy-theory of how a market should be structured to achieve efficiency, justice, freedom, and maximum well-being for all, given the reality of *scarcity*. This theory is intended by its supporters to be a first approximation of the real world market economy. As such, it is perceived to be analogous to a road map, accurate enough to get you there but likely requiring some puzzling over a detour.

AN UNBIASED SCIENCE

The history of economic thought reveals a struggle over what it means to practice a pristine science. The struggle has resulted in an uneasy acceptance that economics can be a science of unbiased explanations of how a market economy functions. In the process of seeking to produce a pristine science a moral philosophy was lost from the soul of the discipline though not necessarily from a moral sense of many practitioners and public ideology.

For the economists qua scientists, the issue of what people choose to consume is not of moral concern. As a scientist the economist may measure the distribution of income but pass no judgment about its fairness. Conventional economists, as a group, enter their profession carrying with them a range of normative diversity, none of which is supposed to influence the objectivity of their economic analysis, measurement, or predictions. Economics is claimed to be a value-free science.

Thus economics itself is directed at the noble purpose of understanding how scarce means can be economized while providing a maximum realization of ends (human preferences). That is the justifiable purpose of the science. It is not the purpose of this standard theory to determine what those ends should be, nor how fairly they are fulfilled.

Conventional theory seeks to identify forces like imperfect competition, near monopolies, and influences external to the market (legal restrictions) which seem to impede production and economizing efficiency. It seeks, also, to develop theories that explain economic instability and theories that explain economic growth, all under conditions of scarcity. Conventional economists, who are hard-headed realists but not necessarily hard-hearted scrooges, assert that scarcity compels the denial of desires. Humankind cannot have all its wishes come true. Some desires of necessity must be foregone. Nature makes it that way. Many suffer severely and some die as a consequence of global scarcity. Regrettable as this is, choices must be made: some will only forego luxury as others suffer severely. Others will do very well in fulfilling their chosen ends. These conditions are the cause for this

work to depart from fundamental theory's normative neutrality and confront scarcity as a moral as well as a technical economic matter.

THE CURSE OF COSTS

The means of meeting human desires are difficult to come by. There are costs involved. It is not their money costs, but their *real* costs, which are of theoretical or philosophical concern for economists. Real costs are the alternatives given up by the world's populace, so that other alternatives may be realized. Unfulfilled alternatives resulting from diverting scarce means (skilled labor, energy, material, technology) to satisfy other ends are the real costs. The more costly each fulfilled choice, the less the fulfillment of other human values, needs or desires. By substituting less scarce means in place of more costly means whenever possible, fewer ends must be relinquished and the economy can provide greater fulfillment of that which is valued.

Economic efficiency enhances the realization of the collective values of the society. It is seen in conventional theory as increasing the wealth of nations and the globe. Evaluating valued alternative ends is not the concern of scientific economics, but it is a concern of this present moral philosophy of economics.

It would appear at first blush that technological progress would increase output and thereby decrease the intensity of scarcity. Thus, it would follow that with continuous technological progress, scarcity would slowly diminish and Karl Marx's fantasy world would ultimately come into being, bringing his halcyon condition: "from each according to his ability; to each according to his needs." There would be no need to coerce economizing. There would emerge true freedom, where everyone would be at liberty to produce and consume without constraint, and Marx's agony of history would have come to an end.

The view that technological progress will diminish the intensity of scarcity is deceptive. Progress certainly does create affluence for its beneficiaries. New technologies doubtlessly do increase both productivity and affluence. But that is not to be confused as an overall diminution of scarcity. In fact, much technological progress may increase the intensity of scarcity. Many new technologies generate new lifestyles with rising expectations, as the history of the automobile demonstrates. More demand for steel, rubber, petroleum, fabrics, paints, highways, and bridges followed the innovation of the automobile. A similar effect follows the application of the miracles of medicine. Increased numbers of the populace live longer, requiring more and better care, which medical know-how and technology make possible. Saving lives is one reason we are now concerned about overpopulation. Conventionally speaking, "wants are insatiable" and new technology generates new desires.

ECONOMIZING-RATIONING

Scarcity makes rationing of means inescapable. Many rationing mechanisms are possible, but not all are desirable. We do fight for a share: to the victor goes the spoils. We queue up and wait: let the prize go to the tenacious. We use the first-come first-served method. Many of us know from experience with public campgrounds about free permits for first arrivals with reserved space once admitted, or seven-day camping, or two-hour parking limits. We use a rationing mechanism like rules-of-the-road, where drivers must choose to drive through congestion or leave earlier or later. We use the elevator, where vertical travel is money-free to the rider but rationed by standing room only, and late arrivals wait for the next opportunity or use an alternative, the stairs.

Competitive examinations, academic records, aptitude tests all to some degree ration enrollment to academies, graduate schools, and prestigious colleges and universities. Finally, a familiar rationing mode is one we have all lived through. It is the family, in which rationing

is done through love and affection, threat and exchange, status and custom, bickering and reconciliation. Scarcity helps make the family a stress-provoking, learning institution.

Adam Smith's followers have theorized that for the vast majority of products and services, the competitive market economy is the mechanism that most efficiently rations scarce means among competing ends. It rations at all phases: from the first allocation of raw means; through organizing production; distributing the output; and finally, conserving in consumption. Prices and revenue-income induce both producers and consumers to ration (economize) their use of virtually everything.

An easily overlooked quality of this economizing phenomenon is that the participating individuals need not be, and likely are not, aware of their role in this grand overall rationing process. Most feel free to make their own choices. Yet each of us is coerced by income and by prices to participate in the rationing process independently of our awareness of our fit in the scheme of things. (Smith referred to this as the "invisible hand.") How now, *in the theory*, do all the participants do all this effectively, though largely inadvertently? They do so, in theory, because they are individual rational maximizers in a system that induces them to do so, though it is (in Smith's words) "no part of their intent." Without awareness, we rationally play our small role in such a way that the whole could not economize the scarce means more efficiently in creating the fullest possible wealth of the populace (given the distribution of income). Consumers, theoretically, shape the quality of wealth through dollar votes in the market.

Prices are scarcity cues in fundamental theory. They quantify the different degrees of relative scarcities among all means. They reflect true costs. They make precise maximum economizing calculations possible. And all this requires that prices be true and accurate measures of real costs and relative scarcity.

How then, in fundamentalist theory, are prices properly formed as true measures of relative scarcity? The answer forms the core of all conventional economics. It is competitive price theory that explains, in detail, how prices are properly formed and how they are rationally applied in economizing scarce means for maximum fulfillment of ends. Accurate scarcity identifying prices are formed by supply and demand in competitive markets where no participant has the power to influence events to his/her own special advantage. Prices are market set and individuals rationally maximize by means of these market-given conditions. The theory of the competitive market provides an image of what the market economy should be, to automatically set prices that would be true measures of relative scarcities.

"ECONOMIC MAN"

A further condition necessary, in fundamentalist theory, for a market to establish prices that are true measures of relative scarcity is that the competitive market must be populated by economic agents who are motivated by gain, and who rationally calculate how to maximize that gain. The Western mind which readily assumes that we think in this fashion was born of an age of consciously-expressed rationalism by thinkers such as Adam Smith. The Western world has enunciated human distinction from other creatures by virtue of our advanced capacity for rational thought. We assert rationality's superiority as a way of knowing and acting. We expect each other to practice such thinking. The rational economic man is assumed to be us. Rational agents calculate maximizing money income, given their talents and resources owned. Rational man also means that, given their incomes and existing prices, they will consume that pattern of goods that will maximize personal satisfaction, whether satisfactions are derived from helping crippled children or being hooked on smoking cigarettes.

Conventional theory is structured and applied on the assumption

that these "economic man" qualities are inherent and operative in everyone's human nature. Those who appear different are maximizing their own unique subjective desires for leisure or the bizarre.

GENERAL EQUILIBRIUM

In this competitive theory, economizing is maximum at every juncture. It gives rise to an ultimate state in which no change can be made in allocation of resources, in combinations of factors in the production process, in quantities or qualities of goods produced, in the distribution of income, in consumption patterns, or in saving-investing-and-growth. That is, no change can be made without reducing the efficiency of the utilization of scarce means and without reducing the satisfaction of consumers' desires.

Although everyone cannot have everything they would like, because scarcity makes that impossible, the market automatically accomplishes the next best feat. Maximum satisfaction is achieved in a world where total satisfaction is impossible. Economists call this achievement "equilibrium," not because it is just, but because the system automatically gravitates to its own maximizing zenith. From the perspective of the application of this fundamental theory, any outside-the-market tampering with either means or ends, or with the natural laws of supply and demand, or with our natural rights, will diminish this automatic maximizing equilibrium.

The completed picture is so magnificent it feels as worthy of admiration as our nation's Constitution. This beautifully constructed competitive theory provides a powerful intellectual foundation to our society's dominant public economic philosophy and ideology. As a result, it serves as a standard behind what people believe to be morally right or wrong about our economic system. Does the evidence support the ideology founded in this theory? The pattern of thought is clearly far more a logical construction than empirical observation warrants.

ECONOMIC IDEOLOGY

Deeply cherished and widely held societal beliefs of how a political or economic system should function form a public philosophy or ideology. Such an ideology provides public support for or against public policy. It is unlikely that a political or economic system could long endure, especially in areas penetrated by the modern age, if there were not an underlying ideology which supplied intellectual, even emotional, support. Ideology is a necessary contributor to social stability. Chaotic, conflict ridden societies lack a uniform persuasive ideology. But an ideology that legitimizes common practices is not necessarily founded in reliable truths or appropriate morality. Much ideology across the globe is founded in dubiously reliable *insights, oversights and illusions.*

The ideas of competitive market theory have profound ideological appeal in the West, and increasingly in nations around the globe. Core ideas explaining the virtues of competition provide theoretical and philosophical bases which support market economy ideology. Further, these ideas legitimate the global spread of free markets. They stand behind efforts to resolve international trade disputes in terms of free trade, open markets, and a "level playing field" for a global economy. This theory is believed, in varying degrees, by most descendants of the Western Enlightenment.

I intend to critique this basic belief system in an effort to winnow out the reliably insightful from the illusory, in order to increase the prospects of successfully coping with the economic problems perceived on the horizon. That said, I am convinced that the West has been a unique and fortunate product of the historical emergence of free societies and political democracies. We have evidence for believing in, and having confidence in, freedom and democracy. Competitive economic theory seems to explain how democratic-like principles function effectively in the free market. Science and rational thought seem to have revealed humanity's dependence on the beneficence and inevitability of the impact of natural laws.

The rise of individualism in the Western world may be contrasted with tribal emphasis upon duty, rigidly prescribed relationships, and traditional expectations. In the West there arose a strong sense of independence and faith in self-reliance. "God helps those who help themselves." Competitive theory seems to explain how this maxim works effectively to create both personal wealth and the wealth of nations. This general climate of opinion is a fertile environment for the ideas of competitive market theory to grow powerful in our public ideology. Both the theory, and especially the ideology, are buttressed by persuasive and appealing argument and selective evidence.

To be adaptive in this era of dramatic and costly change, it is well to know how and why we believe as we do. In spite of my belief in its past moral superiority, as a totality competitive market theory is neither fully true nor morally adequate. Its appeal, however, is based on evidence as clear as watching the sun go around the earth. That is, the theory is ultimately based on a logical illusion constructed out of observed "truths." Introspection, discussions with friends, sources of public information, and economics education, all lead us to accept competitive market theory as gospel truth. Its evidence and appeal are powerfully persuasive.

THE APPEAL OF SMITHIAN ECONOMICS

The Realism of Scarcity

Those who reflect on global economies know we cannot all have all we would like. The concept of scarcity makes sense to us, because it realistically faces a fact of our individual lives, and provides an explanation of the need for an efficient and comparatively fair rationing system. It seems more humanitarian for everyone to have all they need, but not enough exists for that, if expectations are the quality of life seen in affluent nations. Thus a rationing system is unavoidable. The market mechanism deals with this rationing reality and appears, among affluent Westerners, to do so in a fairly equitable, free, efficient, and workable way. But there are serious moral questions about the well-being of the rest of humanity, as well as substantial portions of the West. Regrettably, the hardships the great majority of humanity suffers as a result of scarcity cannot be eliminated with good intentions alone. No matter how honorable or humane the idealistic goals, the directions taken must fit within the reality of economic scarcity and the natural processes necessary to turn good intentions to good account.

As an example, commercial advertising does not weigh the larger consequences of scarcity. As one of its functions, advertising conditions the public to the flow of innovations. It does so independently of their contributions to human well-being. Advertising also increases desires and hence intensifies scarcity. This is an inherent pathology of actual market competition. Defenders of these commercial practices assert that expanded demand for a product results in "economies of scale" (in production) and hence lower prices. Here again the cumulative nature of technological innovations is neglected as a major causal force and commercial activities are given first-order creative credit. Such issues must eventually be confronted in the development of this moral philosophy of economics. Tragically, given the challenges the world faces, the prospects for reducing the severity of general scarcity seem dim indeed, in spite of areas of hope. There is a profound need that advertisers' capacity to persuade be directed to more moral purposes.

The Appeal of Logic

Competitive theory and its ideology possess a persuasive logic. The logic is tight and convincing. It has been refined over more than two hundred years of analytical fine-tuning. But it is convincing only if its foundational presuppositions are accepted as virtually the exclusive determining forces which generate Western economic achievements. This means placing virtually exclusive emphasis on self-interest in human nature as the means of making our market economies successful. Oversights are crucial here. Overlook the long history of technology, neglect the puzzle-posing problem-solving qualities of human nature, bypass the inherent bonding qualities behind social cooperation, accept the assumptions of competitive economic theory as exclusive forces determining the wealth of nations, and the logic of competitive theory seems unassailable.

The Appeal of Evidence

Competitive market economies clearly have been more successful than traditional or command economies. Western economies are the economic envy of much of the world. Historical evidence of the success of free markets can be correlated with the rise of democracy, freedom, and unmatched standards of living. But is the free market the necessary cause of these achievements, or a facilitating condition? The evidence also reveals that the successful still face the challenges of the plight of the mass of humanity as well as a threatening future for our descendants.

The Appeal of Human Nature

Competitive market theory comports well with human nature, as we experience living in the Western world. We know economic man by introspection. We think and feel that we must compete and get ahead in order to live well. We know him/her by observing others. We see the orientation in behavior and hear it in comments. We all recognize it is human nature to like more of the good things, with less work attached to getting them. We want to be free to apply our talents and resources in ways most rewarding to ourselves, to take the job or do the work we like best. We prefer higher incomes over lesser. We know we like to have free choice in the market to buy what we like. We prefer more for our money, than less. We prefer to decide for ourselves how to use what we see as *our* income and *our* money. We prefer not to have a bureaucratic state making decisions for us. We earned it. We believe we deserve it. This self-interested, rational individual questing to get more by getting ahead is at the center of competitive theory, energizing and directing the entire market system.

These desires to live well and free are not an impediment to our humanitarian sentiments. We know that in our private lives we are more altruistic and not so miserly as Scrooge. We are privately motivated by more than money. Rather, we know we can express a variety of humanitarian sentiments in our own way, and to whatever extent we are capable. Thus, we know we are basically decent people and caring of others. We embrace these qualities as individual virtues to be encouraged in our children. They have been described by Robert Bellah as "habits of the heart."

All these qualities, including self-reliance through an honest income, coexisting with altruism, are the human nature we think we know and cherish. But do all these fine qualities assure us of a proper path of progress into the future?

The Appeal of Efficiency

It is widely "known" and vigorously defended by public ideology, that a major virtue of competition is "efficiency." This is widely believed even though most people have never heard the professional arguments of competitive market theorists that, under scarcity, the market will automatically reach the pinnacle of economic efficiency at general equilibrium. In fact, the public ideology is free to interpret efficiency rather loosely, as long as the economy gets us what we are accustomed to expect. In general it seems to do this; perhaps we in the West who have prospered even get a bit more than many might have expected.

Ideology is confirmed. But is it efficient to fail to empower the masses of underutilized humans around the globe?

The Appeal of Beneficent Natural Laws as Governors

It is widely assumed in the West that the market economy functions efficiently in response to a natural order, governed by natural laws. The rightness and inevitability of natural laws is a belief so subtle in our Western psyches that we scarcely realize how implicitly we invoke the idea. Like inalienable rights, these natural laws are just there; we all know it. They are self-evident truths. We know, covertly but certainly, that they provide orderly organization for the economy, tend to induce substantial employment of people and resources, and guarantee freedom of natural rights for society's members. The more successful we are, the more confidently we know that natural laws of economics are beneficent. How else would all these good things happen in free market economies? Certainly not by state imposed rules or planning.

The market, we affluent Westerners believe, is socially beneficial because it is both efficient and just. It provides maximum possible goods and services, at the lowest possible prices and least sacrifices, under conditions of reciprocal justice where rewards equal contributions. Therefore, if the economy seems not to work out that way, some group must be erroneously interfering with the natural rights of freedom, or the natural laws of supply and demand. Labor unions and their policies have transgressed nature itself. Large corporations are unnatural giants stepping out of the small scale, natural competitive order. Labor and corporations have a natural right to be free but not so powerful. Meddling politicians, too, are evil, or naive enough to think they can improve on nature's natural order by imposing rules where nature knows best. They play God and tinker with His natural laws of the market. But on occasion, things seem to go drastically wrong, and we think something ought to be done about it because there is evil in the world. How best to deal with these issues? That is the present quest.

The Appeal of Automaticity

The free market automatically performs its multimillions of complex tasks, tasks which have baffled and defeated all efforts of large-scale socialist planned economies. Little wonder our ideology communicates that it is undesirable for governments to impose restraints on this natural economic order, which the theory demonstrates to be efficient and just, as well as automatic. That which planners are demonstrably incapable of achieving, the market does superlatively by doing it automatically. Thus, it is not only unnecessary to impose government rules; doing so is a detrimental interference with an efficient, just and natural automatic mechanism. We will later look closer at this belief, as it may well be, in part, structured on illusions.

The Appealing Promise of Maximum Economic Growth

Public economic ideology accepts as true that maximum growth is automatically guaranteed if the economy is left to its natural laws. This is the case if governments do not tax away the source of savings, investing, capital expansion, and hence the means of economic growth.

This appears true, at least to those in positions of power, because of the following logical linkages. The rate and quality of economic growth are determined by sovereign consumer preferences. If some preferred goods are purchased in increased quantities, the prices and profits in these industries rise. Entrepreneurs offer higher interest rates in payment for money capital, in order to install real capital to meet the rising demands and to gain premium profits from these industries. The increased goods are there to be purchased because saving makes growth in capital formation and greater output possible. We automatically register and achieve, through the market, the growth we want.

We must not tax away the source of savings from the incomes of the rich, otherwise we kill the goose that lays the golden eggs.

The Appeal of Progress

Growth is progress. Not only is there more, there is better. Better is judged by consumers' increased satisfactions. Consumers' desires are subjective preferences, objectified in market demand. In response to demand, preferred new products are produced. Those products less desired are rejected in the market. Hence only the preferred goods and services proliferate. The economy produces and sells cars rather than buggies. The less desirable products decline. The quality of progress is thus assessed and determined automatically, naturally, and democratically by market vote.

Is growth necessarily progress, and if perceived as such, is that "progress" human betterment? Does the traditional real market, or the competitive utopian market, answer this question? The analysis unfolding here is that neither does. A moral philosophy to direct economic progress to humanitarian betterment is a desperate practical necessity. There is where this quest is headed.

The Appeal of Distributive Justice

Reciprocity—the exchange of equal for equal, quid pro quo, tit for tat, or an eye for an eye—appears to be a universal expectation, among all peoples, regardless of their culture. Only the content, structures, and criteria of that equality differ. It dominates our sense of economic justice.

In the Western world, as it modernized from medieval society, the church and guilds lost control over determination of the just price. So how, now, does our economic ideology determine whether an economy is providing justice? Ideologically, we know a just price is set by supply and demand in a competitive market where none of the parties have power to influence price to their own advantage. Here a reciprocally fair and just exchange arises automatically. The competitive market sets the prices of factors of production where their payments equal their contribution to production. This tendency of natural forces to gravitate toward homeostasis achieves a natural reciprocity equilibrium.

My father always answered prospective employees when they asked what he would pay them: "I'll pay you what you're worth." And my Irish mother regularly reminded us: "fair is fair." Competitive theory says this is so. You earn your own way, are paid what you are worth, and live within your means. Fair is fair.

The Appeal of Rights and Freedom

We of the West know we have a natural right to freedom. Public ideology tells us so. That is why America celebrates the Fourth of July. Competitive economic theory logically proves that our rights and freedoms are provided and protected by a market economy. Consumers are sovereign in the market as they are in the polity. Private incomes empower the freedom to influence political outcomes. Market freedom and political freedom are mutually dependent. They actualize the exercise of natural rights. But is the *powerlessness* articulated in competitive theory matched in the marketplace and in the polity?

REASSESSING THE UTOPIAN MYTH

Avalanche-like social change challenges all societies around the globe. Changes are inevitable. History is not likely to have reached a permanent Nirvana just as we got aboard. The big questions are those of understanding the system, the forces that change it, and of inventing and implementing a reliable moral philosophy to guide humanity successfully through an unknown future. Conventional economic ideas and ideological beliefs are guideposts that seem to have served the West well. They are not to be qualified or modified lightly. But neither are they sacred writ.

My argument is that the history of economic thought and public ideology has, with noble intent, created a utopian myth by which we try to assess the success of our attempts to seek the nature and causes of the wealth of all nations. If this competitive model is a theory and philosophy substantially out of touch with the world as it is, how then are we to assess economies? And how are we to resolve issues in theory, in moral philosophy and in practice? The argument I have been making throughout is that competitive economic theory has become a benchmark of economic effectiveness.

But economic self-interest does not adequately address the world's problems. Neither the democratic one-man-one-vote, nor the dollar-weighted economic vote, necessarily correct recognized wrongs or potential threats to humanity's well-being.

When rational reform must be contemplated, as in environmental protection or monetary and fiscal stabilization policies, the public's ideological support of the free market economy often takes precedence over public well-being. Reform proposals run counter to the following kinds of arguments: it will curtail growth, be inefficient, create unemployment, generate inflation, deprive us of our rights, and hurt the poor. Seldom in the public debates surrounding public policy proposals is it asserted that protecting individual self-interests or special privileges of power are the primary concern.

The insight that the competitive economy is the source of Western success can be accepted as a logical truth only by giving the market virtually exclusive credit for the achievements of a larger, dynamic culture. The cumulative character of knowledge and technology must be overlooked or discounted as a major positive force. Our treasure of natural resources must be slighted. We must also discount our national character of workmanship, honesty, questioning, and cooperation as an important factor in that success. They must be emphasized and preserved.

Further, for the narrow interpretation that the natural laws of the competitive market are the primary source of the wealth of Western nations, the historical evidence of the role of a stable and contributing national state must be neglected. Recall that Adam Smith advised us of the occasional necessity for the crown to provide infrastructure. His foresight has been manifest in publicly provided assistance to the competitive market with public works such as canals, harbors, docking facilities, public education, land-grant colleges, aid to railroads, research of many kinds, and public-private facilities such as a central banking system. Easily overlooked, also, is government's costly role in providing and protecting the institution of private property.

Under conditions of freedom and private property power we face moral issues concerning the well-being of humanity, now and into the future. Are the ends being "maximized" rationally chosen or morally defensible? It is a very basic moral issue for a book in search of a moral philosophy of economics to raise the question as to whether the social objective of an economy should be that of maximizing consumers' satisfaction, as expressed through the market. The market may or may not result in the best moral outcome. Farmers may produce cancer contributing tobacco, use rent and profit incomes to lobby legislators to preserve competitive market freedom that maximizes consumers' (smokers') satisfactions. They might even go further and obtain subsidies that provide "parity" incomes that support them with a standard of living appropriate to preserving the family farmers' valued way of life. This is, of course, stepping out of the bounds of conventional competition and should not be done from the perspective of that theory. However, it is done, and is very covertly justified by beliefs based in our obsession with status rights derived from medieval ghosts in our ideological closets.

For the well-being of humanity, thoughtful people must construct a moral philosophy that will provide practical guidance for directing change in ways that will rely on accurate insights, identify oversights and discard illusions. Consider the following cases of "market failures."

MARKET FAILURES

Competitive price theory can be counted among the major insights founded in Western philosophy, but its profound relevance must not mislead us to ignore its oversights, even illusions. Since the inception of this theory, some economists have recognized that too much can be expected of the organizing capacities of free competitive markets. Markets fail. They fail to automatically meet important social expectations; fail to adequately serve human needs that the existing production processes might very well be able to provide. These failures have been an immediate cause of human agony throughout modern history and some have been severe enough to threaten entire economic and political systems.

Competitive theory and its economic ideology have proven inadequate to deal with substantial real world occurrences such as depressions or poverty in the shadow of conspicuous display. Reality has forced us to rethink economic policies in order to come to terms with these market failures. This is so whether those failures are caused by internal market deficiencies, external "acts of God," or the inadequacies, innocence, or evils of individual participants.

Market Failure: Crises of Economic Instability

Markets' failures to provide economic stability (full employment of equipment and labor) have haunted the West at least since markets emerged out of medieval tradition-bound economies. The history of the competitive market is one of periodic disasters identified as economic crises, general gluts, or depressions. There have been agonizing periods of massive unemployment, epidemic bankruptcies, and monumental losses of output, with tragic denials of human needs while idle industries, labor and resources stood available to be put to work.

One early-day puzzle poser, reflecting on past unemployment crises, tried to comprehend how the economy did as well as it did. Decades prior to Adam Smith's *Wealth of Nations*, Bernard Mandeville, in *Fable of the Bees*, suggested an explanation with the startling message that private vice was public virtue. This was so, he asserted, because the private virtue of parsimony and saving diminished total demand for goods and services. Neither land nor labor could be put to their full use. Fortunately, Mandeville said, private vice—luxurious expenditures by the idle rich—achieves the public virtue of putting this land and labor to work. The non-productive landed aristocracy gave work to the needy poor.

This explanation of a stabilizing vice by the idle landed aristocracy was not exactly satisfying to the Enlightenment. It was not at all appealing to growing democratic thought or the rising commercial class. Without explicitly speaking to unemployment, Adam Smith nonetheless explained how economic stability would be brought about automatically. "What is annually saved is as regularly consumed as what is annually spent, and nearly in the same time too; but it is consumed by a different set of people." Savings, that is, are re-channeled from consumer use to investment use.

Jean Baptiste Say, writing in the early years of the nineteenth century, argued that full employment was automatic. Supply, he explained, creates its own demand. Clearly to Say, people produce only because they desire income for consuming. And they save because entrepreneurs pay interest in order to obtain money to invest in capital formation for profit. Thus there is no glut created by savings, and full employment is guaranteed—automatically. With the passage of a century these ideas of beneficent natural laws became part of public ideology. The multitude believed that instability was a temporary condition, during which all prices re-equilibrated to a general full employment equilibrium.

The world's experience has been devastatingly different. History is replete with economic crises. Indifferent to the ideological certainty that markets automatically tend to full employment, the Great Crash of 1929 struck. The twentieth century's infamous economic collapse was followed by more than a decade of the Great Depression. It was a human disaster. Statistics are bloodless when compared with the personal reports, eyewitness accounts, and personal experiences (which caused your author to study economics). There were virtually no double income couples at that time, where at least one parent might earn a paltry depression wage. This was before unemployment compensation or social security. Banking and business bankruptcies were personal tragedies for everyone. Depositors' lifetime savings were lost in bank closings. Conscientious men returned to their families from job hunting weeping because they were unable to provide housing, clothing, food, or health care for the ones they loved. They had no place in the sun. They felt inadequate, unworthy, unwanted, and rejected. Eventually they saw no hope. Their ideology as the breadwinner was so sacred a belief that the fault of their failure was felt as a sin on their souls. It was not uncommon for individuals with advanced degrees from prestigious universities to feel fortunate to have a job driving a taxi or clerking. I once hired a mature man with a Yale degree to temporarily clerk vegetables in my father's store for $15 a week. It helped feed his family.

In fact, economic crises were both catastrophes of theory and of public policy throughout an entire century and through the Great Depression. In spite of the evidence before them, economists believed all along that such vast economic failures could not last. Say's Law of Markets told them so. The logic of theory reassured lawmakers, the public and theory itself, that what was happening was about to gravitate back to a full employment general equilibrium. Automatically. "Prosperity," the unemployed were told, "was just around the corner." Natural laws work that way. Full employment maximizing equilibrium was the norm toward which economic laws caused the economy to gravitate.

Conventional theory dominated. Yet serious crises of unemployment have historically threatened the very existence of "free" markets, governments and capitalism. The twentieth century in the Western world reacted with waves of socialism, communism, fascism, and all manner of ideological radicalism. The brutal and bizarre movements of German fascism, the Nazi Party, and its ultimate military aggression arguably owes its rampage largely (certainly not exclusively) to the economic instability and insecurities of the time.

But economics like other areas has its brilliant minds that dare to think differently. In 1942 the English economist John Maynard Keynes (1883–1946) published *The General Theory of Employment, Interest and Money*. He dismissed competitive theory's assumption that the market tended to equilibrate automatically at full employment. He provided, instead, an explanation of the causes of economic instability and the periodic crises that threatened capitalism. He proposed policy correctives to the causal conditions as well. To do so, he had to demonstrate the inadequacy of prevailing competitive market theory and its practices, as they relate to the problem of unemployment.

He began by noting that "classical" theory *logically* shows an automatic tendency to a full employment equilibrium. But, he argued, the reasoning is inadequate for the "general" case. That is, the theory of the time was inadequate to understand the *system* as a *totality* which rises and falls as a whole.

As we move into the twenty first century, the world is threatened by economic circumstances and market failures that may prove far more disastrous than the Great Depression and more difficult to solve.

Market Failure: The Environment and Externalities

Seeing the market as an extremely useful social instrument that can contribute to human betterment is prudent. Expecting it to perform effectively without deliberate human guidance is sheer folly. We face market failures other than instability and unemployment. They must be confronted with theoretical and philosophical understanding and practical solutions.

As with the illusion of sun circling the earth, we face another distorted vision of reality. Prices do not automatically reflect all costs. The free market does not and cannot cope with the depletion of the environment automatically. The grave threat here is that competitive theory and its public ideology have (covertly at least) a "nature-knows-best" philosophy, based upon the illusion of beneficent natural laws favoring mankind. Thus, it has been assumed for a couple of centuries that markets have been responsibly managing our economic affairs. Perhaps even more likely, and certainly as dangerous, is the possibility that many costs, external to the market but in the long run harmful to the economy, have in fact been overlooked. This happens notwithstanding any assumptions about markets and with or without anybody monitoring or being in charge.

It has happened in economies with central planners in charge as well as in market managed economies. Awareness and sufficient understanding of our relations with our natural habitat is a long-run first-order necessity. Protecting the environment to protect people requires setting rules. Some rules must be "absolute" prohibitions, such as protecting the ozone that protects our climate. Other environmental costs we may be forced to live with and absorb slowly, such as the impact of continental drift. Still other environmental costs, such as depletion of oxygen-restoring forests, may best be corrected by legally forced internalization of money costs that tilt the price system in ways that save the oxygen-generating trees.

Markets, properly constructed, may be one of the most effective mechanisms for organizing the continuous process of adapting our human niche in the natural environment. This adapting involves constant coping with scarcity, and markets have proven their capacity to coerce rationing (economizing). They must now be called upon to coordinate human dependence on nature's environment by corrective coercion of human nature's sometimes wayward ways. And it must be accepted that corrective action must take place under conditions of very uncertain probabilities and equally uncertain assessment of the magnitudes of future costs.

In the long run, conserving the environment, and using it appropriately as an Essential Economic resource, seems certain to become one of humanity's greatest challenges. The environment is essential to every physiological, social and economic endeavor. Environmental misuse is inevitably costly to the Essential Economy and to the wellbeing of humanity. However, environmental pollution costs are either totally neglected or inadequately registered, *automatically*, in prices. Such costs are identified in economics as "market externalities" and referred to as "social costs." They are external to the price system's automatic control. Many future environmental costs are likely beyond our current capability to calculate precisely. By no means are such costs external to the functioning of the essential real economy. They are real costs to society.

Because such costs borne by the operating economy fail to show up in a timely fashion as money costs, there are inadequate price cues to guide or coerce the unwary, the indifferent, or the irresponsible. This not only creates a high order of economic inefficiency, it can become another human disaster if adequate global steps are not timely taken.

Regrettably, concerns for the environment are often concerns with uncertain cause or consequence, uncertain magnitudes, and uncertain correctives. Therefore, the impact on the preservation of our present and future habitat lies outside present means of market money measurement. This leaves potential monumental problems outside well established rules that govern both market and public fiscal management of the economy. This lack of measurable specificity tragically provides individual rationality a basis to justify inadequate action. Yet there is no way the real economy, as distinct from the market price sys-

tem that guides it, can resist internalizing the true costs and reaping the destructive consequences.

Our individual economic rationality of minimizing money costs and maximizing money incomes resists internalizing external costs into the price system. Consumers who are rationally maximizing their satisfactions purchased by their limited incomes fail to internalize these external costs because the rationing cues (prices) are incapable of automatically identifying and predicting consequences of externalities. Thus environmental, social, and future detrimental consequences of present consumption decisions have no automatic corrective feedback in the market.

Consumers, as citizens, resist introducing true costs into the market, either because of the illusion of individual autonomy, narrow self-interests or ignorance of the implications. Individual businesses, rationally but irresponsibly, respond by the self-interested logic that added costs increase prices, reduce sales and profits, and create unemployment in their sector. Exactly. These are the kinds of things the price system should do to economize scarce environmental means. The resultant unemployed labor and other factors of production must be shifted, preferably by the market, to production of products less costly (destructive) to the environment and hence to long-run societal benefit.

Our language already possesses common sense aphorisms for confronting future uncertainties: "better to be safe than sorry" and "a stitch in time saves nine." Stated more academically, under conditions of uncertainty, the market must be designed with strategies that will reduce the probabilities of human disasters and will provide morally meaningful direction for humanity's lifetime cooperation with nature's unforgiving laws.

More Market Failures: Pathologies of Competition

Further bad news about a competitive market is that winning in the market often pushes Adam Smith's moral sentiment of self-interest to the point of pathology. Smith was well aware of the trader's penchant for conspiring against the consumer, but he saw the corrective for this anti-social behavior to be competition. This insight involved an oversight. It overlooked the possibility that competition itself can have pathological consequences. It also failed to recognize that the stringent conditions for theoretical competition did not and certainly cannot now exist because of the nature of the underlying industrial processes. This need not mean that the pluralism associated with competition should be eliminated. Instead, free, unfettered acts of competition must be modified to serve the public interest as well as private profit. Briefly put, the competitive market itself has inadequate monitoring mechanisms or feedback devices to correct wayward practices.

Competition turns out to be a two-edged sword. One side contributes to the unparalleled success of Western market managed economies. The other side is a pattern of pathologies with which most of us are familiar. For example, competitive advertisers can engage in deception or induce bizarre consumption, such as women's "sophisticated" steps to smoking cigarettes, excessive alcohol use, dangerous speeding in prestigious fast cars, children hooked on sugared breakfast cereals, and the like. It is instructive to note posters in malls designed to discourage teenage pregnancies. The message is surrounded by shops that advertise the wares that tantalize the practice that brings about pregnancy.

Perhaps it is true that in competitive sports, winning isn't everything, it's the only thing; but not so in some segments of economies. There, winning can be losing if the competitive market is the only referee. Salmon fishing in Alaskan waters became so efficiently competitive that winners started to destroy everyone's source of success, including their own, by eliminating the supply of salmon. To preserve a supply of salmon Alaska has created protective rules. Any fisherman with a winning-is-the-only-thing philosophy, who transgresses the explicit rules, is denied the right to continue fishing. The fish are preserved to be rationed in turn by the price system to all salmon lovers who are willing and able to pay the price. Both salmon and market rationing of this delicacy are preserved. But not automatically.

Pathologies of competition are increasingly global in scope. No longer is socialism or communism the center of international concern. No longer is the cry "kill a commie for Christ," but instead, may the best capitalism win. Rather than a military metaphor of fighting an economic war, we have a sports metaphor of a level playing field among all competitive economies. Competitive price theory is ill equipped to explain how freely competing economies over the globe are to be persuaded or coerced to establish and meet very practical, humane objectives. There are severe pressures to reduce money costs of production, or fail in the competitive race for international economic survival in the modern competitive mercantilism environment.

These competitive pressures contribute to the neglect of the natural environment, the maintenance of rain forests and control of acid rain, workplace safety, the welfare of low paid child labor and low status women, low wages and long work weeks, and avoidance of the money costs of unemployment compensation, retirement benefits, and medical insurance. International competition, among competitively managed market economies, leads to an advantage for the less humanitarian policies. Modern mercantilism threatens to repeat the horrors of the working conditions of the Industrial Revolution and its accompanying competitive global market conquests.

Instead of evangelizing religious sectarianism (the Crusades and more recent missionaries) the West is evangelizing democracy and competitive market economies. This may very well be another moral step forward. However, these global movements must be carefully monitored by constant philosophical inquiry into the nature and causes of the well-being of humanity. Much will depend upon how effectively modern technology, democracy, and competitive markets are adapted within other cultural and natural environments. Much will also depend upon how clearly we of the West understand the sources of our own successes and the moral quality of that success. And much will depend upon recognizing the role of rules in correcting "free" markets' pathologies.

The point of these observations is to reflect on the possibilities of illusionary justice in competitive theory. We are not in a world of divine rights of kings, owners, entrepreneurs, or CEOs. We are in a world of rules of man's own making. To be just, the rules should make lives more worth living. We can remake those rules to make living less costly and less precarious under conditions of change.

In an effort to think rationally about achieving economic well-being for humanity, we are inadvertently confused by quite common illusions.

ILLUSIONS

We are already familiar with our capacity to rationally perceive illusions as reality. A flat earth and the sun going around it was a conspicuously reasonable theory, but none the less it was an illusion. Economic illusions may well be more common than we suspect. Without contending that the following are total and proven illusions, I use them to illustrate how probable illusions may be.

Money and Other Economic Illusions

Consider a current money illusion: the expressed horror of national debt. Public ideology tends to say that national debt borders on being evil. It is often illustrated with a cartoon of a stooped man carrying a burden on his shoulders that is about to do him in. However, economists say sometimes it's bad policy, sometimes not. Whether it is bad or good to run a national debt is not determined by the fact of the debt, just as sinning is not determined by the fact of sex. In both cases, being good or being bad is determined by the circumstances and consequences. If interest rate and money supply policy fail to provide full employment, then a nation suffering severe unemployment must not allow itself to be haunted by the national debt illusion. We do not normally apply the "no debt" principle to businesses, as it would deprive them of a major means to capital formation, growth and possible progress. The same is true for individuals needing to borrow to obtain career education. At the national level, debt may well be necessary to borrow a nation's way out of depressions, build a military establishment to fight or prevent wars, cope with national disasters such as hurricanes, earthquakes, tornadoes, or massive banking failures.

The government prints our money supply and I have a twenty dollar bill here to prove it. But reflecting on the role of the banking system in creating our money supply should dispense with this widespread illusion that our money supply is printed in Washington. (Our *cash* supply is minted, yes.)

The Keynesian analysis has exposed yet another economic illusion: that the supply and demand for savings is equilibrated by the market-set interest rate and this guarantees that full employment prosperity is automatically achieved.

There is the "give me the facts" illusion. But the facts require theoretical interpretation and normative evaluation. This observation does not deprecate facts. It does suggest that theory and philosophy are essential to evaluate the meaning of the facts. There is certainly the illusion that when the national income dollar data rises, and we view statistical measures of assumed economic growth, that the economy really is experiencing economic growth. More illusionary still is the sense that increasing national income means economic progress. Although increases in sales, labor's income, and profits are generated by the need to clean up after tornadoes, hurricanes, forest fires, floods, urban fires, earthquakes, auto accidents, epidemics, and the like, surely these do not contribute to either economic growth or progress. They are desirable correctives, but interpreting the resulting increase in national income data as growth or progress is an illusion.

A familiar illusion is the political statement that "we can't afford it." That's an analysis stopper. Again, it depends. It frequently depends on our priorities or commitments, not simply on total accessible funds and facilities but whether they should be prioritized differently.

Prices as Precise Quantitative Illusions

We must not lose sight of a terribly important unverifiable presupposition that lends substantial (probably unwarranted) weight to competitive theory. There is no known way of demonstrating that if prices were set in a utopian competitive market they would establish *true* measures of relative scarcity. The idea is an element in a logically constructed utopian myth. It is not a perversity limited to economics, but it is especially dangerous for economic policies, as the discipline is frequently perceived to be scientifically-mathematically solid.

Prices appear to have a quantitative precision that is meaningful when they are added, subtracted or multiplied. Indeed they can be so manipulated. Prices are so perceived because they appear to measure precisely meaningful quantities. Indeed we individuals are foolhardy not to check our bank balances, paychecks, interest rate on our mortgage, and so forth. Because money is quantifiable we face the tempting illusion that money prices have similar precision for managing the market economy. Because money has the institutionalized power to make claims on the output of the real economy, it creates an illusion that money is the source of that wealth (an echo of the mercantilist illusion that a nation's wealth depends on its accumulation of bullion).

Does a worker's wage (price of labor) provide a mathematically accurate measure of the just price for the work performed? Is a fair wage a price that measures the value the worker adds to the value of the product? Is an accurate measure of the exchange value of a worker's contribution to output also a true measure of the relative scarcity of the worker's skill? Or does the wage rate reflect the power of the corporation, or the bargaining power of the worker's union? Are the products in the market fairly priced at their cost? Do they measure the scarcities of goods and provide mathematically precise cues by which we accurately maximize in the economizing process? Or is price a precise number of an illusionary quality, or quantity, of a presumed concrete meaning that is nonexistent? What is the monetary value of the use of the book I check out of the library (or borrow from a friend) for free?

Prices, expressed mathematically, appear to represent phenomena that are as clear, absolute, concrete, precise, and accurate as the quantitative notations by which they are presented. This is another illusion. Competitive theory and ideology tend to sanctify market prices, thus putting them outside the reach of deliberate modifications that should improve the wealth of nations and well-being of their citizens. (Examples: Taxing gasoline to ration it more stringently for posterity, requiring that wages and fringe benefits be adequate to make life at least minimally livable.)

THE FAILURES OF THEORY

Flaws in theory can be terribly destructive of human well-being. Theoretical flaws have led to human sacrifices to please the gods, the Inquisition, the trial and conviction of Galileo, and the spectacle of communist-baiting U.S. Senator Joe McCarthy. Mistaken theorizing has resulted in tragic delays in finding and managing solutions to the disasters of economic depressions. It is difficult to live with theories and impossible to live without them.

Given their vulnerability to illusions and the inevitability that insights will suffer oversights, we should consider our theory-shaped beliefs with respectful caution. Reflecting on the past inadequacies of competitive theory as a policy guide, and the unreliability of the market in automatically providing humanitarian beneficence, it seems incumbent on a philosophy of economics that it examine this theoretical touchstone skeptically, though certainly not with hostility nor out-of-hand rejection.

It seems unnecessary to belabor further the failures of market managed economies that, so conspicuously, have served far better than any other managed economies. However, much more analysis is essential to formulate means of improving humanitarian economic well-being.

CONCLUSION

In spite of market failures and competitive pathologies, there are underlying processes an effective market can manage relatively well. Roughly established market prices can serve as cues that coerce rationing of scarce means. Private property contributes to pluralism and creative adaptability. A monetized market is a necessary mechanism for effective management of any modern economy. However, competitive theory as an explanation of automatic success of the market in managing the economy, in spite of its fruitful insights, suffers serious theory deficiencies and distortions. It creates a logical illusion that the market is the economy, that it is efficient, fair, and dependable as a guide into the future. An analysis of market failures, externalities, and pathologies puts an end to the illusion that humanity can rely exclusively on competitive market theory as an explanation of the causes of the wealth of nations.

There are understandable reasons why competitive theory, as with social theory in general, encounters such difficulties. In part the reasons are in the very nature of social theorizing itself. We will examine such complications in the following chapters where we will rethink economic theory. The aim is to construct a more reliable, less illusion-haunted moral foundation to guide our economic thinking and practices. However, we, too, are not above oversights and illusions.

5

The Essential Economy
and a Workable Market

Western economies conquered some of the problems left over from the power and rigidities of mercantilism by liberating markets and technology from inappropriate rules dedicated to inappropriate purposes (such as restraining trade to accumulate bullion for the crown, as if it were wealth for the nation). However, these freer markets have failed at times to adequately organize economic production to meet serious needs of the society, or even to meet needs of the production process itself.

Many assume that Adam Smith had demonstrated the total lack of a constructive role for government anywhere in economics. That is not entirely so, for "According to the system of natural liberty, the sovereign has only three duties to attend to. . . ." They are the defense of country, the administration of justice, and the maintenance of certain public works. These he considered "plain and intelligible common understandings."

Neither theory nor philosophy from Smith explain how "plain and intelligible common understandings" identify that there is some intensity of public purpose that needs to be met, even if the market does not automatically call it forth. Smith had to have recognized (or covertly assumed) that there are logical technical necessities for an economy to function effectively. In spite of Smith's insights, he seriously neglected the role and needs of technologies interlocking with humanity and nature. Instead, he focused on labor, the division of labor and market exchanges. He emphasized the important role of the market in *managing* this essential production-consumption-production linkage. But he neglected theoretical analysis of that more fundamental essential process that links labor, know-how, technology, resources, and consumption. Thus he neglected what will be called here the **Essential Economy**, without which there would be no economy for the market to manage.

THE ESSENTIAL ECONOMY

As there is no well developed theory and philosophy of the Essential Economy upon which a public ideology might have been melded into our daily lives, I seek to vivify its qualities and implications. A distinction must be made between the essential forces operative in the real economy and the power system managing those essential forces. It is like the distinction between the technological operation of a car and the owning, perhaps loaning, of that car. That is, it is imperative to distinguish the causes of the wealth of nations from how those causes are owned and managed. The *basic causes* of the wealth of nations and well-being of individuals are the functioning elements of the Essential Economy. The *managing mechanism* is the "workable market."

Smith, at least covertly, must have assumed the nature of an Essential Economy and based his sense of the system's needs on some form of tool-like network, an "instrumental" or "techno-logic" activity. What there is, is a cause-and-effect interdependence, an ecology-like mutual dependence of essential technical linkages necessary to make the economic system work. Build no lighthouses, and ships crash on the rocks while trying to find their way into harbor. Certainly the lighthouse is a public purpose need, knowable by an instrumental relationship. By the same techno-logic, we human participants in the economy need food, health care, knowledge and training to contribute effectively to production, distribution and consumption. Thus, Smith's contributions could be both profoundly important and seriously inadequate to explain the nature and causes of the wealth of nations.

The Essential Economy is the *first-order cause* of the wealth of nations. It includes the fundamental technology-driven production processes. The private-property market system is the *second-order cause* of the wealth of nations. Both perform necessary functions.

The basic, first-order cause, the Essential Economy, is that pattern of cause-effect that links technology, knowledge, skills, values, and resources necessary to get the job done. That means getting the products and services out and into the hands of producers and consumers, who need them to maintain and enhance their contribution to the success of the economy, including the well-being of its participants. The Essential Economy does the actual work of producing real goods and services, getting them distributed for real capital formation (as distinct from portfolio assets accumulation) and distributes goods and services for necessary consumption (as distinct from distributing money income) to enable the continuing work of creating and producing. The Essential Economy functions through the contributions of nature, labor skills, technology-knowledge, and organizing-managing skills, which are the prime causes of the wealth of nations.

As noted, the Essential Economy is critically dependent upon knowledge and technology. Knowledge of technology tells us what our options are for producing the output that becomes the source of national well-being. Without these knowledge-skill-technological options, there is no output. It is in this sense that the Essential Economy is seen as the first-order cause of the wealth of nations and the private property-monetized market is seen as the second-order cause.

The Essential Economy may be further visualized as that aspect of a society where individuals, technology-knowledge and environment are mutually linked like the parts of an effective machine, or a complex living organism, or an ecological system. Elements of the Essential Economy must be mutually networked in a functional way for it to produce effectively. There are activities so fundamental to the functioning of an economy (education, transportation, food) that they must be provided, whether by private enterprise, some form(s) of voluntarism, or public tax-supported or subsidized operations (like education). The economic factors of production are the instrumentalities that produce national wealth. The wealth of nations may be morally judged by how effectively the Essential Economy provides for human consumption needs and the economy's production needs. On the other hand, the wealth of nations is diminished when the market misdirects resources to social status display and sybaritic titillation.

NEEDS

From the perspective of the Essential Economy it readily can be seen that each individual has needs which must be met in order to do his/her part in production, distribution, consumption, growth and progress of the economy. The economic system also has needs if it is to better meet the needs of individual participants. The linking or networking of all these needs in an operational way *is* the Essential Economy.

In spite of the imperative quality of economic needs, they do not play an explicit role in the dominant (standard) economic theory. Wants, desires, preferences do, but not needs. Consumption—the satisfaction of one's personal wants and preferences—has been dealt with as a private, subjective matter. In that theory, needs are not explicitly at issue. Private utility is at issue. Utility is manifest as demand (when coupled with purchasing power) in a world of scarcity where private preferences (not needs of individuals nor needs of the system) must be economized. But the nature and role of needs require special attention in seeking moral guidance for monitoring the economy. Recognizing needs helps clarify the distinction between a healthy Essential Economy and the economic pathologies of the private property, market managing system.

There seems to be a pervasive sense that because all individuals only think, feel, and act through their own unique subjective selves that there is no way of viewing human needs from an objective, public purpose, rational perspective. Instead, freedom and free will in the market become *hallowed will*, not subject to theoretical evaluation for public purposes.

Humans do have needs and needs are especially distinct from frivolous wants. At the extremes these qualitative differences (sheer wants and essential needs) are certainly distinguishable. The present analysis will have a muted message for those lacking the "original and most fundamental moral passion" of empathy if they are unable to distinguish between the need for sustaining food and shelter and the whimsy want for embryo lamb tongue pickled and served on the afterdeck of a sumptuous yacht by a retinue of servants. If there were no scarcity, it would not matter. It is *scarcity* and *needs* that make economizing matter, technically and morally. Certainly needs have a higher moral priority than trifling wants. The intensity and importance of consumption falls in a range between frivolous wants and essential needs. There is, of course, a great range of competing needs that are not readily distinguishable as to relative importance to the economy. Eventually, this issue must be confronted by a moral philosophy of economics. Given the fact of scarcity, all needs compete for peoples' time, energy, understanding, skills, and power to utilize economic resources. These conditions set us to rethinking managing economizing.

MARKET MANAGEMENT OF THE ESSENTIAL ECONOMY

The Essential Economy is largely (not exclusively) managed in all advanced industrialized capitalist cultures by private property and a monetized market. This management power system is being continuously adapted, either to benefit the privileges of power (great and small) or to better meet the needs of people and the needs of the Essential Economic system. (Of course inherent empathy and compassion support provisioning for these needs.) The most fundamental role of market management is rationing scarce means for a multitude of competing, as well as mutually supportive, alternative "ends" that are also scarce means.

The Western economies that have succeeded so admirably (compared historically and cross-culturally) have not been described well by mainstream economics. These Western economies have not been organized by a utopian competitive market. Nor have they been organized by a market that deviates from pure and perfect competition, described as "imperfect competition" by professional economists. Since competitive theory is an abstract myth, the real market does not and cannot deviate from a nonexistent utopia. Nor was this utopia ever an historical reality. Perhaps most importantly, the Essential Economy is not *automatically* managed by a Newtonian mechanistic nature-knows-best market. The Essential Economy has, however, been managed by a market that has worked within a range of successes and failures. I am calling that managing mechanism the "workable market."

THE WORKABLE MARKET

Instead of a Newtonian, automatic, equilibrating market we have a Darwinian evolutionary, innovative market adapting to the changing needs of individuals and the evolving production-consumption process. The Darwinian market is a rather inelegant, pluralistic, changing system. In fact the picture is somewhat chaotic. That is what we would expect of a monetized market managed economy made up of semi-autonomous, private property enterprises in constant flux. It has a quality of pluralism in continuous transition. This quasi-chaos of a pluralistic exchange economy contributes to its creativity, adaptability, and potential for both good and disaster. Although it is more amorphous and more complex, it is far more realistic an alternative explanation of managing the Essential Economy than that conceived by competitive price theory or imperfect competition.

The workable market-managing mechanism is a rather grossly organized, moderately flexible, and quite widely tolerated pattern of rules, within a power system engaging in exchanges of goods and services through negotiated contracts. Markets are patterns of socially evolved rules, allowing individuals degrees of autonomy from rigid restraints on the Essential Economy but not free of restraints and guidance. This workable real world market, rather than being an ideal utopian system, is an evolving crude mechanism that assists in organizing and managing the Essential Economy. That market is not simply a competitive price system organized by natural laws. It is rather an unrefined pattern of man-made rules, giving a roughhewn order to the Essential Economy.

Rules are made at all levels: family, corporation, union, trade association, and government. Federal and state legislatures, government agencies, and the court systems are final arbiters of all rules that can't be resolved within or among private property institutions (conflict of schools with students' families, among professional athletes and their sports commissions, between unions and management, etc.). The competitive market doesn't resolve moral conflict, but relative power enters into the negotiating process. These normative rules, as they are accepted, become values we live by. This evolving system provides an ambivalently acceptable workable market, meaning the community can usually live with it, even prosper.

PLURALISM IN WORKABLE MARKETS VS. COMPETITION IN COMPETITIVE THEORY

Pluralistic workable markets differ from Adam Smith's competitive market. The latter theory calls for pure and perfect competition with perfect knowledge. Pluralism is not so Platonically perfect, neither is it an imperfect and inefficient deviation from the Smithian ideal. Economic pluralism is a quality of multiple enterprises producing similar and differentiated goods and services, having varying degrees of uniqueness. Each enterprise has the autonomy and flexibility (within rules) to create and innovate what it does or produces and how it does it. Under pluralism there is likely to be competition, in the sense of tactics to win consumers' dollar votes for the products or services offered. Firms are legally largely independent of each other. And legally they must avoid any collusion that will impede innovations, or that results in capacity to set prices which the political and court system considers unreasonable, or that in some way controls the market detrimentally to the public good. All this may result in progress or tactics that are pathological.

Pluralism, publicly organized by means of private property and privately negotiated contracts in a monetized-managed economy is positive and important for several public purpose reasons. This kind of pluralism contrasts with the rigid tradition of chieftains, feudal customs, the central planning of socialism, or monolithic corporate power. It avoids a cumbersome and rigid single, central power system.

Pluralism contributes to experimentalism, adaptability, and progress. It helps to limit the power proclivities in human nature, property rights and potential market power, and thereby reduces (does not necessarily eliminate) the extent to which a few are in a position to unnecessarily "exploit" the many, even while serving some extremely well (the pharmaceutical industry). Pluralism dilutes market power and permits self-interest to innovate cost efficiencies and provide more and better products and services at lower relative prices. It creates conditions for a substantial degree of autonomous, flexible, mutually adaptive decision-making conditions which possess qualities approximating the illusionary beneficent automatic market. This flexibility provides an important degree of individuality and some freedom from frustrating administrative directives, although it cannot escape rules.

It provides a market feedback system which encompasses the virtues and frailties of consumers' rationality and irrationality.

Monetized market pluralism provides an institutional means of managing real saving and investing necessary to economic growth and qualitative progress. Central to economic thought, market pluralism provides a means by which pricing becomes a mechanism of economizing-rationing. It is an evolved messy mechanism, though not a deviation from a maximizing competitive ideal.

VIRTUES OF THE WORKABLE MARKET

The workable market has many of the characteristics for which capitalism has rightfully been praised. It is not however perfection, only workable. Concern here is not with why it works badly, but how it works quite adequately. It is like setting aside the question of why we get sick, as we raise the more puzzling question of the nature of life and how we successfully get well and stay alive. What then are the virtues of the workable market?

The workable market provides the Essential Economy with experimental flexibility through pluralism. All quasi-independent enterprises, managed by this market, have degrees of discretion to experiment endlessly with every aspect of their operations which are not constrained by somewhat fungible social rules. This provides an environment for human creativity and cumulative knowledge to generate a dynamism toward economic progress.

The workable market is a means by which money power is distributed and redistributed. It provides individuals with varying claims on output of the Essential Economy, making possible more universal individual participation in this kind of economy. It provides a distributive "reward" mechanism, which creates an atmosphere in which the human addiction to an amorphous reciprocal exchange justice can be somewhat acceptably met. Corrections are regularly made through social devices that fail to conform to competitive ideology, as we will see later.

The workable market is not brittle (as the stringent conditions expected by competitive theory demand), but it is readily adaptable to moral monitoring by social pressures to reform specified practices. Thus the workable market, as a system, adapts to lawsuits, boycotts, court decisions, administrative and legislative rules. This does not mean all individual units thrive, or even survive. But the demise of some helps make the market work. It winnows out those enterprises that cannot successfully survive while meeting social expectations at the standards society's rules require they achieve.

The workable market is adaptable to private power needs, economies of scale, and public ownership as an economizing mechanism. This *real world* market, which is less abstract than the competitive market, manages the Essential Economy in ways that adapt to changing needs for managerial power to achieve technological effectiveness as part of that Essential Economy. Massive communication, transportation, giant industrial production, and widespread distribution systems, all illustrate the Essential Economy's need for flexible market management empowerment, rather than the powerlessness required by competitive theory.

Conventional theory does not allow for this necessary power. Imperfect competition theory sees the existence of market power as inefficient and inferentially unfair. Workable market theory sees market power to be acceptable (justifiable) only in so far as it effectively contributes to managing the techno-logic, cause and effect relationships of the Essential Economy, including effective provisioning of human needs. Nations of the world struggle over how to monitor this market power. (As I write the USA courts struggle over Bill Gates's Microsoft power in the industry, and the European Economic Union denies General Electric-Honeywell the power of consolidation.) The decisions are scarcely "plain and intelligible common understandings," nor efforts to establish powerless pure and perfect competition. They are an evolutionary, innovative, adaptation process. Humanity is groping its way out of the past and into a future.

While flexible pluralism, distributive justice, societal adaptability, and technological and managerial efficiency are important attributes, the Essential Economy must still confront the necessity of economizing effectively. Prices and a market, in spite of serious shortcomings, seem well fitted for performing this economizing role. The workable market works because it provides individuals and groups with price cues and quantities of monetary power by which they can command and direct portions of the Essential Economy (as if directed by an "invisible hand"). These price cues, together with income, impel individuals and institutions to economize scarce means at all phases of allocation, production, distribution, consumption, growth and progress.

However, the explanation of how these economizing cues are formed as scarcity prices is vastly different here from the competitive theory of supply and demand under pure and perfect competition, or even from imperfect competition. Here, prices are not explained as determined by supply and demand in a mechanistic Newtonian mode. Rather, prices are *changed* by supply and demand changes. Prices function in a Darwinian evolutionary adaptive sense by forming prices that function effectively as scarcity economizing cues without having to conform to an impossible ideal of pure and perfect competition.

The question must be faced: How do evolved workable markets set economizing prices and thereby assist managing scarcity reasonably effectively in a world of change? Prices never were established by markets as defined by competitive theory. Rather, over evolutionary and historical time, exchange transactions evolved from varying cultural responses, resulting in institutionalized markets defined by acceptable rules, values, and procedures. These codes arise historically out of human experience, and they change with new knowledge of materials, technology, products, contacts, and contracts. Market exchanges are then reconventionalized and habitualized anew. They are conventionalized and rule governed. Of course, it is legendary that when different cultures initially come in contact the exchanges take on the appearance of being bizarre (Manhattan island ostensibly purchased from the Indians for twenty four dollars in trinkets).

The market rules are correctives from stealing, raids, plunder, extortion, conning, or the potential violence from power threats. On the other hand, power monitors the rules and customs by applying other conventionalized sanctions (the state's administration of justice through property law, the courts and police). Here, power is essential to preserve institutionalized rules of orderly exchanges. This process has evolved into the present Essential Economy being managed by a workable market pluralism. Rather than the effectiveness of the economy being exclusively judged and monitored by consumer demand in a competitive market, it is, in a very subtle way, judged and monitored by public rationality derived from the cause-effect technologic observable in the Essential Economy itself.

HOW PRICES ARE SET IN WORKABLE MARKETS

In Smithian times when enterprises were small, conventionalized rules and sociological relationships governed trading transactions in small communities. Prices and incomes were a product of custom, status, and power. There were, of course, changing supply and demand forces inducing modifications of custom-prescribed exchange rates in the sociological patterns of local markets. But basically, sociological conventions dominated small-town markets of trading neighbors. The reality was not anything resembling competitive theory's freely equilibrating pure and perfect competition among impartial maximizers, indifferent to local conventions and their personal status in the local or exchange community.

As the Industrial Revolution transformed the size and sociological intimacy of economic units, the power shifts were *not* toward pure competition, where no unit could influence market prices to its own advantage. The "great transformation" from predominantly localized agricultural economies to industrial economies was accompanied by discontentment and substantial strife. It resulted in the rise of large corporations, unionization and collective bargaining. It was a shift from sociologically intimate and customized buyer-seller relationships, to a more indifferent, power-dominated influence on market price patterns. Here too, supply and demand shifts had an impact on changing prices otherwise dominated by power bargained contractual agreements and convention in the markets. Thus, prices never have been established by markets as defined by competitive theory.

In summary, in the unreal, abstracted world of perfect competition, all prices always tend to true measures of relative scarcity. They have an absolute cardinal quality that indicates a perfect scarcity cue. However, in the real world, there are multiple causes establishing workable market prices. It can never be known what an ideal, precise, scarcity price would be. Instead, seen from a Darwinian perspective of evolutionary adaptation under workable markets, multiple-factor-caused prices will respond to changes in supply and demand resulting from the evolution of new products, processes, preferences and policies. Thus changes in supply and demand change prices but do not determine prices. Again, prices are determined by convention, power and potential supply and expressed demand.

All this may sound very much like prices being set in markets of imperfect competition. There is more than a subtle difference. This analysis does not see prices set by conditions deviating from pure and perfect competitive conditions as theories of imperfect competition do. Instead it sees supply and demand causing prices to deviate from traditional pricing and power pricing (or the "invisible handshake"). Viewed in this way, changing prices over time set crude economizing cues in market-managed economies under workable markets.

In general, there are two conditions shunting prices from their historical tradition and power determined state. As demand presses increasingly on limited supplies, prices will tend to rise (as conventional theory tells us). This will *tend* to discourage using those increasingly scarce factors of production. Alternatively, due to technological progress in producing a product, coupled with a desire to make more profits from more sales in an economy of pluralism, prices will *tend* to decline as technology reduces the cost of inputs. That is, prices of specific products (computers) tend to decline as the costs of producing them declines, and output (of computers) becomes less scarce over time. Thus under workable market management, prices adjust to changes in scarcity over time. Increasingly costly (increasingly scarce) goods will be rationed more tightly. Decreasingly costly (less scarce) goods will be substituted for increasingly scarce goods (soybean products in place of animal products, and possibly in place of petroleum; spun glass wire in place of copper wire). This pricing provides workable economizing cues and an indeterminate degree of economizing effectiveness. It seems to have worked in Western type market managed economies as judged from the perspective of historical and cross-cultural comparisons.

THE ESSENTIAL ECONOMY AND GOVERNMENT

Caution! When focused on market managing insights, there is a tendency to overlook the more basic contribution of reliable knowledge and technology. The market envisioned in competitive theory lacks means to cause prices to reflect all the true costs (externalities and consequences of competing) involved in economic processes. However, the instrumental, techno-logic of the Essential Economy provides insights into some of the external costs that should be internalized into the market to make economizing more effective and more long range. With this knowledge, the power of governance can impose external real costs (by taxation for example) on market pricing. In this way social costs external to the market (such as depletion of resources, clean-up costs of pollutants, correction of work related injuries, social costs from disruptive change and the enormous social costs from competition itself) can be internalized into the workable market. These costs may be penalized by taxes (for example) to be borne by contributors to the problems (so that they may be coerced to economize and respond to the scarcity of the environment or the destructiveness of their production processes). Of course it will not be perfect because perfection has no known meaning here. Improving can be found to have both meaning and complications, as will be seen later.

Even when monitored costs are imposed by governance or collective agreements, the remaining supply, demand, and price settlement can then be left to the workable market. Prices under these circumstances would then "automatically" adjust supply and demand and tend to "clear the market." All prices would not be perfect measures of relative scarcity of all means of production at any given time. That is both unknowable and undoable. Rather, prices would tend to adapt to changes of relative scarcities, and encourage substituting less scarce means for more scarce means, thus economizing over time. This would not be a utopian perfection nor a Newtonian mechanistic equilibrium of geometric precision. There would be Darwinian adaptation with real world economizing cues. Prices would crudely reflect the changing pluralistic and adapting organic system that has managed the Western Essential Economy as successfully as it has for so long.

VIEWING THE MARKET AS IT REALLY IS

Competitive economic theory provides fundamentalist ideology with an unrealistic standard for judging economic effectiveness. This core theory and philosophy suffers oversights and illusions that cause fundamentalist thinking, founded in it, to be hazardous to human well-being, as market failures illustrate. The myth of a totally free market is an impossible dream for managing the Essential Economy for the long-run wealth of nations and humanity.

Unqualified private property rights are unworkable too. Everyone lives next door to everyone else's private property. How our neighbors use their private property creates a rational, common public purpose concern. Together, an utterly free market and unqualified private property cannot do everything fundamentalist supporters of the utopian market claim for them. The problem is not simply because there is scarcity. The market cannot simultaneously set prices that automatically provide accurate reciprocal rewards equal to contributions and also set prices that are true measures of the scarcity of all means; and at the same time businesses cannot remain small enough to be powerless, while organizing and managing our modern international industrial-communication-transportation systems. Competitive, private economic institutions cannot simultaneously motivate people to choose the most appropriate potential aptitudes, and to learn those skills, and to know where they can best be used for both private purposes and public purposes. Such a utopian market cannot, at the same time, on its own provide for both individual needs and public needs. It cannot coerce competitors to follow socially responsible practices to protect the environment or preserve threatened resources (fisheries or forests). It cannot do all this, and also have powerless players necessary for the market to set prices that are true measures of true scarcity (which cannot be verified as knowable).

QUANTIFICATION, DOLLARS AND SENSE

Quantification is another of the worthy wonders of the world. But the fact that money numbers are quantitatively precise should not delude us into believing that they are therefore accurate measures, or even meaningful measures, of something analogous to an engineered skyscraper or Golden Gate Bridge. Because dollars and cents are measurably precise, that is not evidence of accuracy of meaning for the effectiveness of the Essential Economy. It seems a "plain and intelligible common understanding" that a life-saving drug priced at a few dollars is morally more valuable than a million dollar jewelry piece. However, they exchange in the market in terms of relative purchasing power and relative prices, reflecting relative status power and relative scarcities. They do not necessarily exchange on terms reflecting relative usefulness in meeting private or public *needs*.

Because money is empowerment to make claims on the real economy, it creates the illusion that money is the source of wealth (the old mercantilist illusion). It certainly creates empowerment for individuals and institutions. However, the Essential Economy, not money, is the source of wealth creation. The money economy performs necessary management functions of that real source of wealth. From the perspective of the economy as a system responsible for the wealth of nations, the more obsessed we are with the money measuring instrument, the greater the danger of neglecting the effectiveness, justice, efficiency, general well-being, progress of the Essential Economy.

Behind the monetary numbers, there are historically developed rules, as well as a power system. Thinking accurately about philosophical economics is not determined by mathematical precision, though closely related to logical tightness. Meaningful quantification can contribute substantially to the effectiveness of the Essential Economy. But it must be faced: philosophizing about economics is more analogous to thinking about the life-and-death significance of decisions by jurors, judges, and legislators dealing with human lives through the law. The more reliable, including quantifiably accurate evidence available, the greater the probability of legal effectiveness. It is not a guarantee nor a necessary condition.

Still, it is a useful function of money to provide a symbol by which we can make comparative decisions (however effectively) and thereby ration scarce means. Workable market data must provide useful information for comparing relative scarcities when decisions are made at the public policy level (money costs of prisons versus money costs of prevention), or the individual level (money costs for personal health versus money costs for a night on the town). Being less costly in money terms is crudely symbolic of being less costly in real terms for those possibilities that must be relinquished. But when external social costs (environmental destruction) and internal costs of competitive pathologies (misleading advertising) are poorly reflected in money costs, then real costs and economic effectiveness are both detrimentally skewed.

CONCLUSIONS

It is my objective throughout to enrich the analysis of our Western market managed economy, though it is to be a rather inelegant reconstruction. There is good reason. A market managed economy is not smoothly organized and administered. In fact it is downright messy. The picture is of necessity somewhat chaotic. It is what we should expect of an economy made up of semi-autonomous enterprises in constant flux. It is a quality of pluralism. It is, in part, this quasi-chaos of an exchange economy that contributes to its creativity, adaptability, and potential for both good or bad. We must rethink economics in terms of an Essential Economy questing for progress, fairness, justice, efficient economizing, and appropriate reliable knowledge. The solution is not to coerce the economy to fit the theory but to restructure current theory to discover and deal with overlooked elements of the real economy.

Our concern here is analysis and evaluation of the overall system as a means of contributing to the well-being of all individuals within it. The techno-logic, cause-and-effect instrumentalism of the Essential Economy brings to focus the moral imperative of what should be done to meet the most pressing needs for all. Scarcity, however, qualifies all technological cause-and-effect logic and derived good intentions. Economizing within the Essential Economy is still inescapable.

The Essential Economy managed by a workable market has gotten us where we are but historically at very high humanitarian costs (market failures). Still, it does seek better conditions over worse in a progressive way. This is the workable market of the real world. It is not automatically monitored to adequately meet needs, to distribute resources, products, and services justly, to preserve the environment for posterity, to generate edifying quality standards of living, or to invent and implement humanitarian life styles. These markets are crudely and randomly monitored but not morally monitored. It is essential that informed impartial spectators develop and apply a public purpose rationality derived from a moral philosophy. To this we turn.

6

The Organizing Animal

Kenneth Boulding, one of the twentieth century's distinguished social thinkers, has provided fruitful insight into three major modes by which all humans transact with each other in all functioning social systems: **Threat** mode, **Exchange** mode, and **Integrative** mode. They are the way humans organize themselves at all levels of endeavor from family to business enterprise to global interaction. Boulding's line of thought and the power of his insights can elucidate the relationships among the Essential Economy, workable markets, and moral appraisal. This present work will freely modify and supplement his insights.

To get a ready familiarity with Boulding's modal concepts think of the family and rearing of children. The **Threat** system uses the power to punish, by spanking or deprivation, in order to induce conformity to parental wishes or societal expectations. No negotiating here. Parents are the final authority within the family organization.

On the other hand, the **Exchange** mode introduces bargaining, with reciprocal responses to offers and counter offers in negotiating children's responsibilities for carrying out necessary functions of the household that benefit all members, some more than others perhaps. But agreement is secured because each realizes a net benefit. By the exchange mode, in a rather traditional family, it is determined who sets the table, washes the dishes, dries, puts them away, so Mother is free to prepare favorite desserts and Dad can relax after a hard day's work "bringing home the bacon." Other patterns are being negotiated in this mode to better fit modern family needs.

The **Integrative** mode is the linchpin giving moral direction to social organization. It is more complicated and amorphous than the other modes of organization. In general, the integrative mode of behavior in a well functioning family seeks to determine what it is that should be done for members of the family and how to do it best. It seeks to pull all the needs and potentials of the family and each member together in some kind of inclusive process of improvement. The means of achieving this integrative cooperation are woven into the fabric of the family by setting good examples, using persuasion, and convincing through rational illustrations of proper, in contrast to improper, behavior.

Appropriate behavior is internalized within the family fabric through dialogue, reading, working, playing, thinking together, and general sharing of family experiences. We teach by setting examples and giving rational reasons. We teach and learn how to tie shoe laces, run the lawn mower, use the dishwasher, drive the car, entertain guests, say "thank you" and "please," tell the truth but modify candor to suit the social situation, keep family secrets, control frustrations, hostilities and anger, cultivate a degree of consensus of what is meant by "fair is fair," and so forth. It is also a self-corrective mode. It is a means by which disputes are mitigated and family functions move along with varying degrees of success. All is done in an atmosphere of empathy and understanding reinforced with kindness, love and affection. If all this is done well, we learn and feel a sense of responsibility to others.

Each of these three modes—threat, exchange, integration—is an abstraction from the organic whole. No one of them alone is likely to create a functional family. Yet degrees of each make up the reality all functional families experience. Aspects of these modes may be pushed to a pathological degree. Frustrated beating, with neither love nor explanation of how to behave effectively, is likely to have pathological consequences.

To each mode can be found a moral connection. The **Exchange** mode is conducive to negotiating individuals' contributions to a family in which all participants are better off than they would otherwise be. It is a positive-sum game; all are winners. The **Threat** mode has a moral thrust in the use of power to hold cheating and selfishness in abeyance, curtail conflict, legitimize rules, interpret and enforce these rules in the interest of community cohesion. The **Integrative** mode has a massive moral thrust. It is basically the moral benchmark for both the **Exchange** and **Threat** modes. When **Threat** or **Exchange** fail to contribute to social **Integration** of members, the family is faltering.

The **Integrative** mode provides guidance for coordinating the level of social organization, whether family, corporation, state, or globe. It provides moral direction for both private-purpose rationality (how to behave) and rational public purpose (how to organize).

These three modes of social organization generate philosophical insights into the organization, management, monitoring, and inducement of an efficient, effective, justice seeking, and progressive Essential Economic order. The organic nature of the Essential Economy managed by a workable market system can now be more fully visualized in terms of threat, exchange, and integration, each with its own changing qualities.

THE THREAT MODE: INSTITUTIONS AND POWER

The capacity to threaten is social power. And power is the capacity to get things done, good or bad. Power-threat is an essential mode of social organization and adaptation. The threat system epitomizes a "necessary evil." As an old Irish proverb tells us: "You can accomplish more with a kind word and a shillelagh than you can with just a kind word." In its generic form, the threat mode is a social mechanism with the capacity to apply devices that shape others' behavior: letter grades, pass or flunk, give or withhold permission, hire or fire, reward, promote, punish, fine, withdraw license, and so forth.

Should we apply principles of evolution in combination with cross-cultural comparisons, a reasonable hypothesis is that in the process of minimizing conflicts over scarcities, our emerging species invented norms of how every interaction should be consummated. At any given time, place and culture the power of threat is derived from the customs and beliefs of the society (how control of properties is transmitted from one generation to the next). These conventions of power provide a more adaptive mechanism than constant resort to physical force and weaponry for determining essential social action. Members of the culture function within these rules and have viewed them as God's design, the Natural order, or Natural rights. And they, or we, offer our lives to preserve our "freedom" to conform to these rules.

All norms emerge from inherent human impulses expressed through culturally evolved traits that become society's customs and individuals' habits. These are the rules we live by. They form the institutions that shape, direct, create sanctions and enforce cultural patterns by which social stability is maintained. They may also become the object of conflict, especially under conditions of change (intellectual property rights on the web), or when divergent cultures come into contact and compete for the same resources. I suspect that many customs and beliefs were explained and carried out for wrong reasons (human sacrifices) as likely the illusion-ridden individuals had limited reliable knowledge of causes and effects for designing their social practices. This probability will account for some of the dramatic differences among cultures and for the easy identification of idolatry, mysticism, and superstition in other cultures while we may overlook them in our own culture.

The **Threat** mode is called into play to subdue individual deviation or group challenges to what is "known" to be the right, the good, the true, the only way. Such beliefs are reinforced by ceremonies and rituals, stimulating emotional attachments at a time and in areas where there may be little reliable knowledge upon which agreement might be rationally founded. That is the way we evolved. Ritual remains a substantial component of social order, even today.

Distasteful as threat may be, it is necessary because human natures have evolved with considerable diversity. Humans possess a rather random distribution of propensities within and among individuals. These impulses are clearly not equally distributed among all individuals and not rationally distributed for good mental health within all individuals. Pharmaceuticals increasingly mitigate some of human nature's inherent predilections that can be pathological for individuals in the modern world. The **Threat** mode, with its evolutionary origins, has become a necessary control instrument when some of these impulses become socially aberrant and threaten community cooperation in meeting fundamental human needs. These predilections are likely to create conflict, especially under conditions of scarcity. Throw out four pieces of candy to five kids, for example. Consider rising international expectations and changing values in a world of scarcity where global communication can dramatically expand what everyone may want. There must be order before justice; otherwise chaos (war, terrorism, daily violence, looting) will never allow a social or economic system the opportunity to provide (or improve) justice. In a civilized, commercial context, the power of threat must be viewed as not only an essential instrument for managing the Essential Economy; it is even the power to induce economizing in production.

COMMON SOURCES OF POWER

There are several forms of power that function in an economy.

- Property ownership power. It provides quasi-exclusive rights with the legal capacity to demand a reciprocal exchange for permission to use. Patents provide such power.

- Knowledge power. "The pen is mightier than the sword." It is the capacity to influence events through logic, evidence and persuasion.
- Skills power. Superstars and surgeons. A refined skill highly sought can command respect and rewards.
- Hierarchical power. Administer or manage, give or withhold permission, hire, fire, promote, reward, take away.
- Networking power. "It's not what you know but who you know."
- Business success. This can lead to market power, especially in heavy fixed cost industries where pluralism is constrained because of the high cost of entry or early-comer dominance.
- Political power. Various means of influence in the governance system (getting the votes, chairing committees, length of tenure).
- Accumulation of assets convertible into money power.
- Entrepreneurial power combines many of these forms of power.

With so many means to power, and widespread existence of power, it is readily understandable that there can be frustration and denunciation by those subject to it.

PATHOLOGIES OF POWER (OR THREAT)

Our inherent impulses are vestigial remains of a harsh past. In human evolutionary time, the distribution of evolved power propensities seems to have had species survival value. At other periods, history reveals the quest for power has led to gigantic evil and massive social pathologies. Regrettably, history and anthropology provide considerable evidence of a range of rather long-lived social orders that were downright gruesome, such as ancient Egypt, India's caste system, and Russia both before and after the Communist revolution. Power-threat remains a vestigial device of domination, exploitation, and self aggrandizement.

There is a tendency, even in a democracy, to think of our rights and freedoms as bestowed by the Deity or Nature, as in the divine right of kings or our Natural Right to life, liberty and the pursuit of happiness. Confused again by our illusions. We do not have rights and freedoms, as if enunciated from the heavens for our benefit. We live within nature and societies of *human-created* rights. They are not "my" rights or freedom. They are society's invented rules, which members can bestow or withhold from each other. The existence of private property is one such set of rules. Our predecessors fought and died to be free from traditional "oppressive" feudal-cum-mercantilist rules and to establish new rules more congenial to their new potential well-being. Social progress normally includes the reduction of the abusive use of obsolete threat modes. But this insight cannot be extrapolated to conclude an ultimate demise of power and threat.

The use of power-threat, however, can be either socially responsible or pathological. Though it can be, and often is, brutally abused, it is necessary to provide order and direction to social systems. Thus there is a dual quality of power-threat. Threat is an essential mode (by no means the only mode) of implementing direction and order in any social system such as family, business, corporation, union-management relationships, government protection of property rights, and so on. It exists virtually every place one turns in economic and other social activities. Power-threat is accepted because order and getting things done are supportive of the causes of the wealth of nations, as well as essential to implement an existing economizing system and whatever expectation of justice accompanies it.

To enhance management of the Essential Economy, governments provide and protect property rights and property power, backed by the threat system of governmental rules, courts and public police. In the context of the market, the power system of property is a social instrument for the *management* of getting production out as well as a legal right to self aggrandizement of owners and the management hierarchy. In this way power serves as a tool-like instrument, while still exhibiting vestiges of medieval-like privilege. Power is a necessary condition for social order. It is not a sufficient condition for moral order. Property ownership is also the major threat mechanism that provides pluralism of power by which business enterprises manage to get things done quasi-autonomously. In the West, the dominant users of private property for economic power are the corporations, some of which are more powerful than most nations.

PRIVILEGE POWER AND INSTRUMENTAL POWER

Power is used in two often contradictory ways: for **privilege** and for **instrumental** management. Privilege power is the capacity to play in the game to *win*, to come out ahead of the less powerful, to command the advantages it makes for the self. Instrumental power provides the capacity to *manage* the elements of the Essential Economy.

Privilege Power

The employment of morally indefensible power is commonplace. Communist states are not the only societies in which power has been abused for the personal privilege of the elite, to the disadvantage of the many. Private property power, as currently utilized, distracts from its instrumental function of managing for the Essential Economy's public purpose. It continues its historic role of providing self aggrandizement to owners and management hierarchy. In this special sense government-backed property rights bestow the capacity of preserving privileges, even as they divert scarce means from needs of less privileged citizens.

Adam Smith's resolution of the problem of excessive self-interest by means of numerous small competitors in the market simply fails to confront the instrumental necessity for power. Rules, and not beneficent natural laws of competitive markets, are designed to protect citizens from negative consequences of the necessary power system.

Should all rules be expected to work well? Not unless we know how to always select and project correctly all the consequences of all alternative rules. Only social experiments, often costly, have helped us find our way. Life is a continuous, near random pattern of inescapable experiments. Even standing pat is a gamble. "If it ain't broke don't fix it" is far more dangerous than it sounds. It may assume an eternal Platonic perfection. It may assume we know when and why something works and when it is broken. With twenty-five percent unemployment in the nineteen thirties, we didn't know for sure that the economy was broken. Traditional experts told us that it was self equilibrating. Prosperity was just around the corner.

Fundamentalist economic ideology says that no new government rules are needed to correct our economic ills, except get closer to Adam Smith's free competitive utopia. Anti-trust rules were legislated to preserve competitive powerlessness. But these rules are now open to reconsideration as power is increasingly recognized as the necessary capacity to get technological things done on a national and global scale. As powerful, quasi-autonomous organizations are managed with self-interest motives, they are open to the pathologies of power. Correcting the privileges of threat and power through new rules becomes an essential moral objective for a philosophy of economics.

That such threat-coercion should create discontentment confirms Freud's thesis that civilization suppresses many human inclinations. It is the price we pay for living in civilized societies. Proper suppression of human inclinations is not, of itself, evil. In fact it is morally essential. Human predilections can and do create pathologies. A moral attribute of civilization must be an obligation to keep the natural power-threat tendency channeled toward serving the humanitarian needs of the integrative mode of social organization. Pathologies from power do not call for the elimination of the threat mode. Rather, they call for clarification of morally responsible rules, for administering the threat systems in behalf of the integrative system of the Essential Economy.

Instrumental Power

As distinct from privilege, power also has a techno-logic (instrumental) function for managing the Essential Economy. Even socialist and "communist" societies have had some form of instrumental property-like power to get things done.

Power is also utilized to change the rules, or legitimize privately negotiated contractual changes, as the Essential Economy changes (e.g., from a horse and buggy, pen and paper world to an airlines, computer, internet world). Rules, laws, sanctions, fines, licensing, accreditation, pure food and drug inspection, airlines safety rules and review, mine safety, trucking rules and inspection, supervision over moving toxic material, explosives, and contaminating materials, all call for rules and compliance enforcement. All this is legitimized ultimately through the instrumental device of a governmental threat-power system.

Again, this necessity to monitor the use of power requires a more appropriate means for economics than competitive theory provides. Certainly, the price system contributes substantially to the success of a market managed economy. However, starting the philosophical-theoretical analysis with a powerless, competitive, "first approximation" of that market contributes to the illusion and confusion that the existing market is an ultimate standard of a moral and efficient economic system.

The nature and role of power, like freedom and justice, requires philosophical and theoretical clarification. This is essential to guide us in seeking public purpose rationality in pursuit of the wealth and well-being of humanity. Though government threat systems are the legitimizing authority for rules and policies at any given time, they are not the ultimate *moral* authority. Appropriate reliable understanding behind rules and policies provides "ultimate" moral authority. We live, however, with insights, oversights, and illusions. It leaves us in a very uncertain world at a time when the pace of progress escalates and the costs and dangers of change intensify.

EXCHANGE MODE: SOCIALLY ORGANIZING ECONOMIES

Boulding's second mode of social transacting—**Exchange**—escapes some of the pathologies of power. But power matters here too. The Essential Economy is managed by exchange among those who participate as quasi-autonomous economic agents (as individuals or groups). The central quality of exchange is negotiating (contracting) mutually agreeable exchanges of possessions (including talents) and negotiating rules of their relationships (labor-management contracts) in which all parties feel they derive benefits they would not otherwise have. Exchange involves negotiated reciprocal give and take. Justice here is perceived as reciprocity of receiving and contributing, while all involved feel they have gained in the process. There are very positive contributions of the workable market exchange mode that a moral philosophy of economics must embrace.

- Exchange in modern markets is a positive-sum game. All who participate can gain. Anyone who doesn't gain in a specific exchange is free to opt out. But this does not guarantee that all have adequate alternatives, know-how, or are in a position to participate effectively in the complex modern Essential Economy or in the market exchange process that plays a role in managing it. In this very serious sense, there are those who are, in degrees, shut out of the system and are neither free nor empowered to participate adequately. The problems of these individuals require resolution, not simply admonition that they are lazy or indifferent and undeserving. A moral philosophy of economics should be expected to face this problem with a commitment to seeking solutions, not delivering condemnations. The present analysis offers no guarantee of agreeable resolutions to all such problems. In like manner medicine still seeks solutions to as yet intractable health problems.

- The market exchange mode also has the important virtue of providing a system that is quasi-automatic. It creates the illusion of natural laws beneficently guiding an automatic free economy. The exchange mode does have a quality similar to an automatic market. The functioning of a multitude of quasi-autonomous individuals mutually adapting within the rules of the market is fundamental to the success of Western market managed economies. Individuals mutually accommodate in billions of daily transactions and administer an organic economic process beyond the comprehension of any overall authority.

- The exchange mode makes pluralism workable. And pluralism increases the probability of innovations which solve existing problems, meet many needs, and provide instruments that improve the comfort and conveniences of daily routines. Pluralism and exchange even provide means to occasional peak experiences. Of course, all exchanges are not moral winners. Some agreed-upon exchanges are evil. Racketeers have their own conditions of exchanges.

- Finally, a major quality of the exchange mode is that it taps deep-seated sentiments that have highly complex consequences, some imperative for the relative success of humanity. We see this daily, for instance, in the nobler dimensions of business and industrial enterprises that manage the feeding, housing, health, communication, recreation, and transportation by which most of us live.

Given these attributes of the exchange mode, its shortcomings are not a justification for denial of the very positive economic advantages of exchanges. But of course we are rightfully offended when there is deception and deviation from instrumental principles of the Essential Economy. Thus moral monitoring of exchanges is often necessary.

AN ANTHROPOLOGICAL PERSPECTIVE
ON EXCHANGE AND RECIPROCITY

The field of anthropology glows with fascinating accounts of exchange systems. Exchange functioned in most corners of the globe long before the market was monetized and eventually described by Adam Smith. They doubtless evolved over a million years or more from proto-man to modern man. Recall, Smith noted a human "propensity to truck, barter and exchange." A study of anthropology certainly provides massive evidence of such a universal, inherent inclination to engage in elaborate exchanges.

Some exchanges appear very practical or utilitarian, such as inland peoples exchanging fruits and nuts for water-edge peoples' fish. Other famous exchanges appear highly ritualistic and status validating such as the Kula exchange of the Western Pacific (necklaces for armbands) and the potlatch of the North West coast of North America (blankets, canoes and destructive displays). The accounts of these exchanges portray the multitude of social forms different cultures evolved in the practice of reciprocal "truck, barter and exchange."

Adam Smith was likely correct in his insight that self-love and the propensity to truck, barter, and exchange are powerful forces in the market exchange system. However, a multitude of anthropological reports suggest a wide range of drives is operating. "Dumb barter" between tribal deadly enemies, where traders never dare meet face to face, is one extreme of exchange for limited utilitarian needs. More generally, exchanges contribute to fulfillments of many of Abraham Maslow's needs, such as belongingness, respect, self-esteem, and self-actualization. It is all a satisfying fulfillment of the inherent curiosity to explore, exchange, and consummate a reciprocal agreement. The process usually creates powerful bonding glue (not necessarily affection) for the parties involved.

Reciprocity sentiments are highly motivational and readily encompass self-interest, gratitude, and duty. Certainly these penchants contribute to conscientious performances. This same reciprocity sentiment in economic activities can result in resentment, get-even "conscientious withdrawal of efficiency," and even tit-for-tat destructiveness, as witnessed in bitter labor-management disputes and regular litigations of disputes among commercial interests.

Here stands one of humanity's monumental dilemmas. We are conditioned by cultural norms and genetic drives to expect reciprocal responses in endless social circumstances. This expectation gives rise to intense commitment to cooperate when reciprocity feels fair. When the response feels unfair, it is followed by resentment, even overt hostility and mutual destruction. Most of us are familiar with this observation of the obvious. But it has a kicker here. In the evolutionary process, a simple, instinctual tit-for-tat, or one-good-deed-deserves-another response made a substantial contribution as an inherent survival strategy (hunting and sharing). As humanity emerged through inherent genetic mechanisms to advanced cultural inventions of technology and social customs, there were no nature-given standards of when fair is fair in reciprocal exchanges. Nor are there effective inherent restraints against an "eye for an eye and a tooth for a tooth."

What is reciprocally just in exchange is simply not a knowable phenomenon, but it is a very real feeling. What it *really* should be, to be reciprocally just, is an illusionary pursuit. Adam Smith was unable to solve this problem of a reciprocally fair labor exchange value (the skilled labor problem). It cannot be solved, not even by the fiction that all are equal in merit and deservedness. Such an assumption laid the foundation for Karl Marx's theory of exploitation. Certainly there are pathologies of power and what we might term exploitation; but these issues are not resolved by assumptions of equality any more than the competitive market can be characterized by the assumption of powerlessness. There are moral possibilities but not if we are in a quest for absolute and measurable certainty or nature's automatic resolution.

Thus we are faced with having to develop a moral philosophy of economics that embraces the importance of exchange, accepts the reality of reciprocal sentiments, and does so without demanding naturally-formed, precise quantities for exchange justice.

THE INTEGRATIVE MODE

The integrative mode provides a sense of proper relationships from which moral expectations may be derived. Boulding notes that "while the integrative system is less orderly than the threat system or the exchange system and it is harder to find good models of it, it nevertheless has a perceivable unity of its own." With an emerging picture of the integrative mode before us, pieces of the jigsaw puzzle of a moral philosophy of economics may begin to display clearer character.

MORAL FOUNDATIONS OF EVOLVING NEEDS

The integrative system is an evolving, essential process of instrumental and empathetic relationships which increasingly provide for human needs. This process can point the way toward humanitarian standards of general well-being. The integrative mode is a product of the evolution of qualities of inherent human nature and concomitant cultural creations. These qualities include such sentiments as friendship, love, affection, empathy, bonding and cooperation. They also include a genetic predilection to language, rational knowledge, and instrumental problem solving. These inherent predispositions have generated cultural means that emerged as fundamentals to the Essential Economy.

Exploring the integrative mode is more like the field of human health care than like exploring the equilibrium of the solar system from which model competitive theory is derived. All parts of the human body relate in multiple ways to all other parts. The moral imperative (what should be done) for the field of medicine arises from the question: "What is good for the patient?" Endless inquiry is needed to know how to treat patients' problems better. Patients' complaints are not viewed as exclusively private and subjective even though they have that quality. Wellness is an economic and social benefit. Patients are free from medicine to live their own lives but must live by the rules of wellness to improve the probabilities of good health. As knowledge is by no means always reliable, we can expect as normal that corrections in medical insights and practices will likely arise regularly.

The **Integrative** mode for viewing economic morality presents an analogous organic picture. That view, regrettably, is not now part of the self-conscious public domain of explanation or ideology. All parts of any integrative system relate in multiple ways to all other parts, as do the organs of the human body. All parts also integrate with each other within the Essential Economy. The productive resources managed by the market exchange structure, along with the governmentally supported power system, form an interdependent system. The moral imperative (what should be done) in economies arises from the question: "What are the economy's, the environment's, and the consumers' needs?" These are the needs of economic well-being. Endless reliable knowledge is necessary to know better their nature and distribution. Needs are not exclusively private and subjective although they often have that quality.

Individuals, to be "free" and successful, must discover and learn to live within the rules of technology, social cooperation, and nature's environment. As instituted rules change regularly with new knowledge and technology, the probability is that we face a continuous search to know what the "right" rules should be. How do they integrate the Essential Economy? How do we know the nature and causes of improving the wealth of humanity?

An unheralded source of conceptualizing "true" wealth, other than the technological options provided by the Essential Economy, is analogous to the integrative mode of functional families. Here, a quality of wealth is the manner in which we humans treat each other. This treatment is a product of human understanding and appreciation that has been muddled by inherent differences of sentiments among us, by the tendency to push our impulses too far, often into zones of pathological behavior, and by our failures to recognize and cultivate delicate prudence in all matters of human intercourse. Adam Smith was deeply concerned over "propriety" in his *Theory of Moral Sentiments* but failed to suggest that its cultural cultivation is important in determining the nature and causes of the humanitarian wealth of nations. That omission is a probable reason why economics is often misconceived as only "materialistic." This materialistic conception is incorrect, misleading, and a dangerous put-down on a subject of limitless humanitarian significance.

The integrative mode reflects family-like, sympathetic concerns for the fulfillment of others' individual needs. As Abraham Maslow has noted, these needs emerge in two categories: basic biological needs and uniquely humanistic needs. Basic biological needs are safety, food, thirst quenching, sleep, sex, health, shelter, body covering (clothing), information, belonging and dependency. Without these basic needs being met, our species could not exist at all. Distinctly humanistic needs are love, self-respect, the need to understand, aesthetic experiences, and self-actualization. They include a zest for experiences, creativeness, a desire to be a good human being with a sense of accomplishment. Maslow reminds us that these are needs of healthy people. Individuals do not necessarily, or even normally, give precedence to basic biological needs over humanistic needs. A moral philosophy of economics must, in quest of justice, examine how the system can economize among these many needs.

Human needs have a special place in the integrative mode. Another's needs should be respected over one's frivolous wants, as would be expected in a functional family. Meeting another's needs is imperative to making the Essential Economy work effectively, for others as well as to our own advantage. Here, self-interest and public-interest have a common mission. Private rationality and public rationality coincide in the integrative mode by satisfying both basic and humanistic needs. Here, rationality and the sentiment of love can coalesce as they do in a well functioning family. Thus, one of the standards of social health should be how well the Essential Economy meets the basic and humanistic needs of people. Adam Smith certainly could have found this congenial as he observed, "Humanity does not desire to be great, but to be loved."

THEORY AND PHILOSOPHY OF TECHNOLOGY IN THE INTEGRATIVE MODE

The role of technology has been seriously neglected in economic theory's explanation of the nature and causes of the wealth of nations. This is an oversight equal to neglecting the many qualities of human nature itself. An exploration of the nature of technology is not simply to identify competitive economic theory's neglect of its central importance in the Essential Economy. There is an issue of moral significance here. Technology and its techno-logic are essential in conceptualizing how the integrative mode provides a moral model for judging how well the workable market (power and exchange) manages the Essential Economy.

Technology is a far more humanly intimate part of the **Integrative** system than economic philosophizing has emphasized. Human nature and technology are as intimate as they are because in our pre-human distant past they co-evolved, selecting each other. Man emergent designed technology, and technology emergent "designed" mankind emergent through natural selection (mutated hands that could better manipulate stones as tools and weapons had survival advantage).

This was so, much as in the future intentionally or inadvertently we may redesign humans by means of genetic engineering.

Technology and its accompanying knowledge of how to make and use it seem to be so much a given that its importance for moral philosophy may be virtually overlooked and its practical importance taken for granted. Yet we are sustained by it and we are threatened by it. We are also changed by it. In sum, it contributes to the economic organism's growing pains, pleasures and purposes. Knowledge-technology is an inherent companion, without which we would not exist at all as human.

The quality that reliable knowledge and the multiple forms of technology (tangible tools, symbols, language, mathematics, and computer software) all have in common is their clear and explicit rules of procedure, which have a demonstrably high probability of successfully performing as intended. This high probability is confirmed by the relative certainty of ascertaining causes of failure and knowing how to fix them.

Technology conforms to natural processes. It operates by a natural cause-and-effect "techno-logic." When technology fails there are techno-logical cause-and-effect steps to take to locate the cause of the faltering. Plane crashes are examined in meticulous detail to ascertain the cause of failure, so that redesign or improved training will reduce future failures. Tools and technology, then, are instruments invented by humans (and in an extremely limited way by other species) and have a quality of demonstrable cause and effect repeatable success in operations carried out by following techno-logical rules of procedure. Slice the bread with the serrated edge of the knife; it works better than a spoon. Don't try to take an overloaded airplane off a runway that's too short. It requires technical knowledge and practiced skills to operate technology successfully.

Disagreements over how to operate technologies are resolvable. Either one pattern is a demonstrably superior way to land a plane, or drive a car, or fasten a shoe, or different patterns are demonstrably equally successful, or dangerous. If you drink don't drive. This admonition, within certain degrees of reliability, can even be quantified with an alcohol content level count in the blood. This is *not* an assertion that technologies are not used dangerously or for evil. It is an assertion that views contending that technologies can have deleterious consequences are based on the same form of instrumental cause-and-effect demonstrable techno-logic as underlies rules for how technology should be operated. If this was not the case, criticisms of technology could be seen as unjustified prejudice similar to racial or gender bias.

There is a techno-logic to the use of language, mathematics, computer software, and rules specifying appropriate procedures for reliable results. Rules are sometimes tools, not tangible but "tool like" in their logical cause and effect functions. The integrative system and its Essential Economy are governed by techno-logic rules. However, the threat-power system's market management of the Essential Economy is not only governed by techno-logic rules, but it is also governed by vestigial, mytho-logic rights derived from illusions and bestowing privilege by imputing a positive contribution. Adam Smith spotted that illusion and noted that the landed aristocracy reap where they have not sown. In seeking a naturalistic moral guidance for the Essential Economy it is methodologically fruitful to be skeptical as to whether governing rules have an instrumental or an illusionary foundation. What gives instrumental techno-logic its significance as moral authority is its real, not mythical or illusionary, capacity to contribute to humanitarian purposes and the wealth of nations.

KNOWLEDGE-TECHNOLOGY, MORAL STANDARDS, AND THE INTEGRATIVE MODE

Knowledge-technology, as discussed above, provides a powerful socially organizing and bonding force. Daniel Boorstin's global *Republic of*

Technology: Reflections On Our Future Community explores the process of knowledge-technology integrating the peoples of the globe for mutual benefits that are derived from coordinated use of technology. The use of technology is a social force, in harness with biological-psychological bonding, that forms the **Integrative** mode. Technology is a powerful force integrating humanity. However slowly, but over time, people discover that they share a need for technologies for defining and fulfilling many of their needs (agricultural procedures, automobiles, railroads, medical care). The quality of technology and the logic of its use generate a public rationality, public interest, and public purpose. We see this response to technology and science manifest in "rising expectations" throughout the world. These form a common quality of the integrative mode that provides a dependable standard of what is considered good—that is, morally better.

Progress in standards of living is the result of redefining human needs in terms of advanced technological-instrumental options (quality of health, housing, diets, education). Instrumental logic and evidence in a similar manner transform human values (quality of lifestyles, size and nature of families). All these values and relationships can progressively contribute to longer and more fulfilling lives.

None of this is intended to dodge the regrettable reality that knowledge-technology is also a surreptitious force easily overlooked as it becomes disruptive and at times is shaped into frivolous and even dangerous instruments, many of which are weaponry. Later on, the costs and benefits of technology to humanity will be analyzed with suggestions for coping with the dangers.

Technology does not act alone, even though it possesses a quality of analytical independence from the analysis of power. Technology functions within and under the influence of institutions such as private property, monetized markets, national states, ideological and religious differences. Institutions matter, for better and for worse. They form power-threat systems and define rules of the exchange mode.

However, the historical evidence in David S. Landes's *The Wealth and Poverty of Nations* arguably demonstrates that knowledge-technology, as a totality of benefits over detriments, has been a progressive force.

Changes in knowledge-technology generate the necessity to reevaluate and mutually accommodate the rules and values we live by, that we may together live better. The standards by which living better is evaluated are determined by how effectively the Essential Economy contributes to meeting both basic and humanistic needs. Even the standards themselves are a product of technology-induced values (housing, transportation, education) and reliable knowledge of the manner in which all these ingredients are organically organized in a mutually adaptive mode.

TECHNOLOGY AND HUMAN VALUES

There is here no expectation of finding a pattern of absolute values that will guide us without error through eternity. Rather, the moral quest is to develop the means to create adapting values, rules and standards that will provide guidance for humanity as it evolves with our culture into an uncertain future. All we encounter has emerged out of natural evolutionary forces derived from natural laws. Our search for moral answers is inescapably both bound by, and opened up by, the possibilities we may construct out of the laws of human nature, our natural environment, the fabric of culture traits, all woven in creative patterns by the geometric progression of technology and human knowledge.

Technology in conjunction with human nature is a major force in the economy. It now becomes evident that it is a major ingredient of all social systems with its focus in the integrative mode. Technology, and its cause-and-effect logic, generates and transforms human values. Technology has the capacity of contributing to comfort and convenience, security, self-esteem, self-realization, the need to understand, experiences of scholarship, travel, inventing, discovery, and so forth. It provides means by which needs are increasingly identified and more fully met under constraints of scarcity. Even so basic a passion as sex is enhanced by printed results of research, as well as mechanical and chemical technology. These make sex more fulfilling, and allow for sex with reduced fear of disease or concern for families too large to be provided proper nurturing. These technologies contribute to safer childbirth and survival.

Certainly the change to valuing smaller families from valuing large families constitutes a fundamental moral transformation. Benefits learned from technology are substantially responsible for this transformation of traditional family values. We can observe that loving and cohesive family values need not be restricted to biologically related individuals. Many crave for the opportunity to adopt a child. The new world of technology defines what is essential to rearing responsible children who will grow up to be self-reliant and adequately affluent to take care of fellow humans, and aging elders, relatives or not. This transformation of caring values is providing, through Social Security, an institutionally enhanced independence during modern maturity. Much of the past's assumed loving intimacy toward the elderly may be lost in this transformation. However, I suspect that it may be a small price paid for the advantages of health care and extended, more fulfilling life experiences. All these values and relationships contribute to, and are ingredients of, the integrative mode of social organization, moral meaning and hence wealth of humanity.

Now that we have examined the three modes of organizing social processes (**Threat, Exchange, Integrative**), how do they apply to constructing a view of a moral philosophy of economics?

7

Moral Sentiments and Economic Justice

The world changes at an increasing pace giving rise to confusion and conflict over divergent modes and standards of determining what is right and just in novel contexts such as the internet, weapons of mass destruction in meeting of East and West, reports of approaching environmental limits and thus limits to sharing humanity's niche. Moral foundations differ among individuals and cultures. How can we find a basis for moral agreement and a sense of justice? It is the task of this chapter to explore further steps to develop a morality by which economic justice may be better perceived and more practically applied.

As noted repeatedly, fundamentalist ideology suggests it is not possible to repeal the natural laws of supply and demand. It is best we leave these natural forces alone and, inferentially, live with the wisdom of the beneficent natural laws governing market economies. This is the way to freedom and justice.

This book takes a very different view of the reality imposed on economies by natural laws. Everything we humans do is in some way shaped by that which natural laws make possible or unworkable. But nature is not rigidly forced upon us in ways that disallow human creativity. To the contrary, creativity itself is nature in action. The consequences of natural laws are filtered through human knowledge, technology and invented social organization. Natural laws are not automatically beneficent; humanity has been inventing correctives throughout our emergence. This interpretation is not an escape from nature into a supernatural realm. It is learning (inventing) how nature can be better turned to humanity's advantage.

Recognition of humanity's multiple inherent inclinations provides insight into the positive, as well as the negative, influences of nature on economic behavior. As noted previously, there is far more to humans' economic motives than self-reliance and self-interest. Other inherent inclinations contribute to the causes of the wealth of nations and help judge the economy's moral effectiveness. These inborn impulses are vestigial remains of a harsh and brutal, as well as a nurturing and compassionate, evolutionary past. They are the reasons we humans can be so brutal, so cautious, so loving, so creative, so confused.

EVOLUTION AND MORALITY

Humans are here because we evolved. We did not evolve to live the good life, or a purposeful life, or a meaningful life. We evolved as a surviving, self perpetuating species. However bizarre some cultures may appear, it is obvious that a society would not exist unless the knowledge, technology and social norms provide adequate social order and sustenance to allow for birth and care of enough young until they take over and perpetuate the process. We see that the natural laws of human biology, natural environment, evolved knowledge, technology and social norms were mutually adapted for the society to perpetuate itself to the present. Given such a reality, this book's philosophy of economics is built upon the firm footing of natural laws, not unlike that which Adam Smith sought to do. However, rather than assuming that nature knows mankind's interests best, as Smith assumed, I have looked to humanity's uniquely creative self-preserving qualities upon which to build a moral economic philosophy.

Without an ultimate end or purpose, the human species evolved with inherent mechanisms (foresight, high capacity brains, symbol and tool proclivities) that provided a grasp that exceeded the necessary reach for minimal survival. Thus, we are confronted with the dilemma of what to do with this potential beyond mere survival. Out of this background we generate the questions: Where should we be going and why? What purposes are appropriate to what ends? What experiences are meaningful and why? Here our moral quandary intensifies. No other species must ask itself, what is it we want to do with ourselves or make of ourselves? These questions leave us with further questions. How do we evaluate the numerous paths humanity has chosen and may choose? What is it we might better make of ourselves? How can we decide? With genetic engineering at hand, how (if at all) do we want to transform humanity? Do we choose to keep us as we are with some born fortunate, others born tragedies, and many of us being grateful but wishing more for our offspring? These dilemmas certainly generate the need for moral philosophy. I am not ready to take on redesigning the human species, I have constrained my attention to the simpler questions, those that arise over economic morality and justice.

The insights we have been developing are not purported to pursue utopian perfection but rather a continuation of human experience and learning in the process of human evolution and development. It is a moral quest, and no morality is all-knowing. The goal here is to discover ways of developing values, rules and standards that will guide *improvement*. Our search for moral answers is inescapably both bound by, and opened up by, the possibilities we may construct out of universal laws, human nature, our natural environment, and the fabric of culture traits.

However, just because an innate drive contributed to survival during past evolution, unthinking acquiescence to that inherent impulse is not necessarily morally correct in all present circumstances. This assertion is contrary to Adam Smith's pre-Darwinian view that human sentiments (inherent inclinations) were designed by God as natural laws for the benefit of humanity, and hence should be followed for our own good. Every evolutionary development that facilitated the natural talents of proto-humans becoming human and that provided humans with reproductive and survival drives in the context of that environment does not mean that those predilections are now automatically socially or morally correct. They are not necessarily conducive to the **Integrative** mode of social interacting or to economic effectiveness today or into the future.

To illustrate, the male gender's physical ability to dominate females sexually may be "natural" but it is not in itself a guide to socially effective or morally just practices. Certainly part of the conflict between the sexes arises from this source. The sex drive has been essential to our evolution and survival. Inappropriately directed sexual appetites and physical prowess are conducive to conflict and are not the appropriate arbiters of morality or justice. Often, perhaps always, similar natural predilections are both essential to survival and pathology producing. Hunger and sex illustrate the possibility of pushing any impulse to the point of becoming detrimental. It contradicts Mae West's quip that "too much of a good thing is wonderful!" We can over indulge. We are slowly breaking through old patterns of behavior to sense a morally more correct pattern of female rights. They are not natural rights nor an inherent right to be free. Rights were not built into natural laws or our biology. New rights may over time be structured into our culturally defined normalcy. Although feelings run deep in such matters, what determines moral justice is more a function of mutual adaptation, public purpose rationality, and reliable knowledge than it is a function of inherent sentiments. Morality involves identifying options and negotiating mutually adaptive agreements that shape norms for moral imperatives. This moral determination will be implemented as a result of a combination of cognitive understanding and empathetic feelings of the informed, impartial spectator within us.

In market economies, self-interest and personal gain are readily conducive to both productivity and pathology. Constraints on such inherent tendencies through social agreement create inescapable frustrations and discontents. This gives rise to cries to be free. Sometimes these demands are justified and sometimes they are not. Issues of how to judge better and worse cannot escape inherent impulses but are "resolvable" only through mutually adapted civilized understanding. Though humanity has evolved norms of behavior as correctives to untamed urges, neither nature's impulses nor humanity's norms are adequately fine-tuned for eternity.

MAKING NATURE WORK FOR HUMANS

Once proto-man initiated the invention of culture traits (language, tools and rules) a new form of natural evolution was set in motion. In the process something extremely significant happened. Humans learned to invent their own forms of adapting. Not since pre-man emerged into modern man has pure nature's way been accepted as best for this species. This means that one of nature's creations—humanity—in order to adapt, survive and prosper, must come to understand nature's laws and creations, including our own natural impulses. We have become our own creator of how we will conduct our adaptation, survival, meaning and purposes (or non-survival). It is an awesome responsibility, and it requires an awesome quality and quantity of the right kind of knowledge. It is not so much needing knowledge per se, as it is needing to understand what *kind* of knowledge is appropriate to the challenges nature and our own creativity have imposed upon us. We must determine how to identify and generate that appropriate essential knowledge.

All this induces us to question the inchoate assumption that nature knows what is best for humanity. As noted, the larger forces of nature do not care who "wins," humans, micro organisms or some yet unidentified elements of nature. We have arrived at a point where we can no longer assume that we of the West are the chosen people of

God or of a benevolent, partisan Nature. Yet, in another sense we are all chosen by nature, not purposefully but by the "chance" of natural selection and our evolved self awareness. True, we cannot repeal natural laws, any more than we can simplify the value of *pi*; but we can and do continuously adapt by using these natural laws to our own advantage. The field of medicine provides eye glasses, medications, surgery, and so forth, all of which require understanding the laws of optics, chemistry and biology. We don't repeal or change the law of gravity but we do use laws of aerodynamics to circumvent gravity and enable flight. So too do we shape the adaptive roles of curiosity, inquiry, imagination, creativity, inventiveness, technology, and rules of institutions. Humanity developed civilization by circumventing some of nature's laws and turning others to our own good (or detriment).

Adam Smith identified an important sentiment that is imperative for justice: "sympathetic feelings of the informed, impartial spectator within" us. This impartial spectator is that dimension of human response that accompanies empathy or sympathetic feelings for others. The vernacular would say, "it is walking in another's shoes." The capacity to be an impartial spectator exists in virtually all of us who are emotionally and socially healthy, though I am confident there is considerable inherent diversity among us. Empathy is the source of the individual's conscience; it plays a major role in mankind's moral sense. Those without conscience or empathy for others, who show no sense of guilt or remorse, when grotesque enough, are not unreasonably viewed as psychopaths or criminally insane. This perspective lifts thought out of the straitjacket illusion that human feelings are strictly subjective and outside the reach of public purpose rationality.

MORALITY OF MUTUAL ADAPTATION

Why should we be moral? The answer: to make the human social order work. If one asks, as some do, why humanity deserves priority over other species such as fire ants, cockroaches, bunnies, or beasts of burden, the answer is too simple to sound convincing. There is no reason. Not from the perspective from which the question is usually raised. There is no reason out in the logos or in the larger laws of the universe. Nature very likely has no knowable intended purpose for humanity in preference to other species. Nature allows *Homo sapiens* to suffer entropy, victimization by natural causes, and possibly to die out, as has happened to most of the species that evolved on this planet.

The reason we humans do have this deep interest in the priority of our species is the vested interest we have in ourselves and our fellow man (through our inherent sense of bonding and empathy). The rational self-interest reason we should feel this way is that it reinforces our sense of mutual dependence on each other for our own well-being and those we love or feel empathy toward. We all confront the inescapable necessity to adapt to each other under conflict-provoking conditions over scarcity and perceived rights (human constructs of social order). We adapt peaceably by negotiating mutually acceptable reciprocal exchanges, under the advantages and disadvantages of the differential power-threat system. Or we settle, but may not resolve, matters through violence. For the latter, physical power or technological dominance becomes the determinant of settlement but not a justification of why it should be so. Tension lives on.

I have identified this imperative to increasingly adapt peaceably through the integrative mode as the "morality of mutual adaptation." Mutually adapting is essential to avert the potential excesses of conflict and the ultimate resort to the threat-power mode which is not necessarily morally right or practically best. The morality of mutual adaptation is a recognition of our inevitable interdependence with each other and our environment. It is a morality of mutually adapting in a world in process of change, change which may well continue so long as humanity survives.

Mutual adaptation involves the **Exchange** mode to negotiate harmonizing with others. This mode, remember, is a positive-sum game in which all are winners. The negotiation for mutual adaptation has the moral proviso that it be done so all benefit with some winnings (or minimum losses in cases of disasters). Thus the negotiators do not do so from behind a "curtain of ignorance," where they will not know where they will land in the social order as John Rawls suggested in his distinguished work, *A Theory of Justice*. Instead, the negotiations are to be carried out by informed, empathetic, "impartial spectators." The crucial issue here for advancing all-around benefits is that the mutual adaptation process be informed by the most reliable knowledge of conditions and consequences for all participating parties. This cannot be just assumed, as it is posited in conventional theory. It must, however, be resolved before this emerging moral philosophy of economics is concluded.

Humanity possesses a curiosity that generates new understandings and creates innovative instruments that challenge existing habits, customs, rules and the traditional authority of the established institutionalized threat system. This raises questions of what new values-rules should be identified as morally right (good or better) and how, under changed conditions, such an inescapable choice is to be justified. Past habits, customs, rules, values no longer necessarily provide adequate guidance or justification under changed conditions. For example medications and contraceptives (however reliable) become a justification for modifying traditional cultural constraints on inherent sexual inclinations, and traditional gender rules are changed. With each change, we confront anew the issue of how to determine what is right, wrong, moral, and why. New medical techniques raise new questions over how to economize in the distribution of medical care. The Internet raises new issues over freedom of speech. Electronic money and credit through charge cards raise new problems over causes and responsibilities for personal bankruptcies. Given the limitations of human understanding at any given time and the pace of change, we might well expect, and indeed do confront, confusion, even conflict.

Why should individuals, committed to private purpose, self-interest rationality, support pursuit of public purpose rationality and social empathy as has been asserted above? By choosing what may be the most difficult case to justify, I provide next a generic justification for individual moral obligation to others in general.

FUTURITY MORALITY

Why should we sacrifice for a future in which we will never live? Why sacrifice now to protect the environment for future humanity's benefit? "What has posterity ever done for me?" There are several reinforcing reasons why we should sacrifice for others, even those who can never reciprocate. In our reverie we can, and frequently do, vicariously experience the future. That is how we become aware of it. But why should we become morally concerned? We should do so because there are direct, personal purpose, rational reasons why we individuals should recognize the advantage of accepting moral responsibility to the future. There is the rational self-interest reason of experiencing the inherent emotional satisfaction of our own altruistic acts, such as we experience in the joys of rearing a child, donating blood, and volunteering for good causes. Acting now for the future will give most of us a sense of having contributed to a good cause, others' well-being.

Coupled with satisfaction from altruism is the feeling of empathy for those of the future. This is quite likely a major reason why the moral issue of the future arises in our senses in the first place. For a feeling of empathy, ask yourself how you felt upon learning that the eruption of Mount Vesuvius trapped its victims in their homes as the molten lava seeped in and consumed them alive, or as the September 11 World Trade Center workers were trapped and consumed by flames. We do feel for others as it is one of our most central moral sentiments.

There is a further force behind concern for the future, and that is the inherent satisfaction from posing puzzles and struggling to solve them. It is like the satisfaction from playing solitaire or doing a crossword puzzle. In this case the puzzle is over the future of people like ourselves. Ask yourself how you feel about puzzles posed by depletion of adequate energy resources, fresh water, arable land or the eventual burning out of the sun.

There is yet another powerful rational self-interest reason why we must cultivate values calling for sacrifice now even though there will be no direct reciprocal reward from the future. Encouraging our fellow humans to participate now in future concerns cultivates feelings of empathy toward all humanity, past, future and present. This will cause us in the present to be more empathetic toward each other here and now. This will make our community a better place to live in, and hence provide a more pleasing life for me and mine. My neighbors will be more caring, helpful, loving and lovable. And so will I. Believing and behaving with intentions of bringing benefits to our fellow man synergizes their responding in this beneficial integrative mode.

THE MORAL SENSE

Fortunately for humanity we have an inherent *"moral sense"* upon which a morality of mutual adaptation can be built. It is a natural inclination to do the right thing. It is not inherent knowledge of what the right thing is. We do not intuitively know the right values necessary to cope with all the challenges we face in the modern world. Evolution bestowed a biological predisposition for concerns beyond one's self, beyond the individual's immediate self-interest. A morality of mutual adaptation is founded, then, in an inherent moral sense arising from compelling evolutionary propensities of healthy individuals. This view of a moral sense tends to confirm Adam Smith's insight into the "sympathetic feelings of the informed, impartial spectator." For Smith, that sympathy "seems to be the original and most fundamental moral passion." This compelling source of concerns for others becomes a source of our conscience, and hence plays a most profound role in a moral philosophy.

Further, realization of the need for belonging contributes to a sense of connectedness, as well as improved individual longevity. Individuals who reject bonding in varying degree range from loners to psychopaths. (At the opposite end, we encounter the addiction of the "groupies.") The major point is that through empathy, nature provides commitment and direction that facilitates a pursuit of morality, including self-sacrifice which we admire as heroic. Empathy likely stands behind the popular moral admonition, "Do unto others as you would have others do unto you." This does not tell us what we should want done to us. It does not tell us the qualitative ingredients of moral obligations. However, a generalized sense of mutual "love" and "respect" bonds more caringly and reliably. Adam Smith stated the moral point well: "What reward is most proper for promoting the practice of truth, justice, and humanity? The confidence, the esteem, and love of those we live with. Humanity does not desire to be great, but to be loved. It is not in being rich that truth and justice would rejoice, but in being trusted and believed, recompenses which those virtues must almost always acquire."

There is another inherent moral disposition that is so much a part of our daily lives that it escapes us as a powerful element of our moral sense. It is suggested throughout this work. Humans are inherently puzzle posers and problem solvers. We do heroic deeds, not to be dead heroes, but to save lives, avoid injuries, help others, solve looming problems, clarify puzzling questions, even when they bring forth the wrath of a threat system. (Galileo exemplifies the latter point.) Most of humankind has had the experience of confronting puzzles needing solutions in their routine experiences. By confronting them, they may be pulled to act unselfishly. Parents regularly live lives this way by struggling to make things better for their families. We rightfully expect routine problem solving and reasonable degrees of altruism from healthy individuals.

TECHNOLOGY AND MORALITY

Technology, as well as human sentiments, is a major force not only in forming an Essential Economy but in providing fundamental moral standards for judging how effective an economy may be. For some it seems crass, even anti-spiritual, to cast technology in a moral role. However it is there and belongs there because it contributes to establishing standards of a better life for humanity.

Technical instruments enhance the fulfillment of human needs and are rightfully valued for their capacity to do so. Technology, as we have seen in the evolutionary process, is virtually as intimate to man as our skin. Knowledge and technology have co-evolved with and contributed to the evolution and formation of human nature itself. We are the species that evolved by virtue of primitive technology playing a role in the selection of random mutations that made us human. This co-evolution of human biology and technology shaped our capacities to symbolize, speak, stand, and walk erect, and generated diverse forms of experiencing. Technical instruments assist human bonding through mutual sharing in meeting universal needs and desires in new ways. They provide a dynamic moral quality in a changing world.

Knowledge-technology and the human impulses of curiosity and experimentalism, in conjunction with invented language, have resulted in our advanced rational potential and are an intimate aspect of our humanness. The most valuable product of the Scientific Revolution has been an enhancement of a "techno-logic," cause-and-effect, instrumental mode of thinking. When we apply this way of thinking in conjunction with the integrative mode of human relationships to the betterment of the Essential Economy, together they contribute method to the morality of mutual adaptation. This instrumental thinking contributes to creation and expansion of human values and the nature of needs.

Our techno-logic and scientific knowledge indicate reasonable standards between extreme excess and extreme deprivation. They become values for judging whether lives are reasonably fulfilled in both the underdeveloped and advanced worlds. They are the technology referent that causes the West to empathize with others as "underdeveloped," and induces the underdeveloped to seek the West's level of well-being. Technology becomes a moral imperative for humanity, domestically and globally, spawning "rising expectations."

Technology is also abused as means of dominance, invidiousness, revenge, carelessness, and perhaps other such drawbacks. Even here, recognition of pathologies of tool abuse is the awareness of violating the larger techno-logic of tools' proper humane use in the integrative mode. We invented tools for weapons, as well as for provisioning subsistence. Frequently they were one and the same (hunting for food). Just because they were an inherent product of the survival process does not make weapons of war currently a morally desirable ingredient for humanity. That is why there has been a global effort for disarmament. Technology, by its own techno-logic cause-effect rationality, calls for its own proper use in providing humanitarian needs in the integrative mode (transportation vehicles, butcher knives, medications, telephones). Regrettably, we often mismatched humans have not yet invented social instruments that can reliably resolve conflict without resort to the threat impulse that deprives others of technological benefits or inflicts the excruciating agony technology can deliver.

In sum, technology and its instrumental logic play a powerful hand in forming a humanitarian morality, or it can be subverted to human brutality in response to conflict still inherent in the human condition. Mostly, we have reason to be grateful for technology's adaptive and enhancing qualities, as well as reason to be morally guided by its humanitarian possibilities.

SELF-INTEREST AND FREE WILL

We rear our children or should try to rear them to be morally responsible for their own good. In the process of maturation, individuals normally learn that socially responsible behavior is a necessary condition for realizing their own self-interest. One who is morally reliable has passed the first test of acceptability on the path to prospering. Granted that many seek their narrow self-interest and often succeed through immoral behavior; however, probability favors one's self-interest if behaving in ways accepted as moral. Thus self-interest can and does reinforce the moral sense. This focus on moral conformity creates problems, sometimes severe for some innovators while proving profitable for others (very severe for Galileo, less severe for Darwin, and very profitable for Henry Ford). Such complications led the philosophy of pragmatism to view human life as including a continuum of experimentation, with the results evaluated in terms of consequences. And I am adding that for pragmatism to be a moral philosophy, evaluating consequences must be done in terms of a morality of mutual adaptation.

In the more common cases, deviation from self-interest virtue can be severe enough to cause considerable consternation. It results in some being unemployable and they and the rest of us lose the benefits of their potential contribution. Worse still are the consequences of gross deception, fraud, con-artists who may prosper without meeting appropriate moral acceptability tests. And there is an indeterminate expanse of what I have long termed "legal embezzlement," recently exposed in spectacular corporate and stock market faltering. We are in desperate need of understanding how to cope with such cases. We have less difficulty recognizing the problem and the need.

Free will is an elusive concept which, given proper meaning, is relevant, even essential, for constructing a guiding moral philosophy of economics. Having people in general accept responsibility for their actions is necessary for the effectiveness of the Essential Economy and the integrative system. Democratic societies make the locus of "ultimate" responsibility explicit: *we, the people*. Democratic society or not, individuals do act, and they act within the limits of historical guidance (rules, customs, values), unique natural sentiments, and accumulated knowledge. We do not have a freedom to act outside of our human nature, cultural conditioning, and encompassing natural laws. Within these influences, we each are biologically unique and uniquely conditioned by our culture and sociological settings in which we are reared. The result is that each person has a unique will. It is not a will free of causal determination. Each has the capacity for *discretion*. If it is discretion that is intended by the phrase "free will," then it has a fruitful use in the construction of a moral philosophy. If that is so, then it is my experience that the phrase "free will" is badly abused in the vernacular and badly used in our public philosophy.

The individual is both somewhat lost in the economic process of contributing and receiving and also establishes his/her self-identity as contributor and consumer in the process. Individuals' unique wills provide a creative force of both immoral and moral character. Here we are all inescapably little gods, confronted with the responsibility of continuously designing and redesigning our purposes and the means for humanity's journey. Within this process, we may by discretionary acts of unique human wills contribute to moral progress or falter, without awareness that we should be called to account by circumstances.

Competitive economic theory has asserted a state of freedom for all, as we pursue our share of the scarce goods and services available. The economic system is not, in truth, one of unrestrained individual freedom. No social system can work that way. We morally monitor trading in areas like prostitution, how we process our foods or maintain the safety of our airlines. These rules are established in defiance of an ideological belief that we should be free to choose for ourselves and to use our private property as we like. In reality it is *flexibility* and not freedom that is possible and can be given meaning. Effective flexibility is defined by rules to guide private interest to act in ways that better contribute to the collective well-being of all individuals. How is it knowable, that which contributes to and that which constitutes the collective well-being of all?

Conventional economic theory fails to provide, and even tends to discourage, developing a moral guidance for citizens' reform of the system. This book's moral philosophy of economics is dependent upon unique wills to visualize better prospects over inadequate traditional commitments.

JUSTICE AS JUSTIFICATION
IN ESTABLISHING MORAL NORMS

A moral philosophy of economics inevitably encounters the issue of justice: just price, just distribution of income, justice in determining who does what work, how many hours of work a week, how safe, be paid what you are worth, pay your own way, live within your means, why some must work and others live lavishly on property income, who is taxed and how much and why. The issues of justice or fairness are "endless." In all situations in life we want to be treated fairly. What does it mean? How is this known?

Granted that there are inherent human inclinations giving rise to a moral sense, this does not establish what is fair or just for each class of occasions. We are not inherently provided with enduring answers of what justice should be for the dramatic changes dynamic economies experience. Justice must be founded in appropriate justification. The fact that the market economizes does not automatically provide a justification for its methods or results. Nor does the fact of being the most affluent economy justify whatever it does. The effectiveness of an economy inescapably facing scarcity must constrain consumption by all, induce or compel contribution by the able bodied, and improve the distribution of provisioning for both human and system needs.

Justice is similar to "rights" and "freedom." Neither rights, freedom nor justice exist out there in the logos in a perfect form awaiting discovery. If we seek justice, believing that it has an ideal place in the natural order of things awaiting discovery like some rare archaeological Rosetta Stone, we are foreordained to disappointment. What is considered fair, just or unjust needs to be invented. We are challenged to invent just values, to guide relationships that are as divergent as marriage is from global commerce. In the search for cures of physical ailments, each category of illness requires special medication or treatment. Similarly, for each kind of case in which the issue of fairness arises, we are going to have to invent justice out of the context that surrounds us. And it will change as we seek progress. To improve fairness, justification (not medication) is required. CEO's, politicians, propagandists and advertisers have learned this social justifying device well (CEO's mammoth compensations justified as necessary to obtain the best talent and motivate the most profitable results for the individual corporation and thus provide the best for an economy of free people). It is time the morally concerned elements of society learn to better justify their positions too.

The primary concern here is the issue of justice in the field of economics and how to justify improvements of the economic system. As we are dealing with an evolving process, the challenge is to find adaptive improvements, not a static utopian perfection. Finding and justifying those improvements involves several tightly bound steps:

- Justice requires *justification* of how individuals and groups mutually adapt, or fail to, in the integrative mode.
- That requires *values* to guide practices.

- And this requires *inquiry* to produce appropriate values that have high probability of aiding mutual adaptation.
- And inquiry requires *theory* of how the integrative system functions effectively under conditions of scarcity and change.

Existing economic ideology justifies a traditional pattern of fairness which has much to recommend it. Justification, in public economic philosophy, builds on individual responsibility in a world of scarcity, where each is dependent upon the contribution of others. Self-interest assists self-reliance. All must adapt to the real world. The individual must decide whether to learn, work, and produce. No one can do these things for the individual, (though most can be helped by others). Private property in one's self, in one's output, and in what can be exchanged for that output motivates the individual to produce within his/her capabilities.

This conventional economic philosophy also creates a vision of a best possible world where no one needs to put up with unfair rules imposed by employers, as all are free to work elsewhere or become an entrepreneur. The rules which are fair or just in the work-setting are those negotiated by the exchange mode among free individuals. Thus all win by these negotiated rules.

This justification rationale comports well with dominant economic theory. Scarcity necessitates economizing. Living within the limits of one's contribution to the whole does that. Scarcity coerces economizing while leaving everyone free to consume a quantity equal to what each is most willing and able to produce. It comports well with conventional economics' theory of distribution equal to contribution.

Conventional thinking acknowledges that there will be dissatisfactions. Of course, because there is scarcity, all cannot have all they might wish. However, they can get the most satisfying results possible, given the limits imposed by the scarcity of resources and talents (and distribution of property ownership). This fundamentalist justification argues that we cannot blame private property and the monetized market system for individuals' economic misfortunes. Market institutions deliver the most satisfying results given the existence of limits. This private property, monetized market system of self-reliance is believed to be the best and most just of all possible alternatives. We know that this system is just by the rational way it has here been justified. We can follow the logic of its justification and we can agree with that logic even if we deplore the necessary sacrifices due to scarcity.

Here I have illustrated that we know justice by the logic, theory and evidence by which it is justified. How else? That *is* how we know justice, and when persuasive for most, that is what justice really does mean until an improved version is proven adequately enough to become persuasive. This also suggests how, in the evolution of social relations, it is very likely that concern over "justice" has emerged, even though the process has not been clearly captured in our cultural memory. By this process of justifying, we can reexamine whether and where there are improvements that may be made in the justice of an integrative economic system.

I do not fully accept the foregoing conventional argument as representing justice, as I think it could be better conceived. However, it is a starting place representing an ideal justice for our Western economies. I seek to develop an improved version of justice in a world of scarcity. Difficult as the task may be, we must seek a reliable means of treating each other justly and establish norms by which to hold each other accountable as we progress and change.

When justification is founded in public philosophy based in competitive economic theory, one encounters insights, oversights, and illusions. When economies are in process of continuous change, what is considered just and fair is continuously altered by new standards of human needs and new needs of the Essential Economy. Dominant market theory overlooks the reality that many are not in a position to adapt to change without assistance. Not everyone knows how or is in a position to adjust effectively to changes in the complex modern economy and in the market exchange process. Transitional costs to maintain self and family and to develop new skills (and more) all need to be met at a time when the individual is in the most disadvantaged, unemployed position. Where is justice for the conscientious workers whose lives are disrupted by no failure of their own doing? Our empathies, our ability to see ourselves in the same situation, speak out for new and better justice.

Judging will take place within an ongoing natural and cultural context. That context contains several major inescapable pillars. They are, (1) human sentiments, predispositions and needs; (2) the natural (physical) environment and its ecology; (3) the technological milieu; (4) the institutional setting; (5) a kind of ecological, mutual dependency pattern (integrative system) that organically organizes and facilitates the process; (6) scarcity and the virtues of economizing efficiency and (7) theory that seeks to explain the extent to which the existing system succeeds or falters, and where and how. Revised theory provides the rationale that justifies the justice of alternative options for progressive reform. That which becomes just is that which can be justified as being effective in contributing to the changing Essential Economy's capacity to provide for productive needs of the economy and its human participants. And to be more fully just, such contributions must be achieved at qualitative levels increasingly determined by the techno-logic of mutual adaptation in the integrative process.

JUSTICE AND VALUES

The values of our culture provide the criteria by which individuals judge whether justice is realized for self and others. When facing issues of values, we have been caught between those asserting that values are uncompromising absolutes and those who contend that values are relative to the beliefs of the cultures in which we are reared and where custom makes things morally right or wrong. The dilemma is resolvable. All values are indeed relative but not relative to nothing but believing. Philosophically we are not bereft of footing to build upon. All values must be relative to the laws of nature, including human nature. That is, values requiring beliefs and behavior that fall outside of what is humanly and environmentally productive are worthless or more likely detrimental. (Values insisting that individuals must have the will and capacity to be self-reliant in the free market are insisting on conforming to an illusionary world.) Thus we will do well to recognize that we must live in a world with a basis for moral underpinnings as firm as the laws of nature. Any moral philosophy must be constructed on this inescapable foundation (such as scarcity and human diversity). We look to the nature of common human needs upon which to structure a moral philosophy. At their foundation is a nature-linked logic, in the form of an ecological logic, which is expanded by a techno-logic, and enhanced by socio-cultural instrumental logic, leading to mutual adaptation in an integrative mode.

SUMMARY AND CONCLUSIONS

A moral philosophy of economics not only can be, but must be, constructed on the firm footing of natural laws, as Adam Smith sought to do. However, rather than assuming that nature knows mankind's interests best, it turns out that through the bio-cultural evolution of proto-man to modern humans we have co-opted responsibility for our own well-being. This leaves us facing the question of what it is that we should do about it. That is the source of our moral dilemma. Some of us must invent the answers and some of us must persuasively justify them to our fellow humans, as we in fact do with health care and automotive safety.

The need now is to clarify our purposes and identify worthy idealism for our age. Such idealism and purposes have always been the inventions of mankind. Identifying and proposing purposes has in the past been the role of prophets and inspired classic religious scriptures such as the Bible and Koran. Prophets of how to progress are an inescapable necessity of a moral philosophy of action, warning against present dangers and exhorting a better world. Adam Smith and Enlightenment thinkers have also filled the role of guiding prophets. Beliefs in democracy, individualism, and competitive market ideology were not miraculously handed down on mysterious tablets nor were they a product of genetic evolution. They are ideas generated over historical time by people who happened to have commitments to innovate and articulate social ideas. These prophets of our present Western world are the source of social and moral ideas with which we can build a better society, just as we can build brick homes because past people invented bricks. We are only trying to put another brick of morality in place.

An improvement in economic justice exists, not when the utopian market establishes a general equilibrium of maximum utility under constraints of scarcity, but when the conditions of social organization (institutions, rules, values) and technology assist a greater portion of humanity to experience an enriched realization of their needs. All must be done within the limits of the Essential Economy, scarcity, ecological sustainability—and human nature.

From the foregoing exploration of the evolution of human nature with its biological and technological integration, we can more clearly identify the Essential Economy and the source of moral commitment and guidance for the workable market. If an appropriate moral philosophy is knowable, it is likely learnable and shareable by healthy individuals. Regrettably, humanity cannot be assured that this will come to pass, but with life as a continuous experiment, we had better continue trying.

8

The Meaning of Economic Progress

Many of us admire the wonders of progress while struggling to adjust to the pace and demands of modern life. Progress has become a precious moral value in our public economic philosophy. Successful pursuit of progress has been a longstanding benchmark by which Western civilizations have judged "free market economies" as superior to all others. Scientific economics assesses economic effectiveness in terms of economizing efficiency and growth of domestic product but omits a qualitative evaluation of the content of growth. Is the growth necessarily progress?

The meaning of progress is controversial. There are good reasons for this. The very notion of Western cultural superiority and progress has been under attack by critics of progress. It must be faced: if there are no criteria for judging an effective economy over a less effective economy, we cannot say capitalism is superior to feudalism, communism, or socialism. Nor can it be said that modern Western economies are superior to underdeveloped economies with undernourished children and listless dying parents. We cannot say that technological, scientific, and educational underdevelopment is a form of backwardness calling for correction. We cannot pass judgment about the meaning of improvement or reform. Virtually everyone aware of global conditions knows better.

I contend that Western economies are materially, humanistically, and morally better than all others, past or present. This superiority is a product of progress which should be understood and perpetuated for the future well-being of all humanity. However, our understanding of modern complexities of progress is vague. The philosophical quest for the meaning of progress has not been, and is not now, well developed as moral guidance in the field of main core economics.

More than a half century ago (1944) institutional economist Clarence Ayres, in his *Theory of Economic Progress,* lamented that "the restoration of the concept of progress is one of the crying needs of contemporary social science." I agree that concern for qualitative economic progress, in addition to and as distinct from quantitative economic growth, deserves analytical attention in a moral philosophy of economics.

In defense of the discipline of economics, it seems reasonable to believe that all seminal works were intended to improve understanding of how economies function. Implied or explicit is the assumption that better understanding can lead to better practices. Better practices imply some basis of determining a better economy over a worse economy, or economic progress by correction of economic deficiencies. Better over worse has a moral quality. In a philosophy of economics, exploring the moral meaning of progress is imperative as we seek to find guidance in our dynamic world.

As presented early in this book, Adam Smith taught us how to turn an element of nature to our own account in his *Wealth of Nations.* He showed how to use the natural sentiment of self-interest to our advantage. Recall, selfishness had been viewed in medieval theology as immoral. Smith interpreted self-interest, not as evil selfishness but as a self-reliant motive that energized and organized the market economy and enhanced the satisfactions of consumers. The theory built upon his insight revolutionized our views of turning natural laws to the creation of the wealth of nations. It provided theoretical and philosophical support and guidance to the emergence of market-managed economies.

Even the most renowned curmudgeon and critic of private enterprise penned a tribute to capitalism's achievements. Karl Marx, with Friedrich Engels a century and a half ago, wrote in *The Communist Manifesto*, "The bourgeoisie . . . has been the first to show what man's activity can bring about. It has accomplished wonders far surpassing Egyptian pyramids, Roman aqueducts, and Gothic cathedrals. . . . The bourgeoisie cannot exist without constantly revolutionizing the instruments of production, and thereby the relations of production, and with them all social relations. . . . All fixed, fast-frozen relations, with their train of ancient and venerable prejudices and opinions are swept away, all newly formed ones become antiquated before they can ossify. . . . The bourgeoisie, by the rapid improvement of all instruments of production, by the immensely facilitated means of communication, draws all, even the most barbarian, nations into civilization. . . . The bourgeoisie, during its rule of scarcely one hundred years, has created more massive and more colossal productive forces than have all preceding generations together." Written a century and a half ago, these "civilizing" strides, indeed, seem to have been made.

A century later, Keynes' theorizing to develop stabilization policies was founded in widely held values that having fully employed productive workers and equipment was better than suffering from their underutilization. Knowing, theoretically, how to avoid the human agonies of economic fluctuations and how to improve economic stability through rational reconstruction of economic institutions was indeed a tremendous moral step in human progress. Economies are still in need of continuous reformation for the changing world.

In spite of these rather persuasive insights into human betterment, the moral meaning and practical path to progress remain contested. Progress, in pursuit of the meaning of progress, is enhanced by a vision of the idea's history. Robert Nisbet, in his *History of the Idea of Progress*, provides essential insights into the ideas that shaped our Western climate of opinion. From antiquity there has been a belief in progress, from a primitive past to a glorious future through an unfolding of a beneficent providential design. It has meant "that humanity is advancing toward some goal continuously, inexorably, and necessarily." For some, this tropism is viewed as driven by "an impulse of perfectibility."

Presenting a major exemplar of a secular philosophy of progress, Nisbet asserts that "Herbert Spencer is the supreme embodiment of the late nineteenth century of both liberal individualism and the idea of progress . . . . Lifted from the merely organic [evolution] to the social realm . . . evolution or progress [advances] from the monolithic, static, and repressive type of social organization to the diversified, plural, and individualistic type of social organization. All forms of authoritarianism—religious, caste, racial, moral, and political—are destined to decline and eventually become extinct . . . ." Here, evolution and progress are identical. Nisbet quotes Spencer as saying, "[T]his law of organic progress . . . is the law of all progress. Whether it be in the development of the Earth, in the development of Life upon its surface, in the development of Society, of Government, of Manufactures, of Commerce, of Language, Literature, Science, Art, this same evolution of the simple into the complex, through successive differentiations, holds throughout. . . . The transformation of the homogeneous into the heterogeneous is that in which progress essentially consists."

Further, Spencer contended, "progress is not an accident, not a thing within human control, but a beneficent necessity. And with the same compelling force, . . . humanity must in the end become completely adapted to its conditions." Nisbet furthers the history of the idea by noting that the "Fundamental to the idea of progress . . . is faith in the value of human knowledge, the kind of knowledge that is contained in the sciences and the practical arts, and faith also in the capacity of such knowledge to lift humanity to ever-higher levels of human life." This lifting of humanity is to be achieved through technology and commerce. "All evidence suggests that the surge of technological, industrial, and commercial development in the West commencing in the High Middle Ages and, with only occasional interruptions, . . . touching by the nineteenth century literally all aspects of life, . . . was in large measure the result of near-religious faith in the ascent of mankind from past to future."

In summation, the historic idea of progress has meant:

- Faith in advancement from an undesirable primitive condition toward an ultimate perfection.

- The path of future progress may be unclear but it is inevitable, for it is man's destiny to achieve this ultimate higher purpose.

- The journey is propelled by a providential force, whether an intervening theistic God, a beneficent deistic designer God, a natural evolutionary adaptation-survival process, or some entelechy driving technology-science and commerce to human betterment.

- It will emerge from the cumulative-corrective achievements of mankind.

- It reaches toward a potentially perfectible human condition in which virtue, harmony, happiness, and freedom from familiar ills and imperfections are achieved in a cooperative system of humans adapting within nature and with each other.

Would this were true. But it is constructed on the covert assumption of the automatic human beneficence of natural laws. Mankind still faces questions of how to turn natural evolutionary laws to humanitarian account. What is needed is combined theory and philosophy by which the economic progress of all mankind can be evaluated. The emergence of global ecological concerns is an immediate example. Global peace is another. Population, aging, fresh water, waste disposal, health, gender and racial harmony, global energy supply, global monitoring and governance: all are examples of an emerging global need for a theoretical-philosophical understanding of economic progress. All behavior impacting on these phenomena raises questions of progress or regress, improvement or decline, better or worse.

It would seem self-evident that the pursuit of progress is a noble purpose. However, as noted, the idea is under serious attack. Scholarly literature has led that attack and current events often seem to confirm pessimism over human progress.

CHALLENGES TO THE IDEA OF PROGRESS
BY THE PESSIMISTS

In judging the effectiveness of economies in terms of theory and philosophy of progress it is prudent to pay attention to the critics. They can contribute a desperately needed self-corrective mode of thinking about so profoundly important an issue as the future well-being of humanity.

Skepticism of the prospects of progress has become part of the public domain. The idea of progress is seen either as an illusion, or the reality is viewed as disaster brought on by the self defeating qualities, even arrogance, of the values we have pursued. "Disbelief, doubt, disillusionment, and despair [about progress] have taken over [in the West]—or so it would seem from our literature, art, philosophy, theology, even our scholarship and science," Nisbet notes.

A compact summary of the attacks on progress establishes the logic and weight of skeptical arguments. A major problem in exploring progress is methodological. We lack adequate, incontrovertible, unambiguous, and convincing historical data by which to conclusively and persuasively weigh and judge past human progress; for example, how to weigh human costs of modern wars *versus* achievements of modern medicine. So sweeping an idea as progress "cannot be empirically or logically verified," notes Nisbet. When we seek factual verification in history, we encounter virtually insurmountable problems of selective perception and interpretation, as well as monumental difficulties in quantitative summations of qualitative data for grand conclusions. For all the evidence supporting progress (whatever the criteria), contrary evidence and interpretation can be found in the limitless scope of history, as well as the global scope of current events.

However, our objective in dealing with progress is not to prove past progress (though I am convinced that most of us in the West would rather take our chances of living in the present in preference to a hundred, or a thousand years ago). Rather, the objective here is to determine how to judge the improvement of humanity now and into the future. "Improvement" and "progress" are intended to have the same meaning. If improvement-progress requires returning to some older cultural traits, maintaining other traits, and introducing new forms, then progress requires determining what these are, how to determine better from worse, and how to make the necessary innovations or correctives. Because the challenge is difficult, that is no reason to choose a course of despair. It does require confronting the challenges with the most reliable mode of inquiry available, even if it simultaneously confronts oversights and illusions.

The litany of objections to the idea of progress is long, often touching, and certainly designed to arrest our attention. These objections may well warrant more attention than they get. The pessimistic position asserts that once Western man believed we were God's children assured of guidance by Divine intervention, or alternatively believed in a beneficently planned Natural Order, or felt sure that man's invented technology, truth revealing science, and guiding knowledge would make man free and prosperous. A loss of faith in Divine destiny has destroyed confidence in everything: our institutions of family, schools, business, political systems, democracy, and so forth. Our leaders have proven inadequate to the tasks of making many of us prosperous and free and hence are unworthy of our confidence.

Critics of progress have much more to say. One writes: "Technology-science is not a problem only by virtue of being a captive of pathological institutions. Technology-science creates problems in its own right. Medicinal drugs have negative side effects regardless of the avaricious prescribing medical doctors. Technologies pollute and devastate the environment as witnessed around the globe. Environments are threatened by the products and processes of science. Modern medicine keeps more people alive much longer, often beyond the individual's preference or value to self and others."

And skeptics further contend that as more people are kept alive longer, this contributes to increasing population taxing the environment, a demographic shift to an aging population suffering the agonies of longer, less satisfying, tarnished years, and increasing burdens on the declining portion of the younger population. Is the solution really technology?

The doubters' perception is that technology-science gives rise to industry, urbanization, nationalism, globalization, economic growth, and social change. Technology-science begets industrialization. This begets mechanism and strains humanism. It brings specialization of routinized labor and the "tyranny of the clock." Such regimentation is bureaucracy. Bureaucracy alters the social, psychological and physical conditions under which people work. It is subjugation to system. It demands conformity and stultifies imagination, creativity and the human spirit. It is a recurring source of frustration. We all know the arguments, and many know the bureaucracy experience.

Technology-science and accompanying trade have, with great turmoil, pulled disparate communities closer together into what are now the political organizations of national states. The epitome of political progress in Western national states is the development of democracy. Optimists have seen evolution of political democracies and personal freedom as a crowning achievement of Western progress.

Not so, say the cynics of progress. Democracy and freedom are not as advertised. Majorities tyrannize over minorities. The voting masses, rather than providing quality moral and cultural leadership, use their sovereign power in ways that debase standards and practices of their civilization. Lofty purposes are derailed by fragmented special interests operating through cumbersome political mechanisms by less than noble leaders.

Present and past Presidents report on how powerless they are or were. Authority and power to get things done is diluted in a democratic society from top to bottom. The great leveling process and rights of the individual destroy authority. Teachers' hands are fettered from maintaining the discipline and standards essential to the teaching-learning process. Parents are overwhelmed by children's technological temptations, and either don't know, or in despair abandon, efforts to discipline the youth to the demands of society and the decency of courtesy.

Economic organizations confront personnel reared with democratic ideology inappropriate to the discipline required by modern industrial processes. The serious cases remain unemployable and generate social problems. The great mass work under conditions of conflict rather than cooperation. The very successful are self-disciplined, frequently authoritarian, and sometimes unscrupulous. Much, perhaps most, of that which works in successful organizations seems to defy a considerable range of democratic values and ideology.

Pessimists of progress criticize democracies for other devastating characteristics. Magnificent productions of art, literature, drama, music, architecture of the high cultures of the past are said to be dominated and inundated by modern productions for a low culture of the present. Further, they contend, the near total freedom of expression accorded the artist has resulted in a loss of standards by which the works can be judged. Artistic creations take on a "near randomness for the perceiver." As we can't judge, we suffer what appears to be decline, stagnation, and inertia in the quality of arts and letters.

MORAL INADEQUACIES OF THE MARKET

Another kind of doubt about the virtues of progress is found in market philosophy. Democracy and the Enlightenment have given rise to individualism. The wishes and whims of the individual are given powerful expression in the marketplace. However tastes may be formed, they dictate the character of goods and services acceptable in the marketplace. Critics of progress say the chosen items are not edifying. The contention is frequently difficult to dispute. To put the blame on producers' pursuit of profits does not exonerate democratically countenanced individualism; it only places partial blame. It does not identify correctable resolution.

Affluence under individualism produces massive output and consumption, much without edifying purpose. The result is fundamental dissatisfaction and further frenetic consumption to escape self-inflicted boredom. Consumption becomes a true addiction. It feeds upon itself. In earlier times boredom was an affliction of a minority leisure class. With democratic affluence it afflicts the majority.

All this adds up to moral decay in "democratic capitalism" at the historic junction when the causal forces themselves—technology-science and economic growth (nationalism and militarism set aside)—facilitate globalization, socio-economic expansion, and intrusion and domination of otherwise integrated cultures. Economic growth on a global scale, fostered by "democratic capitalism," suffers from a moral void at the same time it is destroying the integrity of indigenous cultures of the world. No appropriate "moral-cultural order" is providing a replacement. It would not be inappropriate to say, aver the cynics, that a kind of moral chaos befogs the globe.

Taken together, these pessimistic views toward the idea of progress encompass a near total attack on the direction and destiny of humanity.

PROGRESS AND MORAL PURPOSE

For the present moral philosophy of economics, the pursuit of progress is an essential aspect of finding moral purpose. In formulating that philosophy, it is prudent to suspect the presence of past insights, oversights and illusions in this field of thought as elsewhere. Therefore, a revised theory of progress must correct several unnecessary and misleading ingredients common to past ideas of progress.

No Perfect Goal is Needed

From the evolutionary perspective adopted here, I do not assume that there is an absolute Platonic good that exists in the logos as a goal to be reached. Progress as betterment is generalized from human experience in which humanity has sought the better and eschewed the worse. Because these quests for betterment have often taken gruesome turns (for example, fascism) does not mean the quest for progress does not exist or has no meaning. On the contrary, because critics can identify the evil in human sacrifice or fascism, that identification confirms the conviction that judgments can be made meaningfully about deterioration and improvement in the human condition. In much the same way, the idea of economic progress is not envisioned as seeking a perfect, just, and maximizing mechanism. Instead, it is a process of improving but not perfecting efficiency, justice needs and other values.

The response called for in understanding progress is not one of defining an abstract, utopian, good economy. Being empathetic and projecting into the future, we informed impartial spectators assert the necessity of a futurity morality; we want a better life for those who follow us. The option is not to discard the fruitful insights from conventional economic theory nor to define an ideal economic system, as communism was often mistakenly thought to be, or as the competitive market has been conceived. The alternative lies in an evolutionary way of thinking about the issues. We look for a process and not a final achievement. We look to inquiry and not to an ism.

No Teleological End is Assumed or Sought

Neither do I assume that there is an end state toward which evolution and history are being, or should be, directed or pulled. Purpose and direction for the economy are not determined by a final goal. The orientation that assumes such a directing or pulling force is known as "teleology." It is another illusion. Because individuals continuously live their lives with objectives in mind, they do act teleologically (turn on the light to see better; go to college to become a doctor); that is, they act with purpose. To extrapolate individual purpose (teleology) to the evolutionary and historical process creates another illusion. It is much the same source of illusion as mercantilists extrapolating the fact that individuals accumulating money makes them wealthy, and that it is, therefore, the way for nations to become wealthy as well.

Making things and relations among people work better is progress. It is not a progression to an assumed ultimate teleological goal. Rather, progress is a movement from a given condition with degrees of definable deficiencies, inadequacies, or problems to visualized aspirations that it is anticipated will work better. We look to corrections, not final consummation.

Progress Is Not Inevitable

It is not assumed here that progress is inevitable. Rather, humanity in its own interest must invent solutions to the problems threatening us or suffer the consequences of our own inadequacies. Figure it out or run the risk of hardships—in the extreme case, the hazard of humanity's final failure.

GROWING PAINS OF PROGRESS

To further clarify the idea of progress, we can analytically distinguish three phases of progress. **Phase One** is the conceptualization and realization of an improvement over what existed in the past. **Phase Two** is awareness of the flow of consequences following from first phase innovations. Some of these consequences may turn out to be advantageous for humanity; some may prove detrimental. **Phase Three** involves sorting out and evaluating Phase One and Phase Two consequences. This may result in identifying and preserving the advantageous and seeking correction of the detrimental. Understanding and pursuit of public purpose progress is tremendously complicated here by the fact that all three phases are occurring simultaneously and with long-term uncertainty in identifying consequences.

Phase One

Steps to possible improvement, which may or may not lead to human progress, start in individuals' perceptions. Inventing new ways by combining existing tools (interchangeable parts and assembly line) or innovating with rules (uniting for collective bargaining) is a compelling force. If existing instruments (tools or rules) can be made to function effectively in a new way that looks better, someone eventually is bound to try it but sometimes with inadequate insight or concern for long-run consequences.

Though human biological evolution may be relatively slow and uncertain, its quality is creative in development of cultural possibilities. As a consequence, biological evolution and cultural accumulation have been remarkably successful throughout the early evolution and history of humankind. But humans did not evolve at a time, or with the genes, or through a culture, or with an epistemology that prepared them to adapt at the rate required by the present pace of change propelled by the exponential growth of science and technology. Human nature has clearly prepared us well to invent but may not have prepared us adequately for the necessary pace of social adaptation. We are increasingly tested. It is a major theoretical and moral challenge and a probable cause of pessimism about progress.

Technology and knowledge develop because sentiments like curiosity, puzzle posing, seeking knowledge, approval-disapproval, tenacity and workmanship, all mutually transact. They do so in the organic context of the cumulative logic and know-how of tool-using *Homo sapiens*.

Entrepreneurs introduce new products and production processes with the goal of profits and growth as the test of their efficiency and success. Here there is logical linking of technologies causing the wealth and progress of civilizations while the same technological impetus creates a wake of costly change. We pay a price for that progress.

As no activity has an exclusive life of its own in an organic system, the consequences are cause-and-effect linked, well beyond the intended results of the initiation of the innovation. Hence a flow of consequences follows from technological or social inventions and innovations.

Phase Two: First-Phase Steps to Progress Have Second-Phase Consequences

Humans in workable markets engage in innovations of largely independent experiments, which may be first-phase steps to progress. They are inescapably followed by second-phase unanticipated social changes (labor-management disputes over working conditions, for example). This does not mean the innovations were bad or mistaken. It means that all consequences of innovations have not been, and may not be, predictable, beneficial, or acceptable to all segments of society. Some innovations are costly by being disruptive, such as technological unemployment. Some unanticipated consequences are humanly advantageous, such as the many technical improvements that partly liberated females from many kitchen duties and endless child rearing where "a woman's work is never done." Possibly the most significant first-phase/second-phase consequence relationship is that of technical inventions in modern medicine. These first-phase steps may well be immediately identified as improvements and hence progress; but they are followed by second-phase consequences some of which are painful or costly. For example, individuals have difficulty covering new and increasing medical costs under emergency circumstances when the new techniques are technically called for. Here we experience a painful (hence costly) inability of many needy to pay the price, and in the longer run society confronts the costs of population explosion and/or seriously aging population having increased needs with decreased capacity to contribute.

Phase Three

Critics of progress observe consequent costs, and condemn us for losing our moral foundations. There are degrees of truth about these challenges, and the moral implications warrant consideration. But the response need not be abandoning a road of progress, nor going back to a past with its painful problems.

What is required—and generally has haltingly happened—is a third phase. This is the examination (however unsystematic) of the advantages (benefits) and pathologies (costs of second-phase consequences) arising from the first-phase innovations. This third phase involves changes of rules and rights, values and institutions, sometimes so dramatic as to be termed "social revolution" (the emergence of capitalism out of feudalism; the changing role of the female in the Western world).

In this third phase, democracies and market managed economies continuously adapt under pressures of second-phase consequences from first-phase innovations (slaves emancipated but not yet adequately empowered and integrated). New conditions arising in the second phase (intrusions on privacy through the internet) need the hammering out of new rules, customs, habits, laws, and institutions for the new circumstances.

In Phase Three, society responds to identified consequences of initial progressive innovations in medicine (to continue an example). How to make the essential medical system work better? Here we see humanity engaged in Phase One independent experiments that contribute to Phase Two unanticipated social consequences, and that are evaluated in Phase Three by an instrumental logic that leads to corrective efforts, giving rise to private and public medical insurance (with *their* consequences). These efforts, too, have consequences calling for corrections. Such cases have caused cynics to condemn the profit motive (private health insurance) and bureaucracy (both private and public health insurance). Certainly the criticism arises from reasonable insight. But here, as elsewhere, insights are oversights and the many advantages of the profit motive and bureaucracy cannot be dismissed simply because they are not utopian perfection. Human existence was scarcely utopian prior to the domestication of plants and animals. Progress can be made by correcting understandable faults discovered by experience and/or pointed out by critics.

These phases raise issues that are worthy of being addressed, however briefly. Where would we have stood on the innovation of the automobile if we had projected the magnitude of annual highway deaths today? The need for technological assessment and environmental impact studies reflects awareness of the probability of severe side effects as a consequence of technological innovations. Here we face the endless issues of cost-benefit analysis, whether in money terms or by other standards. We see that change becomes progress only so far as it is justifiable in terms of a humanity adapting to the environment, each other, and human nature itself. This is the orientation of ecology applied to Boulding's Integrative Mode of interaction to formulate a moral philosophical foundation to economics.

In the modern world, progress-change is increasingly complicated, as noted by its cumulative, accelerating nature. We can get a sense of the increasing pace of change by recognizing that it took far longer to learn how to put a handle on a stone hand axe than it has taken since then to invent the atomic age. Some of us witnessed the era of the Model T and the early propeller planes when it was common to say "we can no more do that than we can fly to the moon."

As we change at this pace, Phase Two of previous innovations still churns while more Phase One innovations are increasingly introduced. The stabilizing of new rules and new institutions in Phase Three has not been completed while second-phase impacts continue hitting. All phases are now battering us simultaneously. It is imperative for the well-being of humanity that this process become a self-conscious concern in our public ideology, that there is neither guarantee of automatic and continuous success nor an ultimate goal to guide us. There is, instead, the necessity for continuous inquiry and action by and for the species. Relying on individualism alone is a recipe for tragedy. Under the circumstances, it is a tribute to the sympathetic feelings of the impartial spectator within most of us, and the instrumental logic that often guides us, that we have had no more strife than we have painfully endured. There is, however, evidence of severe growing pains. Are they fatal?

APOCALYPSE?

Are these concerns just another form of the ancient predictions of apocalypse? Is it an appropriate moral strategy, under existing uncertainties, to take the stance that such predictions have always been wrong before, therefore they will always be wrong forever, and therefore let us not now tinker with proven values and venerable institutions of the present? Preserve our individualism and freedom of the automatic market.

This is a seriously precarious response, for the reason that sudden, total devastation need not occur. Things could be even worse. Instead of all dying at once, more and more could suffer longer lives in anguish and die slowly in a continuous, long-term decline in quality of existence. Humanity could suffer extensive, chronic conditions from which it might never recover: continued destruction of the ozone; unrestrained polluting; population expansion that squeezes supplies of water, arable land, energy, and food varieties. Deadly, debilitating, and ever-stronger germ and viral strains can threaten to overcome the pace of medical research. Societies' rising expectations clash over the scarce means available for satisfying those perceived needs. Weapons and new tactics for their use become increasingly employed in an intensifying clash of civilizations. It is sobering to remember that demise has been the fate of most species that evolved on this planet.

Still, the optimists' case for modern man has inspiring, enthusiastic defenders. Though I stand with them I think it philosophically unwise to take sides when there is a better alternative. There is a more responsible approach than either an assertion in support or denial of apocalypse. Philosophy, theory, and practicality can find common cause in pursuit of understanding and implementing moral progress.

There is a third way. Much can be made of both the pessimists' and the optimists' positions in constructing a theory of progress, including means to implement that process into the uncertain future. We need the pessimists' negative feedback to forewarn humankind of possible afflictions and potential dangers. And we need creative optimists to invent and implement means of circumventing those possible dangers. More is to be said later on selectively inventing and monitoring a path of progress.

But pursuit of a third way requires recognition that no guarantee of progress can be made. To conclude that there is no point in trying courts unknowable disaster, so solutions must be sought even in the face of differences. Pessimists point to reasonable concerns, optimists seek objectives widely desired, and both positions reflect widely and loyally held values. Objective data—though often proven inadequate at any given time—exists with which to work, and additional data can be available by well-directed inquiry. No permanent success can be expected, only a process of continuous evaluation.

A POSITIVE VIEW OF PROGRESS

Perhaps the most significant theoretical and moral lesson we may learn from technology, and apply to economic institutions, is the previously noted insight into the "techno-logic" of "tool-like" (instrumental) relationships contributing to organizing society's integrative system.

Here, rules are tools for using tools and operating machinery like automobiles on highways and computers on the internet. But the logic of rules-as-tools goes much beyond machinery. Its generalization is a way of thinking about the economy (possibly the Integrative Mode of all social relations). It creates a way of thinking about the instruments of economic institutions (Federal Reserve System, private property) that direct the Essential Economy. This mode of thinking allows the empathetic impartial spectator to supplement an individualistic self-interested rationality with a public purpose rationality. It is a thinking mode that enhances the rationality of how to generate improvement for ourselves and humanity by modification of the existing social order. It shapes more reliable thinking of how to improve social systems upon which individuals depend.

A REASONABLE ASSUMPTION?

This analysis of progress assumes that the reader is disturbed by events such as suttee, the practice of Hindu widows throwing themselves on the flaming funeral bier of their husbands. It assumes that you support modern medicine for the relief of pain over the practice of blood letting. It assumes support for modern agricultural practices over human sacrifice to win the favors of the Gods for abundant crops; modern dental care over decayed and missing teeth; life expectation of 65–85 healthy years over 45 years without adequate nutrition, medical care or comforts and conveniences; homes with glass windows, heated in cold winters and cooled in hot summers, over cabins or caves; and women's freedom from husbands' rights to own and punish wives, or freedom to choose a spouse on mutually agreeable expectations over a choice imposed by others.

Progress means the existence of an economy with unemployment compensation to care for conscientious workers victimized by economic instability over being forced with their families to scrounge and beg;

medical insurance that provides claims on essential services over absenteeism, incapacitation, and even early death. Certainly, it is progress that the aging have social security insurance over their suffering the consequences of retirement plans gone wrong, followed by humiliation and disintegration from poverty, failing energies and pointless lives; and that freedom of religious belief exists in an environment protective of the rights of others, including their spiritual lives as well.

In general, progress assumes recognition of the good and comfortable life for the many over expanding sumptuous indulgence for the few at the expense of the deserving and needy. It assumes the importance of ideas for clarifying the meanings and mechanisms for pursuing these values over resort to financial and political power to preserve obsolete beliefs and instruments of privilege that prevent the advancement of humanitarian practices.

A PRAGMATIC VIEW OF PROGRESS

To find a path of progress requires an ethical pragmatism. The realization of progress (and regress) is seen to arise out of the historical experiences of humanity. Each experience has the potential of being examined as an experiment. From the experience-experiment procedure, lessons are learned as to what seems to meet or deprive reasonable needs. This process generates a sense of what is better and what is worse. Reliability of these judgments has been wanting, but a view of progress has been emerging out of this experiential activity.

Mankind Must Acknowledge Its Own Responsibility

Progress is not inevitable, and humanity in its own interest must invent means of realizing potential capabilities, as well as means of solving the problems threatening us. Progress is, at its core, a moral matter involving judgments of better over worse. Various notions of progress, too, have evolved during the history of human experience. That certainly does not mean that all evolved values should be perceived as proper or morally justifiable. This is so in the same sense that even though inherent drives were instrumental in human evolutionary survival, that does not make them determinants of what is good or progressively better today (impulse to overeat, physical force over justification justice). Progress is not acquiescence to innate drives or all evolved values. However, we have evolved inherent inclinations (a moral sense) which contribute to the possibility of formulating judgments of moral beneficence, debasement and a quest for moral betterment.

The importance of progress was discovered historically with improved insights into meeting and enriching human needs. The very idea of progress is emergent (in an historical sense) with human experiences. In their transactions humans experienced sensations, discomforts, frustrations, satisfactions, conflicts. They encountered problems and created explanations. Ways were invented or discovered by which tensions and problems were mitigated. Satisfactions, comfort, joy, understandings were achieved and found more satisfying than other experiences. This was the experiencing process that gave rise to improvement now identified as "progress."

PRAGMATISM AND PROGRESS

This awareness of pathologies and promise places an intensified practical burden on humanity and an increased need for an applicable moral philosophy to guide us. Pragmatism can be seen to take three forms: populist, crass, and ethical.

Populist Pragmatism

Practically, when not stultified by an absolutist ideology, we have acted in terms of a populist pragmatism. That is the pragmatism of the people confronting existing ideology, which appears to have failed, and doing what looks as if it would work better. Indeed populist pragmatism has both dangers and positive possibilities (for example, unemployment compensation meets needs but can be taken advantage of by free-loaders).

Populist pragmatism is public or private calculated decision making in the face of problems (for example, the Great Depression). It is a kind of desperate, inchoate experimentalism with little refined theory or philosophy pointing the way. Franklin Roosevelt's Works Progress Administration to provide jobs was an effort contrary to both public ideology and competitive equilibrium theory and without the benefit of Keynes' macro-economic theory.

Crass Pragmatism

For the crass turn of mind, a narrow or limited end is the justification for the means used. It is public or private populist decisions to do what would seem to work for calculated, vested, self-interest advantages, with little or no consideration of wider humanitarian consequences. This is a situation in which we quite frequently make the accusation of "rationalizing." Terms such as "opportunistic," "calculating," "selfish," "shrewd," "scheming," even "evil'" identify the nature of these decisions. Our stereotype of a Machiavellian intent vividly illustrates this. Stereotyped, derisive meanings of "pork barrel" legislation, "politics as usual," and "profits for profits' sake" further illustrate the meaning of crass pragmatism. This form of pragmatism gives the term a bad name. It is reason for the correct condemnation of pragmatism on the grounds that *the* end does not justify the means. However, only the totality of potential moral ends (that is, desirable social consequences) can justify means.

Ethical Pragmatism

The commitment here is that pragmatism should be practiced as a moral procedure. This involves the calculation of decisions in an endless quest of how best to bring about consequences that will be consistent with a morality of mutual adaptation.

Characteristic of pragmatism in general is a willingness not to be absolutist or rigidly conformist to public ideology. Characteristic of *ethical* pragmatism is a willingness to deviate from ideology, not for personal aggrandizement but for public betterment. It consciously suspends accepting aspects of venerable theories and ideology while looking for alternative means of mitigating human hardships. For example, ethical pragmatism suspends an absolutist *ideology* of individualism in its quest for the well-being of individuals, their unique needs and contributions.

Pragmatism recognizes that only through experimenting can we learn the results of acting upon specific hypotheses. From these hypotheses, informed empathetic spectators construct theories insightful enough for reasonably predictable success. In this pursuit, ethical pragmatism is explicitly wedded to the *method* of science.

Standards of judging progress, then, arise not from outside experience but from episodes within it. Purposes emerge out of successful experiments, as do explanatory insights, oversights and illusions as to what constitutes and what causes improvement or deterioration. As we do not possess absolute certainty, activities are destined on occasions to go wrong. Social welfare efforts have suffered such a fate. If we are not dogmatic ideologues, we learn from doing.

Self Correction

When it is possible to better explain causes of difficulties, then there are more objective grounds for probable improvement. If we think it may be done better, then we seek means to goals-in-view. Progress is improvement over less satisfactory goals and the pursuit of the more probable of more satisfactory goals. If there are beliefs and practices that impede improvement, then progress will include corrective feedback of the mistaken and pursuit of the more reliable. As we cannot attain a utopia for all times, and as experiences reflect both successes and failures, we grow aware of the usefulness of having self-corrective practices built into our moral philosophy.

PROGRESS: A MANY-SPLENDORED THING

Progress is multi-faceted. There is progress in many dimensions of human experience. Just as growing from childhood to maturity has many qualitative changes we identify as maturing (without knowing what the adult will be), so too the experiences of humanity have many qualitative and quantitative dimensions. These contribute to the moral sense of mutual adaptation and expand the scope of empathy to encompass more and more of human experiences.

Progress Corrects for Deficiencies in Human Endowments

It is a common insight that individuals are differentially endowed biologically, sociologically, and with property, wealth and power. For the individual, these outcomes are randomly shaped by accidental happenings. Infants have not earned their advantageous starts or deprivations. As a black comedian quipped, "I was born a suspect." Society proceeds with these non-rationally distributed endowments among individuals. Progress proceeds by improving the capacities of the disadvantaged to contribute to their own self-reliance and to the general well-being of others. Progress includes the self-awareness of the advantaged that they have a responsibility, not alone to the traditional rights and privileges of their status but to turn their advantages to the public good. Nowhere has there been a more persuasive example of the absence of this deontic duty than in gender relations. The evolution of inherent sentiments seems to have given rise naturally, in all cultures, to universal injustices toward the female.

The Quality of Human Relationships

Progress is improvement in how we treat each other, in how an increasingly fulfilling life contributes the same to others. Adam Smith recognized the sentiment of loving one's fellow man. Recall his saying, "Humanity does not desire to be great, but to be loved. It is not in being rich that truth and justice would rejoice but in being trusted and believed, recompenses which those virtues must almost always acquire." Yet Smith failed to suggest that this cultivation of affection among us is an important determinant of the nature of wealth enhancement. Certainly this sense of loving and being loved is another dimension of progress. Certainly such moral concerns must extend to all humanity independently of gender, race, age, ethnicity, or occupation. Economies have prospects of progressing substantially in this social relations area of the nature of wealth. Here we have room to become vastly richer without vast expenditure of scarce resource costs.

Workable Market Progress

Economizing within the Essential Economy is necessary, and progress includes the workable market economizing more and more efficiently. Progress involves inventing private and public instruments which improve mutual adaptation, mutual contribution and the inescapable need to mutually share in the rationing of scarce means. Progress is improvement of the system of rules, regulations, and laws impacting on this process. Traditional vested rights (males *versus* females, management *versus* labor) must be transformed to liberate and empower those with neglected needs necessary to individual fulfillment, and necessary to improved capacities to contribute to humanity's well-being.

For market progress, Maslow's "peak experiences" should increasingly come from helping others (not necessarily exclusively altruistically) to fulfill their hierarchy of needs. This is done by entrepreneurs organizing the production of edifying and instrumental goods and services. It is done through peak experiences of being effective doctors, nurses, teachers, entertainers, builders, volunteers; by becoming the "movers and shakers" of more effective rules-as-tools, making the work of these other activities better, faster, easier, more economical, more satisfying and fulfilling, less boring, less conflict and tension generating, and generally more humane.

CHANGE IS COSTLY

Progress creates change. At its present pace—and it quickens—change is devastating to many of our most intimately human qualities. Progress is not pain free. The pain of change is the cost of improvement. Cumulative technology evolves the products and processes, and entrepreneurs introduce them with the goal of profits as their private touchstone of efficiency and success. But private net profits meeting consumers' market demand is not a measure of society's net progress over costs of change. Surely pessimists of progress have valid concerns here.

Current change brings disruption of institutional supports, basic values, personality stability, and even physical health. It brings disruption of a sense of security, loss of nurturance from sundered social bonds, and ambiguity of values and moral character. This pace of change threatens to eradicate historical roots more rapidly than they can be replaced with other stabilizing and comforting sources of sentience and meaning for our lives. If the economy is to cope with the social costs of change, those costs must be brought into the market and reflected in prices. Progress under these conditions is a matter of benefits over costs at the aggregate social level.

Have we practical guidance in these matters from traditional competitive economic theory and its fundamentalist ideology? The illusion created by fundamentalist ideology is that there is a price system that automatically causes and directs economic progress to a maximum benefit of humanity. Maximum growth is automatically guaranteed. The rate of economic growth is determined by sovereign consumers' preferences. If some things are wanted in greater quantities, the prices and profits rise, and entrepreneurs offer higher interest to get money capital to invest in the area of increasing demand. The higher interest induces greater savings from those who prefer more in the future over less now. By saving and loaning now, they have more income from interest received in the future. This increases future income and purchasing power. The greater amount of preferred goods is there to buy because saving made possible capital formation and greater output, which makes more goods for the savers' future consumption. We have exactly the growth rate and goods we want, determined by our willingness to forego in the present to get the resulting increase we want in the future.

This growth is seen in economic thought and ideology as progress. Market demand communicates what the population wants most. New products that satisfy these desires are produced. Those less desired are rejected in the market. Hence only the preferred goods and services proliferate. The less desirable diminish. Thus there is automatic progress of growth and quality of life in how humanity chooses to live.

In spite of having an element of reality, this perspective overlooks another market failure—the failure to mitigate the costs of change. This must not be read as a moral attack on seeking profits. Instead, markets need rules, and old rules need not fit new circumstances arising from steps toward progress. The human costs of change are not all registered in the marketplace and, hence, are not calculated in market decisions that are assumed to contribute to the effectiveness of an economy. In fact the actual dollar costs to individuals of making adjustments in a changing world will increase the measures of Gross National Product and signal economic improvement.

With the pace and quality of modern technology-scientific advances (computers, internet, robotics, genetic engineering), the pessimists of progress signal new dangers threatening the reign of humanity. This book's philosophy implies that in a world of change there is no moral justification for displaced, conscientious individuals being required to bear the costs of progress. The benefits of progress are *social* benefits.

The costs of change should be *social* costs, not private costs suffered by innocent individuals. The costs can be borne by the many better positioned beneficiaries of progress.

It is not societies and individuals alone that are being stressed. Technology and environment are in tension. The quickening pace of global economic growth may be destroying the environment at a rate that threatens to reach a point of no return. This can be well on its way before mankind can negotiate an adequately sharp change of course, assuming there is knowledge enough to know what that course should be and how to negotiate the turn.

A moral philosophy of economics must seek ways of achieving improved benefits in excess of costs of change as a way of finding net progress for humanity. Both philosophy and practice must start with the world as it is, or better, as it appears to be.

Humanity "succeeded" in adapting over a very long evolutionary and civilizing history, even before knowing reliably that the earth is round, not flat, spins on its axis, and that the sun does not circle about us. Clearly we can be wrong and get along. Some can be quite right and persecuted for it. Right or wrong, life on earth can be precarious. The only practical alternative is a tenacious pursuit of appropriate reliable knowledge, theory and philosophy to guide public policy and private practice.

9

Thinking about
an Unknowable Future

Our major concern now is to develop strategy to cope with an uncertain future arising from progress and change. The shrinking world is increasingly becoming an interdependent global Essential Economy. Peoples of the planet are drawn together by both the impulse to "truck, barter and exchange" and an equally inherent capacity to learn and appreciate superior technical instruments. Even deeply ingrained superstitions and prohibitions slowly, very slowly, erode as successive generations experience changing technology and ever more reliable and pragmatically useful knowledge. These transformations of people's behavior, beliefs, and institutions contribute to the clash of civilizations, for which competitive market theory provides inadequate correctives.

Progress that brought local unsettling change now brings rising expectations, global transformations, and increased costs of emotional, social, and environmental disruption. Here the Essential Economy is market managed in a world of competition in the pursuit of profits. A costly consequence is that in competing, firms conserve money costs by neglecting human and environmental costs. This creates conflict and dangers. If we are to manage the prospects of progress and the pace, costs, and dangers of change, it is necessary to invent a vision of how to go about it. What strategies are we to follow, under conditions of knowledge insufficiencies, about forming policies for an unknowable future?

FOUNDATIONS OF A GLOBAL ECONOMIC ETHIC

We are not bereft of bases for constructing a global ethic. In spite of seemingly intransigent differences in ideologies among cultures, all have much in common upon which to build agreement. All Essential Economies are based in human nature, natural environments, technology-knowledge, and some form of entrepreneurial organizing-managing. All are faced with scarcity and must ration (in some way) the allocation, production, distribution, and consumption of industrial and consumer products. Some form of market is the major exchange mechanism managing the inescapable economizing-rationing processes of the globe. All function with a threat mode playing a governing role and the integrative mode playing an indeterminate moral role.

Nowhere is there an unqualified option for every individual being free to satisfy whatever passions provide the greatest personal satisfaction. Social order and economizing, of necessity, do not permit such absolute freedom. All enterprises experience real costs in production. All overlook or neglect the totality of true societal and environmental costs. All individuals experience a hierarchy of human needs. All experience socially disruptive costs of progress and change. All in the modern world have to adapt with others within their own culture, and most must adapt indirectly with others outside. All are threatened by the devastating costs of environmental destruction and the clash of civilizations. None can be "free" from these economizing constraints.

Also, in the modern world of change, all economies must have the political stability of a positive state to provide and protect an infrastructure of flexible property management, a monetary system for a monetized market with a central banking system, and a saving-investing system. There cannot be an Essential Economy without an education system focused on developing the manual and intellectual skills needed for economic processes and progress. An additional essential aspect of economies experiencing progress is that they include social reform, as well as personal betterment. Social class systems are destined for modification, even in the West. Ideological resistance can be expected to be severe.

As all humanity shares these many conditions and needs, a potential global ethic has common cause to build upon. Increased awareness of our common interests can be posed as common puzzles to solve.

STRATEGIES FOR FACING AN UNKNOWN FUTURE

Though the costs and dangers of change impact us in the present, it is the uncertain future for which we must now prepare. Since we in the present contribute to those costs and dangers, it calls for our developing a strategy to deal with that unknown future, starting now. As the future is not knowable we can only project possible scenarios of what it may be like that we may better act now. For this purpose I construct three possible courses the future might take: **Most Likely Scenario. Worst Case Scenario. Most Necessary Scenario.**

THE MOST LIKELY SCENARIO OF THE FUTURE

This prospect is a global view from the USA perspective. Most likely future decisions will be philosophically based in a populist pragmatism in the midst of globally divergent ideologies. The economy which now dominates the globe is an evolving Essential Economy with government-structured private property managing markets. These markets are continuously adapted by the global community largely through internationally autonomous governments. All social systems function through Boulding's identified threat, exchange and integrative modes of organization. Virtually no one in touch with the modern world will fail to anticipate that change is inevitable. This is the case, even as change is resisted, at times violently.

Threat Mode in the Most Likely Scenario

Governments will continue to assume responsibility for those services that are privately but inadequately managed in the public interest. Water resources, energy supplies, transportation, forests, and fisheries are likely candidates. An international central bank and monetary control system seems virtually inevitable in the most likely future. There will be some intermediate forms of awkward, transitional, ad hoc, international monetary arrangements tried.

Since governments will continue to be active as the pace of change quickens and the costs escalate, government activity may or may not grow more dominant, but it will be forced to become more active and inventive at the margins of intense concern. Taxes and rules will be applied modestly though explicitly to nudge the market to meet growing concerns over social cost issues such as ecological decay. Governments will continue, in a cautious manner, to innovate institutional systems to provide services neglected or poorly managed by the automatic market. No efforts will be made to construct new grand alternative systems, such as took place in twentieth century Russia, China, Germany and elsewhere.

Exchange Mode in the Most Likely Scenario

Workable markets will continue to manage Essential Economies by setting prices that will be applied in allocation, production, distribution, consumption, and growth. This process will continue to be nudged by taxes and governmental rules.

Integrative Mode in the Most Likely Scenario

Science and its statistics will continue to call attention to threats to health, environments, unmet needs, and brewing conflicts among peoples at all levels. Governments will continue to be held responsible as a means of problem mediation-correction. The citizenry will continue to view the market as the main mechanism for solving economic problems. The irrepressible spirit of humanity will rise in defense and support of fellow man, however spotty.

Somehow, a globe suffering from the debilitating conditions of the Great Depression was able to rise to the challenge of a world war, battering humanity with unheard-of levels of creativity, productivity, and destruction. Certainly that kind of sacrifice, creativity, and productivity can now be and may well be devoted to enhancing the well-being of humanity, rather than destroying it. Regrettably, good deeds may not be nearly so dramatically heralded as brutalities.

Progress will include diminution of the illusions and privileges of unconscionable arrogance of wealth. Progress will bring an increase in the selection of those individuals occupying positions of power who are sensitized to compassion as well as instrumental understanding. These are transformations persisting in a long-run process and will be welcomed by many as justice in both a domestic and a global ethic. Humanity has bonding and empathetic sentiments, as described earlier. Such sentiments, coupled with the inherent impulse to pose and solve puzzles, are where hope lies for life on this globe. Progress will persist in this most likely future, even in the face of inevitable but "manageable" devastating conflicts.

Integrative Mode and Convergence
in the Most Likely Future

As Western market economies under democratic governments are one major model, and China's emerging market under a central authority is another model, the two share one goal, improvement of the well-being of their respective peoples. Both have in common the above list of conditions that all mankind must face. Both will struggle between instrumental power and privilege power. Both will seek means of shaping the market exchange system to most effectively manage the Essential Economy. Both will seek to integrate their systems on the basis of a techno-logic coupled with edifying sentiments of humanness as well as a populist pragmatism. ("It doesn't matter if the cat is black or white as long as it catches mice . . . " Deng Xiaoping.) Both will distrust the other on ideological grounds but cooperate in common terms of self-interest, technological interdependence, and humanitarian bonding. The "global republic of technology" will become enriched by its pluralism and unified by recognition of its instrumental commonalities.

Research and Finding Our Way in the Most Likely Scenario

What we don't know can allow humanity of the future to suffer far more severely than we have experienced in the present. What we seek to know can contribute to human progress with its promise, costs and dangers of change. The research infrastructure of the Western world is largely focused on what the previous chapter called first-phase progress. Western world economic ideology will continue to judge successful research in terms of private profits and monetized standards of growth expressed as gross national product. Of course, there will continue to be research that contributes to all dimensions of human progress (medicine, weather forecasting, ecology, pure science in physics, chemistry, biology and more).

This analysis is unprepared to project the character of research of the non-Western world. However, I suspect that most of the world's new knowledge will result from the Western world's research infra-structure. This, too, will contribute to convergence. It will also cause conflict over rules of private property, reciprocity and excesses of competition. Populist pragmatism will overcome much of the global ideological differences and support convergent public purposes. This will be done as the East and West negotiate exchange agreements in order to achieve benefits from the other's resources, inventions, and better priced products.

Thus far, this scenario of the most likely future is from a very optimistic perspective. It largely comes to focus on Phase One of progress.

Here expanding knowledge improves the lives of individuals in ways that are recognized and embraced.

Phase Two, it may be recalled, experiences the unanticipated consequences of the purposive acts of Phase One progress. Here, the likely future loses some of its luster. China's one child per couple population policy will make our Social Security projections a pleasurable problem by contrast. That population policy, which likely is essential for China, will create a shrinking number of young people to be concerned for a massive aging population. We of the West will experience a similar problem for different reasons. Our success is in extending longevity, coupled with a falling birth rate. This results in a shrinking youthful population faced with a proportionately larger number of healthy and productive older individuals who eventually become elderly dependents. There, of course, will be many other second-phase consequences of progress, as have been noted by the pessimists. The likely future will experience growing congestion, depletion of environment, violent forms of dissatisfactions (terrorism), and other costly experiences.

THE WORST CASE SCENARIO OF THE FUTURE

Here, policies are dominated by competitive theory-ideology. Individualism reigns. It is the most costly and dangerous economic future. It is a vision that the pessimists of progress may be more right about than they actually conjecture. They fear that uncontrollable population growth, growing pollution with environmental decay, and clash of civilizations will lead the human species to the same slow agonizing extinction that met most species that once, like us, evolved and thrived on this planet.

Exchange in the Worst Case Scenario

In this scenario the exchange mode is the ideal and it dominates. Unregulated free markets are the mode of exchange. Competition is free, cutthroat, and there is no concept of unfair competition.

Pathologies are explained in terms of individuals being forced to act as they do because their competitors will defeat them if they don't. This is explained philosophically in terms of "Social Darwinism," as survival of the fittest producing the most fit and hence the best. All is also Newtonian automatic. It therefore needs no adjustments to its tendency towards maximum equilibrium. In this context the content of the free media is defended on grounds that the press is providing what the public wants, not what it needs. Idealism is unrealistic here. It would be fatal for the individual in a competitive market.

The worst case scenario envisions that the free market will be relied upon to automatically cope and hence there will be no need for policy creation or innovation. The ideology based on the logic of competitive price theory is so persuasive that it will prevail politically. Progress will be attributed to a beneficent automatic competitive market. The logic from Adam Smith's economics will be asserted. Natural laws are beneficent for humanity. We are achieving the best possible under scarcity conditions.

Market Management of the Global Economy in the Worst Case Scenario

There are dire consequences from a global competitive market in this worst case scenario. National self-interests will support local commercial interests in a mercantilist-like race to export low priced goods and services. Governments are pressured by this market to be lax on its rules regulating working conditions and employee benefits. Under competitive self-defense, these practices spread throughout the globe.

The modern world depends on large complex enterprises like chemical plants, globe encircling airlines and the world wide web. Existing economic theory is inadequate to explain a global economy built upon the technologies of these modern industries. So far as I know, we do not have a theory or philosophy adequate to the challenges the global economy faces. In this scenario, the world economy is flying blind.

In traditional theory, exchange value or price is assumed to be set in a competitive market by supply and demand among powerless buyers and sellers. This perspective sheds no light on the meaning of prices in "imperfectly competitive" markets for industries like energy suppliers, the oil producing countries, the computer software companies, and most large and profitable enterprises. Private price manipulation largely prevails. It is not done to enhance public purpose but to satisfy management's personal aggrandizement.

In this worst possible future it is assumed that all have freedom of choice to consume the goods and services individuals prefer as they register their subjective interests in the market. However, in that future the probability is that enterprises will develop power in the market through consolidation and advertising. This creates power for commercial self-interests to induce lifestyles having little social or psychological integrity. No rules will be needed to regulate environmental costs, consumer safety, or working conditions. A business must do what it takes to survive.

Exchange markets, assumed to be level playing fields, are markets where bizarre privilege power is assumed not to exist and incapable of distorting impartial justice. No unions are needed to countervail power. No taxes are necessary to redistribute incomes resulting from advantages of power perceived as rewards motivating efficiency.

As government regulations are viewed, in the worst case, as inefficient, unfair, and unnecessary, natural resources (fisheries, oil, fertile land, forests) are depleted to the point of no return. In this worst case exchange mode the strong and the deserving are claimed to be winners in an increasingly harsh survival-of-the-fittest world.

Threat Mode in the Worst Case Scenario

Ideology portrays private property, in preference to government, as the rightful dominant economic power in this scenario. Property power is viewed as a natural right that provides "competition," personal responsibility and concern for economic facilities, and the advantages flowing from managing resources for profit. Everyone benefits in free market exchanges. Here protection of property privilege brings about fulfillment of our preferences. These are the virtues of free private enterprise. It causes all to do their best. And further, justice is justified by the logical nature of these natural achievements. In spite of dependence on government protecting private property rights (perceived as natural rights), anti-government prejudice will view government action elsewhere as "interference" and the cause of problems, and certainly there is no need for global governance to infringe on our sovereignty. The consequence of all this is that we will be free to suffer from creeping chaos leading to global war and/or environmental devastation.

Integrative Mode in the Worst Case Scenario

In this scenario the humanitarian inclinations of the integrative mode are rejected as sentimental, inefficient, and interference, causing do-gooders to do harm. The instrumental techno-logic of the underlying Essential Economy is rejected as a source of moral or practical guidance. Rather, moral guidance is the product of free expression of self-interests of each, monitored by competition. Don't touch private property rights. They protect the self-interests that are automatically integrated by the free competitive exchange market. Public purpose puzzle-solving and sentiments of empathy, of the integrative mode, are twisted to support military research, respect for heroism and remorse for massive war casualties.

Research Infrastructure in the Worst Case Scenario

In the worst case scenario, the research infrastructure is owned by private enterprise and focused on production for sale and profits. Peoples' preferences registered in the market determine the kind and quantity of research needed, which brings the quantity and quality of innovations most desired by the populace. Pessimists' concerns that war is supported by industrialists for profits will be realized. The industrialists will become heroes for their creation of weapons needed to "protect our freedom."

First-Phase Change in the Worst Case Scenario

Products are produced that appeal to every strength and weakness of human dispositions: food, clothes, yachts, pomp and display, drugs, alcohol, tobacco, and the range of familiar and unfamiliar goods and services. These are matters of subjective private tastes that maximize utility. Preparation for war is prudent as it protects our cherished freedoms and values.

Second-Phase Consequences of Change in the Worst Case Scenario

Unanticipated consequences of private innovations are the private concerns of individuals. Because individuals bear the costs, they will adapt to the consequences of change by turning them to their own self-interests. In this way, the market will conquer costs and dangers of change as prices will ration goods and profits will induce technologies that will avert negative consequences. There will be protests against interfering with the free market and individuals' private freedom. Survival of the fittest will make all who survive more fit. All of this transpires both domestically and internationally.

Third-Phase Corrections in the Worst Case Scenario

What is there to correct? The fit and successful have survived and prospered. The remainder received according to their contributions. What other adjustments to progress and change need to be made? None, of course. However, the pace and quality of change is out of public purpose control. Social conflict becomes endemic. The species' future is threatened. As the basic philosophy is to compete to win, it can be expected that there will be a fight to exhaustion. The effort to win pits all against all, and a survival-of-the-fittest struggle guarantees conflict and warfare destructive to all. Thus, in this worst case scenario, the future is universal Hobbesian and Malthusian disaster.

THE MOST NECESSARY INTEGRATIVE SCENARIO FOR CONFRONTING THE FUTURE

This scenario is the most necessary because the most probable scenario contains humanly dreadful elements, and if reality veers at all toward the worst possible scenario it would inflict even greater disaster on humanity. It is unnecessary to gamble so recklessly with so many human lives when the possibilities for human betterment can be considerably improved. Whatever choices we of the present make, we inescapably will be "the makers of our own fate" and the future's as well. It is a formidable responsibility to the future of humanity, fraught with costs and dangers as well as possibilities for progress. Social progress has historically emerged out of tension-provoking conditions. In such a context, the populist pragmatic approach has previously been applied. The populace has suspended aspects of public ideology and tried something that seemed as if it might reduce the tensions by mitigating the causal problems. The FDR administration applied such a "populist pragmatism" in its "New Deal" of economic stimulus, unemployment compensation, social security, and other socio-economic experiments.

As pragmatism is in part characterized by suspending aspects of accepted ideology and experimenting with an innovative policy, it could be said that Hitler's policies, too, were pragmatic. But as it was narrowly and nationally inner-directed and the consequences were evil (defying a morality of mutual adaptation) it was what I identify as "crass pragmatism." Some pragmatic social policies have worked and some have been disastrous. In this pragmatic manner the social history of mankind has been a succession of near random experimentalism. Needed now is an explicit "ethical pragmatism" seeking the morality of mutual adaptation for the whole of humanity. This present work is built upon the anticipation that such an ethical pragmatism will provide the integrative mode with moral method to guide the exchange and threat modes of social organization.

Exchange Mode in the Most Necessary Scenario

In today's world it is increasingly necessary to view the exchange mode—the workable market management of the Essential Economy—on a global scale. Human social adaptation has been on a global level at least since Christopher Columbus, with beginnings going back beyond recordings in the Scriptures. But the most intense and widespread global interdependence and pace of change have enormously increased to the present and will likely become both more intimate and more tension-provoking in the future.

In the event that overpopulation and ecologically pessimistic predictions become an increasing reality, they will confront the human species with a more desperate threat of greater global scarcity than the ideology of economics has previously faced. Prices must be nudged by recommendations based on appropriate research in order to more intensely economize in the allocation of increasingly scarce resources for reasonably efficient production, and to improve justice in distributing the output, and set a pace and quality of appropriate growth and progress. Monitoring and administering the stringencies, causes, and mitigation of these scarcities will necessitate extensive nudging of the workable market mechanism by public policy and power. All this will depend upon and require improvement of appropriate and reliable knowledge.

Threat-Power in the Most Necessary Scenario

Discriminating between instrumental power and privilege power becomes increasingly necessary as the global economy confronts realities of the pessimists' predictions. In this world of increasingly acute scarcities, where reducing privileged unproductive consumption can provide others with more essential needs (food, education, housing, medical care), practical moral steps of institutional progress must legitimately be taken. Here, there is justification for deprivation of the privileged, where whims are sacrificed that others may have more of their productive needs met. Global economic progress will result through meeting basic needs and providing more opportunities for "ongoing actualization of potentials." Progress here is both quantitative and qualitative and contributes to improving a workable wealth of humanity.

Integrative Mode in the Most Necessary Scenario

In this most necessary scenario, the integrative mode needs to dominate and direct. It is necessary that it do so because it seeks, by means of the most effective method of generating reliable knowledge, the essential ethical nature and causes of the total social health of humanity. In this necessary integrative scenario we seek strategies for an ongoing fulfillment of the finer qualities of our humanness.

In a worldwide economy, a global ethic is required that has reliability beyond the limitations of populist pragmatism. Needed now is an ethically oriented pragmatism seeking the morality of mutual adaptation of the whole of humanity. It requires experimentation, as we do not know reliably what the second-phase consequences of purposive policies will be until acted upon. This most necessary integrative scenario seeks strategies for this process of history's unfolding. All this calls for some form of benefit/cost calculations, based on weighing relevant consequences, many of which are qualitative and not readily quantified in monetary terms. We must learn how to succeed, or pay the price of our innocence or ignorance.

That the task of understanding and implementation is extremely difficult is not justification for continued reliance on venerable outdated ideological illusions. We can learn a methodological lesson from the popular legend of the drunk who lost his wallet in Central Park and looked for it in Times Square because the light was better there. Attention must be appropriately directed to critical issues, no matter the difficulties.

NEEDED: A GLOBAL ETHIC FOR HUMANITY

How might the larger philosophy of humanitarian concerns be dealt with in terms of a morality of global mutual adaptation? Here we need a global ethic by means of which understandings may be generated and negotiated. Humanity has been slowly evolving elements of a common culture built on a global ethic in the shadow of enormous conflict. This ethic is not constructed on the certainty of a sacred faith. Rather, it builds upon human limits, penchants to do both good and evil, and the inclinations to explore, explain and bond in meeting human needs through the emerging global Essential Economy.

When markets and individual self-reliance fail to provide steady improvement in the effectiveness of economies to meet neglected human needs, we have in the past turned to family, charity and voluntary associations. These sentiment driven institutions have been and still are helpful. But past forms have proven vastly inadequate to cope with the enormous costs and dangers of rapid change on a global scale. We are at a juncture in history where humanity must rely on and build from our more noble sentiments to fashion a more inclusive economic ethic.

In international relations, the ideology of dominant Western style economies is to seek the strategy of a level playing field. This means that all follow the same rules. That sounds fair. But it has meant treating unequals equally: treating economies with surpluses to export the same as economies struggling to develop; treating debtor economies the same as those with surplus trade balances. Does a level playing field mean no public support or subsidy of exporting industries? Are public education, highways, agricultural support programs, state universities' agriculture research, public weather forecast, and similar devices—are these subsidies? Do these policies subsidize exporting industries and thereby upset the level playing field? What are the rules for an economic playing field to be level? Is this another search for a utopian ideal? While emergence of integrative rules for a global workable market is essential, it is not necessarily imminent.

Money capital moves globally, easily. Talent too can flow easily to the highest bidders of the world. Technology is easily shipped or sent by e-mail. Technological know-how, and simplified, standardized manufacturing techniques are readily taught in lesser developed economies. Low wage, low standard of living, low environmental protection areas are beckoning mobile manufacturing industries. Of course, these compete with advanced economies' industries and labor. This pushes businesses to take the "low road"; that is, lower wages, skimping on environmental protection, fringe benefits, part-time work, and resisting taxation. All this contributes to economic instability and discontent among nations, while there are inadequate global institutions to implement rules or monetary and fiscal policies to stabilize economies and provide security nets for the victimized.

One alternative is to accept the sovereign right of all nations to establish their own rules. Its justification is "self-interest." All could seek rules favoring their own competitive tactics: allow child labor, indentured labor, convict labor, ignore civil rights, provide no fringe benefits, no medical insurance, no unemployment compensation, no retirement benefits, meet bottom of the barrel human needs, neglect environmental protection that has global consequences, and in general, avoid regulations, avoid taxation, and induce industries from elsewhere to move in (or out). This global competition to seduce industries leads to lax rules to facilitate "infant industries" or to attract global enterprises to less developed economies to help catch up. Advanced economies' enterprises confronting this form of competitiveness feel coerced to meet the low standards of competition. Again, the competitive quest to win (even survive) leads to social pathologies.

Neither the level playing field, business tactics, nor national self-interest tactics stand up to Adam Smith's sympathetic impartial spectator's sense of "plain and intelligible common understandings." Nor does the emerging global economy experience the promise of Smith's automatic competitive market. Certainly centrally planned economies have not coped as well. Of course, neither do we have a global political democratic republic with the capacity or authority to provide integrative guidance or common governance. How then do we find intelligible, common understanding among economies ranging from different forms of capitalism to planned socialist systems, to countries dominated by dictators or theologians, or those seriously lacking a consistent ideology, all with very different views of private property rights, intellectual property, patents, profits, and purposes of market exchanges? We do not have a working model to guide us. In this changing world, discovering or inventing a morality of mutual adaptation has become a practical necessity.

FUNCTIONS OF GOVERNMENTS

There is no escaping the role governments have to play in policy formulation. Because this exposition involves philosophical, as distinct from empirical cases, it will not analyze a specific government. Instead, it will deal with a philosophy of generic governance that would apply to local, state, national, and global governance. There will be, however, a distinct tendency to use the United States economy, ideology, and government as a referent.

- First, the primary role of governments is to tell people what they must not do to each other because people don't want it done to them. In the threat-exchange-integrative world, disputes over changes eventually land in the lap of a government. These governments contribute through legislative rule making and courts as rule referees.

- A further role of governments is to provide infrastructure for doing what people don't otherwise do for each other, either because it is not possible or profitable or because there is inadequate voluntary financial or participatory support. Government sponsored large scale infrastructure and social services facilitate the creation of national and global wealth.

- An additional role of governments is to do for marginalized individuals what they do not have the insight, inclination or capacity to do for themselves by helping them become self-reliant, contributing citizens. Other action is necessary where individuals are not socially or humanly redeemable.

- A fourth role of governments is to negotiate instruments (diplomacy, legislatures, the military, courts) to prevent governments from doing the unacceptable to each other or to their own citizens.

These functions will not meet market profit standards of efficiency, as that is not, and need not be, their objective. Governments should be effective, of course. The moral test of the rightful role of government is not a dedication to the past but the empowerment of the people to mutually adapt. Effective governments ultimately legitimize and enforce rules that empower people to become more adaptive and productive in enhancing their own and societies' human needs fulfillment.

These functions of government reflect the wisdom of Adam Smith. Recall Smith's observation: "The system of natural liberty leaves the sovereign only three duties." They are national defense, administration of justice, and maintenance of certain public works and public institutions. These "duties" become major governmental responsibilities in the modern world of dynamic technology, rising expectations, and increasing pace of change without morally monitored direction.

ADMINISTRATION OF JUSTICE

All cultures have rules, customs and laws. Some are self generating, as with common law, collective bargaining or internet etiquette. But there are hackers, con artists, crazies, selfish gougers, and the powerful who "know" they deserve what they can get. In this context of rules, confusion, and abuses, the quasi-autonomous exchange market generally facilitates whatever the level of human well-being is by managing the invention and implementation of technological progress. Regrettably, the justice of who contributes and who benefits is unresolved by this market. However, a social instrument with threat power is essential to maintain a degree of orderliness, even though what is just may remain unresolved. Governments are such power instruments. They decide on reasonable or unreasonable rules of law, evaluate successes and failures, frequently provide correctives, and decide who is right in conflicts over rules negotiated by private contracts. Thus a government ultimately monitors the rules that govern. However, this governing is not the ultimate source of determining what justice should rightly be.

The historical truth is that our markets are products, not of beneficent natural laws but of centuries of largely forgotten "experimentalism." That experimentalism is kept active by changing the rules to cope with management of new technologies emerging from the dynamic Essential Economy. The result is that regulation and re-regulation comprise an inevitable experimental process for a flexible and adaptive market managed economy. Whatever the improvements are in justifying emerging rules and practices within the larger culture, it becomes the function of governments to administer them (US troops enforcing integration of education in Little Rock). Still unanswered in this analysis is the question of what determines what is best, just or moral. It will be addressed in the final chapter of this book.

GOVERNMENT'S MAINTENANCE OF
PUBLIC WORKS AND INSTITUTIONS

Adam Smith noted the responsibility of "the crown" to provide public works and institutions. He did not provide a vision adequate to the needs of a present-day moral philosophy of economics. The search for a global economic ethic illustrates the philosophical gap.

A global ethic must recognize that the Essential Economy and its contributing individuals must have instrumental power to be able to participate. Instrumental power is necessary to make the Essential Economy function effectively. It differs sharply, though not necessarily conspicuously, from power bestowing privileges of invidious status. To perform in the Essential Economy, participants must be educated-motivated to their tasks and have empowered access to food, shelter, clothing, good health, appropriate transportation, and a range of flexibility to adapt to personal and public needs. The more basic of these needs are universally understandable and distinguishable from requirements for status display that deprives the Essential Economy of resources in a scarcity world. These understandable needs provide a starting place for agreement on a global ethic.

TURNING GOVERNMENT'S RESPONSIBILITIES
TO THE PEOPLES' ADVANTAGE

We live in an age of anti-government ideology, and at the same time turn to governments for orderliness and help. The anti-government attitudes can be so severe that it is difficult to explore a strategy of governmental potentials without confronting arguments founded in covert convictions that governments do best by doing least, or at least doing less, not more. Certainly the threat system's socially necessary rules are a substantial source of civilization's discontents. Reinforcing this discontent is a covert assumption that in the absence of governance, natural laws of markets will do best. These attitudes and arguments flourish even among otherwise highly enlightened, responsible and tolerant individuals.

"Some of my best friends" are anti-government prejudiced. And they "know" from firsthand experience. But then, I know from first hand experience, too, in family, business, marriage, friendships, universities, the military, and every institution I dwelled in that everyone, every group and every institution has imperfections. I witnessed them. Preconceptions based in firsthand observations can condemn the human race because "people are no damn good." But we are stuck with being us, and we do well to try to turn us to better account. So, too, are we "stuck" with the necessity of a government threat system and we would do well to learn how to turn it, too, to better account. Critique, yes. Constant debasing criticism and prejudicial ridicule, no.

These attitudes toward governments create semantic confusion, reinforce market fundamentalism and inhibit potential contributions by a "positive state." Government contributions semantically become government "intervention." This semantic morass seems to derive from historical ideology, not analytical clarity. Market economizing coercion is called "freedom" but government protection of individuals from others is called "interference" or "control." Government protection of private property power and privilege is never condemned by fundamentalists as "interference" or "entitlements." This is a semantics of confusion and anti-government prejudice. These dysfunctional attitudes toward governments are detrimental to workable market management of the Essential Economy's pursuit of human betterment. Of course governments, like people and all institutions, can blunder badly. As governments are the super threat systems, they have the power to do super damage. As in all institutions, all innovations are "experiments" and some at times fail. It is another illusion that private failures are not public costs. In a world of scarcity, private failures are just as much a public cost as any economic activity. Failures are another regrettable side effect of progress and can be anticipated as costs of change. We learn by trying and it is inescapably costly. It is also extremely fruitful.

Government power, like market power and power in general, does not necessarily produce a clear understanding of or dedication to seeking the well-being of humanity. Political leaders, like others, have no clear choice of what to stand for other than that justified by traditional theory-philosophy, ideology and a crude populist pragmatism. When currently seeking a source of moral monitoring of progress and change we resort either to God's guidance, natural laws, conventions of the culture, constitutional commandments, or "experts."

Governments, too, must be monitored. Government power systems in democracies may well be under more scrutiny than private power systems. Certainly the U.S. Constitution provides mechanisms to monitor government itself. Even so, we are still left with the larger question of how do we know what should be done as we face the potential benefits of progress and the costs and dangers of change.

THE PEOPLE AND DEMOCRACY

Democratic societies make explicit the locus of "ultimate" responsibility of governance: we the people. A general view of democracy is that it is founded in majority vote. This is another insight suffering serious oversights, even illusions. It is sheer illusion that because it is the expressed will of the majority it is therefore right, workable, good, or moral. It is not the vote, but what understanding stands behind the majority vote, that morally matters. Majorities in southern "democratic" states of the USA supported immoral separationist policies until coerced from outside to change their practices. Majority vote does not make policy right; it only grants policy an acceptable power, even if evil.

It is through widespread appropriate and reliable understanding by informed, impartial spectators that we determine the effectiveness of democracies in guiding responsible change. Thus a democracy must generate the wisdom to discern when to conserve the familiar, how to conclude what innovations provide progress, and how to determine what changes are moral improvements. Sovereign citizens in a democracy carry the responsibility of redesigning institutional rules, not simply for themselves but for the future to cope with the consequences of change.

How is the majority informed with adequate wisdom to stay abreast of the pace and requirements of change? Part of the answer is through open inquiry, public debate, instruments of universal communication, and widespread conviction that all these elements are fundamental to responsible democracy. But democracies are caught in a philosophical bind. Our ideology covertly assures us that natural laws govern beneficently, and thus we can trust in free markets and free citizens to make naturally right decisions. However, knowing what to do in this increasingly complex and rapidly changing world is not only not self-evident, but it suffers severe understanding and information insufficiency. Is there a remedy at hand?

THE PURPOSE OF FREEDOM OF THE PRESS IS TO RELIABLY INFORM THE DEMOCRATIC PROCESS

The media, and its constitutional right to free speech, are singled out here because of the strategic importance of mass communication to our capacity to cope with change arising from the present pace of progress. As is expected, to initiate any policy in a democracy, a major step should be a public debate of the issue. But how is that debate publicly conducted?

National well-being, progress and change are monitored primarily by scholars, the arts, activists, politicians, those who "witness," and the media. Certainly the original purpose of freedom of the press was not to protect the press to say only those things that contribute to its profitability nor to create the impression that governments are incompetent. Constitutional guarantee of a free press should have the aim of providing a public instrument (infrastructure) for enlightened public debate over issues of public purpose concern as well as private purpose concern.

The present objective of the media is out of joint with public purpose press freedom. This is another of humanity's not easily resolved dilemmas. There are serious failings of the media, whose economic objective is profit. The device to profit has become entertainment. "If it don't bleed, it don't read." This diverts the scarce resources of the press, not just from informing but from adequately analyzing issues in terms of public, private and global consequences for humanity's well-being. No small responsibility.

The public cannot know what is better to do unless we have a press committed to explaining the options, providing the rationale for selecting alternatives, and explaining how and why each may go well or badly. This will not satisfy voyeurism, provide a bunch of belly laughs, or produce competitive profits. These observations are not to deny that the press should be financed and certainly better through some form of pluralism than as a monopoly of the state. Regrettably, resolving the media shortcomings is an issue that cannot be further discussed nor resolved here.

TAXATION-SPENDING DIRECTED BY THE INTEGRATIVE MODE

Taxation and government spending are instruments of the threat-power system. Taxation-spending is commonly perceived and condemned as abuse of power by the State. Here it is necessary to view the potential of taxation and spending from a very different perspective. They can be practical means with moral potential, such as providing schools, public health protection, fire departments, public roads, and lifting ghetto kids from context of crime to positive social contributors. The process can be and must be made instrumental to humanitarian edification. It is the integrative mode that must provide moral guidance to taxation-spending. This is done by means of generating knowledge that justifies allocating money power to appropriate use by both the threat and the exchange modes.

However, there is substantial ideological effort to justify the position that taxes should be administered in a way that preserves private purchasing power ("it's the people's money") and leaves large incomes virtually alone in order that they may be invested in private enterprises. This tax avoidance position is assumed to be just because it is perceived as necessary in order that business investments may more fully meet the desires of consumers who know best how to spend the incomes they earned producing the available output.

In the Necessary Integrative Scenario we observe that it is questionable that capital growth and economic progress need be dependent on the money-power privileged. The alternative exists in a market managed capitalist economy. Tax corrections are needed to mitigate the dissipation of scarce resources in luxurious display and sybaritic titillation by those excessively "rewarded." Part of our adventure capital already comes from and can be increased by expansion of retirement insurance for the economy's work force. This adventure capital can be expanded to a level equaling, even exceeding the savings of the current very wealthy. And it would be invested by professional investors. TIAA and CREF are exemplary examples. Justification of great inequality of incomes is no longer applicable in a pluralist discretionary market economy.

Taxation, though determined by power of the state, still preserves the same form of flexibility (freedom?) for individuality as the "free market" purports to provide. Individuals retain the discretion, within existing rules and incomes, to engage in whatever economic activities they choose. Just as the market preserves discretion while coercing economizing, in a similar way, taxes imposed on endangered resources will continue to preserve consumers' discretion. It will do so while nudging the market to favor otherwise neglected public purposes.

Certainly, taxation has historically been horrendously abused and can currently be improved. But both "abuse" and "improvement" require moral standards by which to evaluate the construction of taxation policy. Taxation policy should be based on its consequences, judged by the moral evolutionary, integrative, adaptation mode, not the power of traditional status rights and rationalized reciprocal justice.

AN ELEMENT OF SPECULATIVE IDEALISM

There is much to be said in favor of improving the qualitative content of wealth and continued possibility for progress. We might well revise the content of consumption and visualize it as a means of producing socially healthy activity. There is much room in our inherent human sentiments and sensuality for enrichment of lifestyles without irreparably threatening the environment upon which we are dependent. Conservation through market-enforced economizing need not be condemnation to unbearable misery. We can substitute much natural resource dependent consumption with humanistic fulfillment.

A case can be made for justifying, as real wealth, the condition of peace, love and affection, living in modest but reliable comfort and convenience, all with occasional peak experiences. Inherent human sentiments, as well as promising technology on the horizon, are already expanding the enrichment of consumer lifestyles without irreparably threatening the environment.

The expanding service economy can take many corrective forms. We can replace much material consumption with nonmaterial fulfillment. We can engage in more reading, play, socializing, loving our fellow man, entertainment, dialogue, gardening, dance, arts and crafts, drama, voluntarism, love making, laughter, better health; we can adopt a needy child, become a mentor or tutor for the youth, and much more.

As many have a bent to travel, and travel is costly in real cost terms of energy and facilities, this compulsion calls for resolution if possible. It can be satisfied for the many in the future by vicarious travel throughout the range of archaeology, anthropology, astronomy, and history. It can generate deeply moving experiences provided by emerging technology of broadband interactive communication coupled with virtual reality. We can share virtual time with the most inaccessible peoples of the past, or of the globe.

All can be done without burning more energy or consuming more resources than having dinner at home while watching a home movie. All provides conservation in place of dissipation. We can further conserve while we better serve by contemplating how to make our fellow humans happier, rather than how to make ourselves materially wealthier. And of course, the list of lifestyle options may only be limited by our imaginations and appropriate moral considerations. All this can preserve the creative and adaptive advantages of pluralism and even lend luster to our lives.

Such an orientation was within the range of Adam Smith's vision of moral sentiments. "What reward is most proper for promoting the practice of truth, justice, and humanity? The confidence, the esteem, and love of those we live with. Humanity does not desire to be great, but to be loved. It is not in being rich that truth and justice would rejoice, but in being trusted and believed, recompenses which those virtues must almost always acquire."

Is such an ethic conceivable? The prospects of such a global transformation are indeed dim. To improve the probability, what is needed most of all is appropriate reliable knowledge upon which to build the case.

RESEARCH INFRASTRUCTURE
IN THE NECESSARY INTEGRATIVE SCENARIO

Much information contributing to progress runs the danger of being coupled with serious information insufficiency. This lack of information as to how to cope with the unanticipated consequences of progress is critical. Bluntly, we are getting dangerously ahead of our capacity to cope. Strategy must be invented and implemented, or the costs and dangers of change can overcome our capacity to adapt, let alone progress.

Our research infrastructure requires analysis and revision to support the Integrative Scenario. A strategy for appropriate research is essential. The strategy proposed here is a composite of a Humanitarian Research Institute, an Apollo-like program to design the institute, and a triage strategy to most effectively utilize knowledge from the institute.

The first step is to design a research system that will produce policy recommendations for integrative progress and human fulfillment. This, it must be reemphasized, is a strategic response to the recognition that, under the most likely scenario, humanity's future is indeterminate, certainly not assured. Worse, under the worst case scenario, humanity's future is certainly tragically diminished or possibly virtually destroyed. Complicating the human condition much further, we do not know the details of a moral mission for humanity or how to determine what the details of the morality of mutual adaptation might best be.

We need knowledge now of how to prioritize *where* we need to progress and *how* the costs of change will likely impact. If we are inadequately informed of what is happening as a consequence of the magnitude of change, then there is no way of knowing what is the right or wrong course to follow; we will not know what is practically or morally right or wrong. Desperately, we need a research infrastructure dedicated to the mission of seeking answers to these moral-knowledge deficiencies.

These, of course, involve ethical questions. What should be done? Ethicists, rather than being expected to tell us what should or should not be done in specific moral cases (abortion clinics, prostitution, distribution of income, genetic engineering, cloning) must tell us how to go about resolving these global moral matters. We need to know what needs to be known, and how to know it, in order to resolve what it is that should be done. That is, we need to answer the question of how to know what will be right(er) or wrong(er), better or worse.

Given the magnitude of policy issues that have an ethical component needing reliable knowledge to resolve, the scarcity of total research talent must be faced. There is a severe scarcity of reliable knowledge to supply insights to replace deficiencies in understanding. In a world of scarcity, resources dedicated to determine whether there is life to communicate with in outer space may best be shifted to research of where and how to progress and how to avoid the human costs of change and possible disasters on this earth. As far as we know now, the closer threat is ourselves. "We have met the enemy and he is us." Robotics, genetic engineering, the World Wide Web, energy shortages, environmental destruction and inadequately prepared populations are upon us, not creatures from outer space. They may be out there; they are not known to threaten us as we threaten ourselves. This Most Necessary Scenario must confront our knowable and threatening challenges. The next step for dealing with these difficulties is to pursue an "Apollo strategy" to construct a Humanitarian Research Institute to provide the knowledge needed to improve the possibilities of successfully encountering the future. It is there we turn next.

10

An Apollo Project
for Humanitarian Economics

As we are aboard spaceship earth, it is well that all operating systems be mutually designed for a successful mission. That objective must be made explicit enough to formulate policies to pursue appropriate purposes. That calling, in broad conception, is to understand and achieve progress through mutual adaptation for human fulfillment. A major part of that endeavor is to know the characteristics of the mission and what determines its continuous success. Responding to that need-to-know challenge requires a very special Humanitarian Research Institute and an Apollo-like project to generate the knowledge to design that Institute. We seek an ideal but must not expect perfection, not even in this most necessary scenario.

THE APOLLO STRATEGY FOR PUTTING A MAN
ON THE MOON

The Apollo strategy of interest here was the managerial technique developed for generating the knowledge applied to putting a man in space. Briefly, here is what the Apollo strategy was: Establish a research team to formulate a general design. It becomes a spacecraft needing fuel for power, a communication system, a guidance device, mechanisms to provide oxygen, food, liquid, waste removal, and so forth. Then research teams are established to generate knowledge of how to construct each of these aspects of what is to become an integrated, fully operating spaceship.

Each area's research team (communication, fuel, guidance, etc.) worked on solving its facet of the project. As some areas made considerable progress and other areas lagged behind, an economizing and timing strategy coordinated all parts with all other parts to make the total come together as an organic "mission possible."

The strategy is contrary to capitalism's common sense. The Apollo idea is not to reward the successful teams that have proven themselves by their progress but just the reverse: Shift research funds (thus resources) away from the successful to the laggards, so the laggards can obtain more and better talent (and equipment) to catch up. This must go on as a continuously corrective process until all facets produce a spaceship capable of human space flight and safe return.

CONSTRUCTING A HUMANITARIAN RESEARCH INSTITUTE AND RESEARCH INFRASTRUCTURE

The proposed Apollo program's mission is not modest. It is equivalent to seeking to create a God. It seeks to design a research institute that can construct a strategy for managing the pace of progress, including coping with the costs and dangers of change. The Institute must become a permanent means by which all nations identify the knowledge needed to provide humanity with practical moral guidance without the costs of change being more painful than its gains. Just as utopian Gods have failed us, this Research Institute will not provide perfection or certainty. It will have the limitations of its creators—mankind itself. Here it is not sacrilegious, but virtuous, to critique and correct ourselves.

The first task of the project is to design itself. This involves determining the appropriate areas and kinds of knowledge to carry out the mission. The project can be broken down into component research teams with their tasks flexibly specified for shaping an Essential Economy. It can strive to identify how to know that the advantages of progress are greater than the costly consequences of change.

In a very conjectural manner, I illustrate the many types of essential components which can be identified, understood, and integrated to formulate a justly operable economic spaceship earth. They must be capable of sustaining humanity and formulating a continuous self-corrective mission. Conspicuous components (there may be many more) include optimum population; global communication and understanding; peace; conservation; ecological adjustments and maintenance; human needs; technological needs for the Essential Economy; rules as tools; appropriate and workable institutions; formulating the nature of evolutionary private property; institutions to monitor and project consequences of major activities or cumulative effects of minor activities; institutions responsible for recommending correctives to costly change; an integrated global financial system; a global ethic; a global constitution; taxation-spending principles; effective educational media for communication of publicly necessary knowledge; the role and objectives of the arts and humanities; modes of resolving ideological conflicts; "a common faith" for humanity; and how to fit all in an integrative whole under constraints of scarcity and continuous disruptions from human creativity. All aspects should be justified for their contribution to mutually adapting people to each other and their environments.

This Apollo project for a humanitarian mission can economize talent as well as other resources of the total research infrastructure. Thus each sub-area should be examined and evaluated with reference to all other existing research budgets. The design team should try to develop principles and means for evaluating success of the many sub-projects and their potential contribution to humanity's net advantage.

Some of the research areas will make substantial progress while others lag far behind. As with the initial Apollo project, highly successful areas of research that get out in front, such as advanced medical research in contrast to lagging population policy, should experience budget cuts, while lagging research (population policy) is enhanced. Research resources desperately need to be shifted out of the break-through areas and into the lagging sectors. It seems a plain and intelligible understanding that astronomy and physics, for example, are further ahead in their fields, and *new* knowledge in these fields is less essential for humanity's purposes than the question of knowing how to reduce the costs and dangers of the clash of peoples and civilizations. It is reasonable to shift from seeking to communicate with uncertain life forms in outer space to learning what and how to communicate more effectively among conflicting humans on this planet. Priorities should be reordered from what one author called "humanely worthless research" to humanely essential research.

Much past research has borne a bounty of knowledge of what is needed to meet many basic needs. On the other hand, how to determine distribution of goods and services confronts lagging understanding. An additional area is dealing with qualitative issues such as love, affection, respect, grief, gratitude, joy, security/insecurity, anguish. How can we evaluate and calculate such qualitative benefits and costs in order to economize our time and facilities effectively? Perhaps the humanities and their art forms can contribute substantially here. They seem well equipped to communicate an intensity and understanding of emotional qualities that are bound to be involved.

TRIAGE STRATEGY TO CONTROL
THE PACE AND COSTS OF CHANGE

The Humanitarian Research Institute, in this Necessary Integrative Scenario, will want to provide a triage strategy to gain control of the increasingly costly pace of change. Recall that classic triage is focused on a severe scarcity of medical facilities faced with a mass of wounded soldiers. The wounded are classified in three categories: the wounded who will survive without attention; the wounded who will not survive no matter how much attention they receive; and the wounded who only have a chance of survival if they receive adequate attention. The strategy is to disregard those who will make it without attention and disregard those who cannot make it no matter how much attention is devoted to them. By totally neglecting these two groups, maximum possible attention is available to those who will now have a chance. It is a maximizing strategy. A similar strategy for use of research resources can be applied to getting the pace of change under control. This triage strategy must be applied to prioritize the research infrastructure of the globe.

Currently, research is justified by its potential for advancement of knowledge. That seems reasonable and right. Use of that research, however, often gives rise to unanticipated consequences. This creates the potential for costly and dangerous change. It may be necessary to slow progressive innovations until we can catch up by learning how to manage unanticipated consequences of past developments. Such a condition may be illustrated with pure research cracking the genetic code and for-profit research giving rise to genetic engineering for improving individuals' lives. Innovations from these areas of research also have the potential of causing further human evolution without our having a reasonable grasp of the consequences of what the human species may become. When unexpected consequences are encountered we find humanity facing unanticipated costs, dangers and inadequate knowledge of how to cope. The results can be greater human costs and more severe tragedies than the kinds we see in the historic past and across the globe today.

A triage strategy is necessary to get the pace of change under control that we may have the time and resources to develop the knowledge needed to correct the unanticipated negative consequences of initially positive action. The triage strategy must be founded in three appropriate research categories: (#1) practical purpose research (get along as well as we are without more of it), (#2) curiosity, or pure research (as far as we know we will survive and even progress without more of it), (#3) research providing the knowledge by which humanity will have a possibility of net progress over costs of change (essential to reduce costs and dangers and realize net progress).

Triage requires neglect of the first two research areas (the practical and the pure). This will slow the pace of change. It will also slow pure research that simply satisfies curiosity in its initial phase. The strategy will help if we shift research resources from one (practical) and two (curiosity) to three (net progress) in order to provide maximum research to stay ahead of costs and possible dangers of change. For-profit research devoted to new products can be considered unnecessary costs of business and denied tax deductible status. For-profit research devoted to increasing efficiency and lowering costs of producing, as well as research improving operating efficiency of existing products, should be tax deductible costs of business. This tactic will both slow change-creating innovations and lower true costs in a scarcity world.

Scarce resources are dissipated in far more ways than misplaced priorities in research. But research is a major source of increasing the pace of invention, innovation, progress and change. It is prudent to slow the pace of progress to slow the pace of change and shift resources to increase lagging knowledge that has high probability of net benefit for the world economy. We must divert research resources from the out-front areas of medicine that save more lives that live longer and rededicate the research talents to improve lagging knowledge of population policies and quality of life issues that will give more meaning to those larger numbers of longer lives.

We do not have the knowledge to know with "common understanding" which extant research projects most effectively belong in which of these categories. Determining that is itself a high priority for the Humanitarian Research Institute.

CHARACTERISTICS OF THE HUMANITARIAN
RESEARCH INSTITUTE

Keep in mind that we are considering characteristics of the most necessary scenario. The Institute's focus is on collecting and generating appropriate reliable understanding to guide humanity's uncertain mission dedicated to the well-being of the human race without bias toward nation,
gender, class, race, wealth, power, religious sect, theology, ideology, or
scientific discipline. To not have bias or prejudice is not synonymous with
refraining from critiquing or even condemning. Value judgments, for and
against, must be made and justified with analysis, theory, and evidence
open to public review (as in the case of all proper science).

This Research Institute's actions should be open, honest, publicly
justified, and communicated. All findings and proposals are to be
freely made part of the knowledge commons. Patents, copyrights,
intellectual property, and any similar concept that might, in any way,
impede free access and use of the knowledge generated is unacceptable. This openness is to be written into the Institute's mission.

The Institute will have no institutionalized political, administrative, or market power. Once established, its sole source of financial
power to command resources for its mission will be derived from the
power of ideas to persuade donors of the importance of its purpose.
Funds to finance this institute may be solicited from all governments,
the United Nations, international agencies, public agencies, private
corporations, private citizens, and absolutely any source willing to
contribute on the Institute's terms. All contributions will be accepted
on the condition that no strings are attached.

THE INSTITUTE'S FUNCTIONS

A primary role of this Research Institute is to function as the idea coor-
dinator of all research on this planet for progressive integration and

fulfillment of the whole of humanity. It has the responsibility to compile an inventory of the nature and costs of all relevant research in progress. It will determine the areas where research resources are insufficient to provide appropriate knowledge for adapting to the pace, costs and dangers of change. The mass of research done by private enterprises, universities and other research institutes of many kinds provide the advantages of research pluralism. The knowledge developed by the three categories of research— (1) applied, (2) pure, and (3) net progress (or mutual adaptation)—is the information resource base humanity is dependent upon. This mass of research needs to be evaluated to determine where knowledge is being generated that supplements the objectives of human well-being and that which contributes information unnecessary for coping with the costs and dangers of change.

The Institute should, then, have two sub-courses of action to take: one, encourage all sources of potential research funds (public and private) to help the most necessary and lagging areas of research that they may catch up; and two, establish its own wing that will research in areas of insufficient knowledge not elsewhere adequately attended to.

Determining What Makes Reliable Knowledge Appropriate

In spite of the information overload flooding in faster than it can be digested in some areas, there are serious problems resulting from insufficient *appropriate* information. A profoundly important issue is that of knowing the kind of knowledge that is most needed. That is, what is appropriate knowledge? That, of course, depends on the objective. If it is pure curiosity (#2) it cannot be judged whether or not it is appropriate. Random, yes. Has random curiosity proven valuable in the past? Of course. But we face different conditions now. Its immediate value is not now self-evident. If it is practical applied research (#1) its usefulness is virtually self-evident from the start. However, the second-phase consequences of applied research are not nearly so evident as its initial purpose.

As our concern is progress in mutually adapting and staying ahead of the costs of change in the process (#3), then we must know better what mutually adapting is and how to do it continuously better. *Determining this is the central function of the Humanitarian Institute. It must seek to determine how to achieve integrative progress, while improving fulfillment of the hierarchy of human needs.*

It is the *extremes* of benefits (needs) and costs (pathologies) that may reasonably and economically be explored early by the Institute. Certainly we should not devote research talent to generate knowledge of how to make cigarettes more addictive while needing research resources to learn how to better treat cancer. And certainly we should be researching how to resolve disputes and improve peace among all peoples on earth in preference to exploring outer space.

There are good economizing reasons our research infrastructure not emphasize the marginal issues clouded with shades of gray. These are the areas where, if we can't tell what difference it makes, what difference does it make? On the other hand, the Institute must be charged with identifying the extremely pressing areas where there is high probability for improved public benefits and/or reduced social costs. These insights can provide a basis for recommending where shifts in research funding might best be made.

THE INSTITUTE'S CHARGES

The Institute will have three major charges to pursue. **Charge One:** Identify areas of advanced and abundant knowledge, in contrast with lagging but critically needed knowledge for mutually adapting. Recommend shifting research support from the highly successful, but not currently critical, and recommend that the funds go to lagging areas desperately needed for the success of the integrative mode. This is necessary whether the critically needed new knowledge is in the area of physical science, social science, or the humanities. It will encourage all sources of potential research funds (public and private) to contribute to research in critical lagging areas that they may catch up. It should influence private benefactors, university projects, legislators, government granting agencies, the United Nations and the international community to favorably consider research projects providing appropriate knowledge for human adaptation. Projects focused on global scale issues could be cooperatively researched through joint international ventures. There is precedent in the genome project with USA-Great Britain and the space platform with USA-Russia. Joint international projects might be well suited to develop global standards of trade and principles for a global ethic.

Charge Two: The Institute should generate its own research projects in areas not adequately attended to elsewhere. It will do some of both: do its own research and persuade others to focus research on specific knowledge-slighted projects.

Charge Three: All relevant knowledge accumulated by the Institute should be applied to formulate policy proposals relating to its integrating mission. This information should be forwarded, with recommendations, to appropriate policy-making and implementing bodies. All proposals must be backed by the justifying research findings.

THE INSTITUTE'S MISSION: A SUMMARY

The Humanitarian Institute is dedicated to broad and appropriate objective research in quest of improving knowledge necessary to human well-being for the long-run adaptation to living on this planet. It is especially focused on providing knowledge appropriate for public policy formation. It will recommend policies. It has no formalized administrative or political power to implement public policies.

A primary function of this Research Institute is to determine the areas where research resources are insufficient for providing needed knowledge for adapting to the pace, costs and dangers of change.

Further, the Institute seeks knowledge necessary for proposing solutions in knowledge deficient areas. It differs from applied medical or engineering research designed to benefit individuals in an immediately identifiable manner. In contrast, its focus is on policy issues clarifying why and how any topic of research can be reasonably expected to modify the global organic system and to do so in ways that will facilitate individuals' capacities to adapt, be increasingly fulfilled, and contribute effectively to the welfare of humanity. This includes research into the meaning of human well-being itself. It seeks to develop seminal ideas designed to better understand human progress, how best to achieve and judge it, and how best to cope with the costs of change.

Dedication to humanity's well-being is to be pursued without bias toward any phenomena, including no bias against critiquing and condemning any phenomena. The research is not expected to be value neutral. On the contrary, it is expected to identify and clarify the values that hold the greatest promise for human well-being. It is expected that research will be done with a willingness to be guided by current theories, as well as depart from established wisdom. The approach is not just to win arguments but to develop procedures to resolve differences of understandings. Confrontation from outside the Institute is to be viewed as feedback and not treated as an attack.

Seen from the perspective of ethics, it is not the role of the Institute to simply state what is right or wrong. Its mission is to provide the theoretical, empirical and practical justification for why proposed policies are more right or more wrong than other potential options. This must be done with the neutrality and objectivity of otherwise unbiased science. Its public openness commits it to the same kind of scrutiny as the Supreme Court of the USA. It requires even more independence than the Federal Reserve Board or the Supreme Court. However, it differs from both in a very important way. It has absolutely no power to influence events other than through the power of persuasion through reliable knowledge. Reliable knowledge, like the pen, is not only mightier than the sword in the long run it must be mightier than the almighty dollar. The question is: how is a society to obtain the knowledge to formulate global policy that encourages progress and copes with change? We seek reliable means of generating appropriate wisdom through "science as a candle in the dark."

SCIENCE: THE INSTITUTE'S METHOD OF KNOWING

Still open is the question of how appropriate and reliable knowledge is to be derived. Thus, what method must the Institute follow in this most necessary scenario?

There is no perfection in knowledge; there are degrees of reliability (and unreliability) such as reading the tea leaves, reference to ancient lore, personal purpose rationality, majority vote, rational extrapolation from fundamental convictions or we can learn by refined and expanded application of scientific method. Scientific method does not escape the problems of insights, oversights, and illusions. Scientific method must confront these characteristics within itself. And, of course, it is the method of science that the Institute is to follow.

In the process of proto-man evolving into modern man there certainly emerged a form of *common sense*. This historical development of rational common sense has further evolved into *scientific method*, that is, sophisticated rules of knowing more reliably. Inherent curiosity has led mankind to observe and speculate on nature and man's place in it. Circumstances of geography along with animal and plant types led the Fertile Crescent, the Middle East, and then Western society to the stability of an agriculture based economy. This stable lifestyle allowed for curiosity and creativity to evolve one of our great tools, a written language. This tremendously improved the accumulation and passing down of observations and speculations. This cumulative process evolved through philosophy into the invention of the methods of inquiry being called "science."

Increasingly, elements of scientific method have spread throughout the Western populace, giving rise to a rationality that impacted the seventeenth century Age of Science and the eighteenth century Enlightenment and Age of Reason. This rationality has been woven into the fabric of an emerging rational integrative mode of social organization. These rather abstract knowledge processes evolved concurrently with the evolution and spread of tangible technologies, which reinforced a techno-logic concern for consequences of behavior: If it doesn't work well, look for a corrective. This mode of thinking gives rise to both a private and public self improvement ethos. It becomes an outlook from which disputes are perceived as problems to be corrected. It becomes a pragmatic ethos to analyze problems to be solved in terms of consequences for mutual adaptation and enrichment. The integrative system becomes a self-correcting moral improvement system. All this requires increasing understanding. Out of this history evolved, and continues to evolve, generic science. Its method is a pattern of values guiding scientific inquiry.

We will find a flavor of the evolution of science from the following instructive poem of Sir William Dampier.

Natura enim non nisi parendo vincitur.
(Nature Is Not Conquered Except By Obedience)

At first men try with magic charm
    To fertilize the earth,
To keep their flocks and herds from harm
    And bring new young to birth.

Then to capricious gods they turn
    To save from fire or flood;
Their smoking sacrifices burn
    On altars red with blood.

Next bold philosopher and sage
    A settled plan decree,

And prove by thought or sacred page
    What Nature ought to be.

But Nature smiles—a Sphinx-like smile—
    Watching their little day
She sits in patience for a while—
    Their plans dissolve away.

Then come those humbler men of heart
    With no completed scheme,
Content to play a modest part,
    To test, observe, and dream.

Till out of chaos come in sight
    Clear fragments of a Whole;
Man, learning Nature's way aright,
    Obeying, can control.

The great Design now glows afar;
    But yet its changing Scenes
Reveal not what the Pieces are
    Nor what the Puzzle means.

And Nature smiles—still unconfessed
    The secret thought she thinks—
Inscrutable she guards unguessed
    The Riddle of the Sphinx.

These last poetic stanzas suggest that in quest of reliable knowledge we must not become deluded into a search for absolute certainty or overarching human control. The poem conveys an important insight into science. However, if we expect to find meaning for man in the processes of nature, we will have anthropomorphized nature ("she sits in patience," "she thinks"). Poetic license? An illusion, none the less. It attributes to nature the uniqueness of nature's human product, the capacity of humanity to invent/create meaning for itself. We seek to do so within the limits and with the possibilities available through nature. Those limits and possibilities are a function of both nature and human knowledge. Here we encounter, not a tricky and deceptive nature. We encounter both insightful and deceptive human understanding. It is natural.

There are ancient ghosts in our intellectual closets that still haunt our view of science. Having faith in absolute certainty is an archaic expectation for knowing, even for science. A more reasonable quality of expectation is one of qualified confidence in preference to certainty—probability, not absolute faith.

As previously noted, Adam Smith observed that Newton's science, as method, was the best philosophy man ever invented. The methods of science are, of course, the discovered rules of generating the most reliable knowledge. But there are views, attitudes, and philosophies often surrounding scientific method that this present analysis rejects. It rejects the attitudes of "science for science's sake," "the truth will make us free," or "knowledge for knowledge's sake." All quests of knowledge applying methods of science do not necessarily lead to human betterment. Some scientific findings lead to first-phase improvements, with second-phase unanticipated consequences that may not lead to third-phase remedies. This was, and for some still is, the concern over scientists developing the atomic bomb. Building it was the application of scientific method. Deciding to build it must be seen as the experience-experiment process. The finished product was used as an application of the threat mode. We now can seek to learn from the experience (viewed as an experiment) by examining the consequences from the perspective of the integrative mode and its morality of mutual adaptation.

This is not another anti-technology, anti-science plea. It is a plea that scientific-technological pursuits be closely monitored with a sense that just because science resolved a past puzzle, it does not follow that humanity will be free, humanely enlightened or better off knowing that additional truth, while not knowing how to manage its consequences. It is not the generic *method* of science that is here being questioned. It is the quality of the application of the method that is of moral concern.

ETHICAL PRAGMATISM

Ethical pragmatic reasoning in moral matters requires theoretical, logical, and evidential inquiry into the consequences of policies and practices resulting from the values that drive and direct us. Here again, we face the realization that we are not likely to do anything right(er) unless we know more reliably what we should be doing. Thus knowing what to know and how to know more reliably becomes the strategic, practical, and moral necessity for humanity. Finding our way is dependent, not on all knowledge generated by science but rather upon the methods of science applied to more reliably finding our way. For practical as well as moral purposes, that which is relative is not adrift in chaos; nor is science a guarantee of beneficence. However, all that is relative is relative to inescapable natural laws and therefore dependent on natural conditions upon which essential economic and life processes are constructed. As the specifics of man-nature evolution-adaptation are not known to be mandated from outside this natural process, what is necessary is an internally constructed morality of mutual adaptation linking nature and our fellow man. How that adaptation is best achieved is knowable only through the most reliable knowledge of how to do so increasingly effectively.

We are confronted with the questions of how we understand or explain how the integrative social processes work and break down. This is the endless quest, not for certainty but for more appropriate and more reliable understanding. Thus, knowing reliably is a process of evolving increasingly reliable explanations in open-ended time through unending inquiry.

NEED FOR TIME-BOUND ANSWERS

Though knowing appropriately and reliably may always be improved upon, it is regularly reasonable to ask for cloture of inquiry now, as we live now and must act now in this on-going, open-ended process. Thus we very likely will always be acting with insights suffering oversights, and confusions from illusions. As we cannot wait to the end of time to draw conclusions needed in order to act now, concerns over questionable reliability of knowledge deserve an answer now.

What would be required to provide a currently acceptable answer to such concerns? It would require a cogent argument, based in an explicit theory, supported by demonstrable evidence, that a reasonably informed impartial spectator could follow. This argument could be confirmed or rebutted, in part or degrees, by other reasonably informed impartial spectator's cogent arguments also supported by demonstrable evidence. That would be analogous to the role of a court of law conducted by a judge impartial to the outcome and pleaded by unbiased attorneys before an empathetic jury, all parties dedicated not to winning or avoiding defeat but to finding the truth as best it can be known at that time. A quest for absolute certainty will not resolve this matter. We can have a hung jury and not know what is better or worse.

All this is to emphasize the question: how can we know justifiably what specific policies should be supported or rejected? The Necessary Integrative Scenario calls for a Humanitarian Research Institute to provide the most relevant and reliable knowledge possible to put us on the path to a fulfilling mission for humanity.

VALUES SHAPING INQUIRY FOR MORAL KNOWLEDGE

At the heart of virtually all moral matters is the nature of human values that establish expectations for us and aspirations by us. Values motivate the direction that our thinking and behavior takes. What values are we to use to evaluate the qualities of values being questioned in a world of change? How do we evaluate values supporting or condemning TV programs, advertisements, guns, alcohol, tobacco, abortion, education, liberation of females, income distribution, reward systems, helping the poor and homeless, family size, population of the planet, divorce, and other issues blanketed by systems of values?

Ethically evaluating values is itself guided by a special *pattern* of values: a cluster of core values that are instrumental in generating understandings for critiquing, validating, modifying, or condemning social values as they are transformed in a changing world. Ethical pragmatism rests upon such a pattern of values. They are, of course, the values historically evolved and identified as the essence of scientific method.

Scientific method's pattern of values prescribes procedures and attitudes when seeking reliable knowledge. Science is not an esoteric gift designed by the Gods for the exceptionally gifted. Nor was it born with the Scientific Revolution, important as the period was in developing new knowledge of nature and improved methods of science itself. Science is, instead, a group of values or rules that have evolved over the history of humanity. These values when followed to the most refined degree known at any time have gradually demonstrated their advantage in improving the probability of generating explanations which when acted upon are more reliable than all other explanations derived by any other means. According to Susan Haack's *Manifesto of a Passionate Moderate*, one should see science "not as *privileged*, but as *distinguished* epistemically; as deserving . . . *respect* rather than *deference*. Science is neither sacred nor a confidence trick."

This method of knowing can be humanistically applied as well as applied in physics, chemistry, biology, pharmacy, or engineering. It is the application of the same pattern of values to the quest of human integration and mutual adaptation as that applied to putting a man on the moon or uncovering the genetic code. They are core values in that whatever humanity believes, by following these values, the belief can be confirmed as truer, falser, or having degrees of reliability. As a cluster, they are self-correcting values. They are not sacred writ. They are humanly invented. They are open to improvement. Together, these values constitute the "canons of science."

What are these values that are to be followed in order to best guide procedures for improving the human condition in the most necessary scenario?

Motivating Values of Science

As all human behavior is performed for "rewards" of many kinds, those engaged in scientific inquiry do so for many reasons. The individual's motives, if properly following procedures, do not matter to the reliability of outcome. So long as the values of science are followed the reliability of the results will be the most robust available. This does *not* mean that all results are morally defensible, but they will be the most reliable. Nor does it mean that the selection of issues for research is not influenced by motives.

The scientific personnel selected for the Humanitarian Research Institute should be those motivated to discover how best to determine how to organize humanity in pursuit of both short-term and long-term human well-being.

Attitudinal Values

The investigators selected must be meticulously honest, prepared to suspend vested interest while pursuing reasonable alternatives, and possess humility in the face of challenging persuasive evidence and theory.

Procedural Values

It is the power of knowledge generated by scientific method that makes truth persuasive. The procedural values for determining truth are not esoteric nor magical. They reflect common experiences of facing problems and intuiting possible resolutions by constructing hypotheses-theories that may be verified by appropriate means of testing. This hypothesis testing must be open for others to follow, confirm, or reject or modify. Thus the procedure produces self-corrective conclusions-theories over time.

These values, attitudes, procedures form a cluster or core of integrated, reinforcing and mutually correcting values. The more fully their practice is integrated the more reliable the results. We have not found an absolutely certain way of finding absolutely reliable truth. That expectation is another utopian illusion. However, we very likely will continue to achieve means of improving reliability for a broader range of areas crying out for understanding.

Virtually all humans rely, almost daily, on some segments of this scientific inquiry to get through their day. "Why doesn't this lamp light?" Individuals can and do specialize in segments of these canons. Thus there are degrees of being scientific. Observe first-class craftsmen at their tasks. They practice many of these canons with an artistic flair.

SCIENCE AND SHAPING THE FUTURE

All this epistemological concern is related to development of policy to provide direction for humanitarian progress and minimizing costs of change. This inescapably confronts the necessity of projecting consequences into the future. Can science deal with the future? Here, perhaps more than any place else in science, we cannot demand certainty. We can, however, expect substantial improvement of reliability over autonomous "marginal efficiency of capital" estimates, or majority vote.

Here, the best we may be able to achieve by the Research Institute is development of the most probable case, and most necessary case scenarios. Where these can be modeled they can be projected by thought experiment or computer simulation to provide a vision of likely results. Acknowledging that there will not be utopian perfection, a committee of informed, impartial observers (including outsiders to the project) can examine the work and projections. They can supply direction, with a better-safe-than-sorry caveat, for political processes to implement.

This may not be as promising as our concerns may cause us to wish; but it is an alternative to the dangers of standing pat in a world of change or being led by ideologically supported systems of power. Political democracies will continue to succeed only to the extent they are informed by the values of scientific method in developing reliable understanding.

SCIENCE VALUES, MORAL CHARACTER, AND IDEALISM

These canons of science have emerged as values shaping democratic attitudes and scientific attitudes alike. Their morally proper use, judged in terms of the morality of the integrative mode of mutual adaptation, is humanitarian and reflects the best of human cognitive procedures.

The individual reaches more significant dimensions and qualities of social and moral responsibility as she/he becomes more pragmatically rational. We approach this ideal as we more consciously contemplate decisions in terms of net sums of social consequences. Additionally, these consequences are to be weighed in terms of mutual adaptation among people, and they with their natural environment.

As we review these canons sympathetically as values by which we might aspire to shape personal character, as well as a worldview, we will discover the potential for colorful, interesting, and morally responsible individuals. They can even lead us to peak experiences. Regrettably, few, if any of us, possess such a sterling character. It is a lofty and promising ideal.

These values of science are the most promising values by which the lives of all may be improved, as they are increasingly practiced by all. This is achieved through practicing appropriate sentiments of human nature such as curiosity, love of others, bonding, altruism, the fruitful use and precarious consequences of self-interests, the nature and nurture of self-reliance, impulse of workmanship, honesty, and in general our moral sense. These views of science impose humility and make us extremely modest and cautious. Yet we must act, and because of uncertainty, we must recognize that we act experimentally.

Discernment becomes increasingly difficult under conditions of rapid change. In a world of change, knowledge in some areas becomes increasingly unreliable. Evidence becomes decreasingly clear. Weighing options becomes increasingly difficult. As the margins for discretion narrow toward a point of indifference, the degree of moral importance, itself, diminishes toward zero. That is, if it cannot be known what difference it makes, then what difference does it make? This indifference will persist until additional reliable information shifts the weight of the options. In the meantime, the use of the threat mode, exchange negotiation under existing rules, majority vote, or flipping a coin are all equally moral procedures so long as they reduce social costs of change and conflict.

There is no guarantee of continued economic, social, or humanitarian success; no knowable perfection; no ultimate ideal. We proceed with hope and cautious confidence that seeking increasingly reliable knowledge about the process we have evolved in will improve probabilities of continued success, even progress for humanity. We make no leap of faith that we will find and implement "a true and only way" to find or design the nature and causes of the wealth of nations and humanity.

We have evolved with genetic and cultural means of learning and knowing with varying degrees of reliability. This uncertain degree of scientifically reliable knowledge is the best available basis upon which our morally guiding values must be structured. These values making up the canons of science provide a "constitution" of general principles by which social behavior may be morally monitored and managed. This provides no guarantee that we will develop necessary understanding of natural forces by which to confront scarcity, prosper, avoid suffering, and escape all agonies of humanity. But it is our best bet.

References

This book is largely written in an essay form designed to persuade philosophically. It is not footnoted with academic citations. However the work is, of course, built upon ideas developed in the Western world's literature and history. As there may be readers interested in pursuing the concepts further, I am listing some direct or indirect sources that may be explored. I do this primarily in chapter sequence as the topics are introduced. As the philosophical views in this work may appear somewhat abstract I recommend an excellent scholarly presentation of commonly shared ideas in a very applied context from which I have borrowed heavily without specific citations. The work is *Values, Nature, and Culture in the American Corporation* by William C. Frederick (New York: Oxford University Press, 1995). See especially its chapter seven.

CHAPTER 1. THE QUEST

For a delightful introduction to economics see a book on economics that reads like a novel. It is *The Worldly Philosophers* by Robert Heilbroner, published in paperback as A Touchstone Book by Simon and Schuster and reprinted often during the last half of the twentieth century.

Another good introduction to the mood of this book is *The Moral Sense* by James Q. Wilson (New York: Simon & Schuster Inc., 1993).

CHAPTER 2. ADAM SMITH'S FOOTPRINTS

For an insightful and pleasant introduction to the intellectual atmosphere surrounding the rise of the moral philosophy of economics see Carl L.

Becker, *The Heavenly City of the Eighteenth-Century Philosophers* (New Haven: Yale University Press, 1932; Seventh Printing, 1948).

The present book's moral philosophy of economics evolved from one of the great thinkers of the Enlightenment, Adam Smith (1723–1790). He was a distinguished Scottish moral philosopher well worth discovering or rediscovering. His substantial works that this book is built upon are: *The Principles Which Lead and Direct Philosophical Enquiries: Illustrated by the History of Astronomy*, available in *The Essential Adam Smith*, Robert L. Heilbroner (ed.) New York: W. W. Norton, 1986). Smith's central moral philosophy is spelled out in his *The Theory of Moral Sentiments*, a work written and rewritten over the period 1759–1790. My copy is published by the Liberty Fund, Indianapolis, 1984, edited by D.D. Raphael and A.L. Macfie. And perhaps the greatest and the first work establishing modern economics, Smith's *An Inquiry into the Nature and Causes of the Wealth of Nations*, 1776 (New York: Modern Library, Edwin Cannan, (ed.), 1937). For a time-conserving reading of Smith I suggest Heilbroner's *The Essential Adam Smith*, noted above.

There is a helpful but critical perspective of Smith's views in Kenneth Lux's *Adam Smith's Mistake: How A Moral Philosopher Invented Economics and Ended Morality* (Boston: Shambhala Publications, 1990).

There was a close predecessor to Adam Smith's founding of the discipline of economics. He was a French physician, Francois Quesnay (1694–1774). He developed the first systematic vision of an economy governed by natural laws in his *Natural Rights*, published in 1765.

For a sense of the technological dynamics impacting the Western world coming into the eighteenth century Enlightenment see *Technics and Civilization* by Lewis Mumford (New York: Harcourt, Brace, 1934).

Also on technology and progress, see the early section of the delightfully written *The Evolution of Progress* by C. Owen Paepke (New York: Random House, 1993).

CHAPTER 3. INSIGHTS, OVERSIGHTS, AND ILLUSIONS

To pursue a deeper sense of the moral philosophy of economics being developed in this work, see *Habits of the Heart: Individualism and Commitment in*

American Life, by Robert Bellah et al. (New York: Harper & Row, 1985). It is a book that will provide emotional relief from economic analysis while contributing essential intellectual understanding of the social importance of the nature of individual character.

"Are Men Rational or Economists Wrong?" by Tibor Scitovsky. A chapter in: Paul A. David and Melvin W. Reder, eds., *Nations and Households in Economic Growth: Essays in honor of Moses Abramovitz* (New York, Academic Press, 1974).

Again see *Adam Smith's Mistake*, noted above. Zbigniew Brzezinski, *Grand Failure: The Birth and Death of Communism in the Twentieth Century* (New York: Collier Books, 1990) presents a case which can be interpreted as arguing for not giving up in despair and jumping to a grand alternative system because Western economies falter.

Politics, Economics and Welfare: Planning and Politico-Economic Systems Resolved into Basic Social Processes by Robert A. Dahl and Charles E. Lindblom (New York: Harper, 1953). This is not necessarily a fun read, but it is one of the fine examinations of the relations among political, economic, and social processes.

An intriguing confrontation of a specific case of new technology and the law, by James Boyle, is *Shamans, Software, & Spleens: Law and the Construction of the Information Society* (Cambridge: Harvard University Press, 1996).

See also an extensive look at the power structure and its functioning in *Who Will Tell the People: The Betrayal of American Democracy* by William Greider (New York: Simon & Schuster, 1992).

Looking for a workable market is illuminated by Robert Kutner's *Everything for Sale: The Virtues And Limits Of Markets* (New York: Alfred A. Knopf, 1997).

For one of many works observing that an economy is managed by *rules*, see *The Morality of Law* by Lon L. Fuller (New Haven: Yale University Press, 1969): ". . . law is the enterprise of subjecting human conduct to the governance of rules" (page 106). Also re rules, "We have always set the rules of the marketplace—and often changed them when we wanted different outcomes" (page 281).

One can find a gold mine of recent insights and information on human evolution, human nature, and culture in Paul R. Ehrlich's *Human Natures: Genes, Cultures, and the Human Prospect* (Washington, DC: Island Press / Shearwater Books, 2000).

CHAPTER 4. FREE MARKET THEORY, TOUCHSTONE OF IDEOLOGY: PRAISE AND A CRITIQUE

There is a technical and rather dry read in which a major issue in economics, *scarcity*, is elegantly spelled out. It is worth the close attention it requires. See *An Essay on the Nature and Significance of Economic Science* by Lionel Robbins (London: Macmillan, 1949). The portion of the book dealing with scarcity persuaded me that I could not think realistically about economics unless I coupled my philosophy of technology and the Essential Economy with Robbins's view of scarcity.

This chapter four includes historical analysis of economic depressions. Prior to Adam Smith's *Wealth of Nations*, Bernard Mandeville wrote the *Fable of the Bees* in which he suggested that private vice was public virtue because it provided full employment. Jean Baptiste Say argued in his *Treatise on Political Economy* in 1803 that full employment was automatic because supply creates its own demand.

In 1942 the English economist, John Maynard Keynes, published *The General Theory of Employment, Interest and Money* (London: Macmillan, 1942). (Not an easy read!) He demolished J. B. Say's, and others' theories that the market tended to equilibrate automatically at full employment. For a readable account of Keynes's complex ideas see *The Age of Keynes* by Robert Lekachman (New York: Random House, 1966).

CHAPTER 5. THE ESSENTIAL ECONOMY AND A WORKABLE MARKET

C.E. Ayres, *The Theory of Economic Progress* (Chapel Hill: University of North Carolina Press, 1944) presents a case for viewing technology's importance in what I am calling the "Essential Economy." However he neglects the problem of scarcity and fails to face the rationing role of a "workable market."

The following three books will provide provocative insights into interpreting the nature of Western economies.

Economic Organizations and Social Systems by Robert A. Solo (New York: Bobbs-Merrill, 1967).

Legal Foundations of Capitalism by John R. Commons (London: Macmillan, 1924). It is the voice of practical experience not easily followed but worth the effort.

A conservative interpretation of the U.S. constitution, *The Tempting of America: The Political Seduction Of The Law* by Robert H. Bork (New York: Simon & Schuster, 1990).

The concept of the Essential Economy provides a very different view of the fundamental foundations of economies from that of conventional theory and common ideology. This innovative view is supported by the following works:

Jared Diamond, *Guns, Germs, and Steel: The fates of human societies* (New York: Norton, 1997).

James F. Moore, *The Death of Competition: Leadership and Strategies in the Age of Business Ecosystems* (New York: Harper Collins, 1996).

Kevin Kelly, *New Rules for the New Economy: Radical Strategies for a Connected World* (New York, Viking Penguin, 1998).

Jane Jacobs, *The Nature of Economies* (New York: Modern Library, 2000) and Michael Rothschild, *Bionomics: Economy as Ecosystem* (New York: Henry Holt, 1990).

To escape the preconception that human rights are natural rights, see *The Cost of Rights: Why Liberty Depends on Taxes* by Stephen Holmes and Cass R. Sunstein (New York: Norton, 1999).

CHAPTER 6. THE ORGANIZING ANIMAL

Kenneth Boulding in *Ecodynamics: A New Theory of Social Evolution* (Beverly Hills, CA: Sage Publications, 1978) sets up three modes by which all humans are organized: threat, exchange, and integrative.

Positive comments by Robert A. Solo on Boulding's threat, exchange, and integrative modes can be quickly reviewed in the *Journal of Economic Issues*, December, 1994, page 1196.

Daniel J. Boorstin, *The Republic of Technology: Reflections On Our Future Community* (New York: Harper & Row, 1978) explores the process of knowledge-technology integrating the peoples of the globe for mutual benefits.

Abraham H. Maslow has noted the nature of basic human needs in *Toward a Psychology of Being* (New York: Van Nostrand Reinhold, 1968).

David S. Landes's *The Wealth and Poverty of Nations: Why Some Are So Rich and Some So Poor* (New York: W.W. Norton, 1999) is a rich and colorful work that argues that knowledge-technology has been an important progressive force.

CHAPTER 7. MORAL SENTIMENTS AND ECONOMIC JUSTICE

The Moral Sense is a great work affirming that human nature is a basic source of moral inclinations. It is written by James Q. Wilson (New York: Simon & Schuster, 1993) and noted above for chapter one of the present work.

A significant view encompassing morality is available in *The Moral Animal: Evolutionary Psychology and Everyday Life* by Robert Wright (New York: Pantheon Books, 1994).

Adam Smith, prior to modern psychology, saw morality emerging out of human nature in his *The Theory of Moral Sentiments*. One may wish to read it for a perspective on the history of ideas.

A scholar deserving recognition for giving us another push to make economics a morally self-conscious discipline is Amitai Etzioni with his *The Moral Dimension: Toward a New Economics* (New York: The Free Press, 1988).

As the role of technology in human affairs is a fundamental issue running throughout this entire moral philosophy of economics I suggest some material to read. From the Harvard University Program On Technology And Society (61 Kirkland Street, Cambridge, Mass. 02138) see Research Review No. 3, Spring 1969 entitled *Technology and Values*; also see the institute's *A Final Review 1964–1972*. In addition to an extensive text it contains sixteen pages of references.

C. E. Ayres's *Theory of Economic Progress* (noted above) develops a moral philosophy of technology that is a "must" for someone tantalized by the prospects that technology is a major source of human good.

Further, the works of Victor C. Ferkiss still deserve attention. They are

Technological Man: The Myth and the Reality (New York: Braziller, 1969) and *The Future of Technological Civilization* (New York: George Braziller, 1974).

When the topic of *justice* arises it seems improper to neglect John Rawls's distinguished work, *A Theory of Justice* (Oxford, Clarendon Press, 1972). I confess I am impressed, yet I do not resonate well with his thesis. I fear that finding our way in a rapidly changing future will require continual changing standards of justice and we will need a concept of justice that is practically possible to progressively implement. Rawls's view is open to such concerns but fails to prescribe a practical procedure.

CHAPTER 8. THE MEANING OF ECONOMIC PROGRESS

A perspective of issues motivating continued concerns for market managed economies: *Everything For Sale: The Virtues and Limits of Markets* by Robert Kuttner (New York: Alfred Knopf, 1997).

For those who have not read *The Communist Manifesto* by Karl Marx and Friedrich Engels, 1848, it is a challenging "must" and may be found in *The Essential Works of Marxism* edited by Arthur P. Mendel (New York: Bantam Books, 1961).

Robert A. Nisbet, in his *History of the Idea of Progress* (New York: Basic Books, 1980) provides essential material upon which I have relied extensively.

The Idea of Progress: An Inquiry Into Its Growth And Origin by J.B. Bury (New York: Dover Publications, 1955, original copyright 1932). Another distinguished work establishing the importance of the concept of progress for humanity.

The True and Only Heaven: Progress and Its Critics by Christopher Lasch (New York: Norton, 1991). This book speaks to many of the more pressing issues of today.

C. Owen Paepke develops an enthralling analysis of *The Evolution of Progress: The End of Economic Growth and the Beginning of Human Transformation* (New York: Random House, 1993).

David S. Landes's *The Wealth and Poverty of Nations: Why Some Are So Rich and Some So Poor* (noted above) contributes insights that are imperative to evaluating the nature and causes of progress.

C.E. Ayres, *The Theory of Economic Progress* (noted above) argued in virtually all his work that technological evolution has been the major source and standard of judging human progress.

A book that half a century ago defended the place where this author, with caution, stands today: *The Case for Modern Man* by Charles Frankel (Boston: Beacon Press, 1958).

David W. Marcell, *Progress and Pragmatism: James, Dewey, and the American Idea of Progress* (Westport, CN: Greenwood Press, 1974) presents a persuasive pragmatic view of progress.

Critics of technology-science's ability to bring dependable progress provide necessary caution. See for example: John Swaney, "Obsolete Technology Mentality: "Technology, Virtue Itself?" *Journal Of Economic Issues*, June, 1989.

CHAPTER 9. THINKING ABOUT AN UNKNOWABLE FUTURE

This moral philosophy of economics contends that the future is descending upon us at a furious pace and we must find a way to cope with the threatening dangers of change. For help see *Preparing For The Twenty-First Century* by Paul Kennedy (New York: Random House, 1993). In searching for the nature of reliable knowledge to guide us, see Karl R. Popper, *Objective Knowledge: An Evolutionary Approach* (Oxford, Clarendon Press, 1972).

On the *environmental* debate see: An extremely optimistic analysis of the environment in *The Skeptical Environmentalist: Measuring the Real State of the World* by Bjorn Lomborg (Cambridge: Cambridge University Press, 2001). And for important responses, see *Scientific American*, starting with the January 2002 issue.

An important book on environmental concerns has recently been published by the Earth Policy Institute. It is *Plan B: Rescuing a Planet under Stress and a Civilization in Trouble* by Lester R. Brown (New York: W.W. Norton, 2003).

For an analysis of the importance of the historical evolution of science and technology see Jared Diamond's *Guns, Germs, and Steel*, noted above.

See the human importance of the evolution of methods of science argued by Carl Sagan in *The Demon-Haunted World: Science As a Candle in the Dark* (New York: Ballantine Books, 1996). And for related discussions see his chapters 24 and 25.

To flex our minds to the need for taxation and government spending see *The Cost of Rights: Why Liberty Depends on Taxes*, by Stephen Holmes and Cass R. Sunstein, noted above.

CHAPTER 10. AN APOLLO PROJECT
FOR HUMANITARIAN ECONOMICS

For a distinguished presentation of science as the foundation of reliable thought see again Carl Sagan's *The Demon-Haunted World: Science As a Candle in the Dark*, noted above.

I find a pamphlet by George Simpson entitled *Science as Morality: An Essay Towards Unity* a fascinating, daring, and important speculation worthy of attention. It was published in 1953 by The American Humanist Association, The Humanist Press, Yellow Springs, Ohio.

For an advanced and sophisticated level of scholarship dealing with science, see the magnificently responsible work by Edward O. Wilson, *Consilience: The Unity Of Knowledge* (New York: Alfred A. Knopf, 1998).

The Jerome Levy Institute of Bard College is worth contacting for bold insights into economic issues: Blithewood, PO Box 5000, Annandale-on-Hudson, New York 12504-5000.

The poem 'Natura enim non nisi parendo vincitur' (Nature Is Not Conquered Except By Obedience) can be found on page vi opposite the Preface, in A HISTORY OF SCIENCE, Sir William Dampier, 3rd edition (London: Macmillan, 1945).

"Science is neither sacred nor a confidence trick" (page 94) is from Susan Haack, *Manifesto of a Passionate Moderate* (Chicago: University of Chicago Press, 1998). Her book is a fine modern read.

In searching for the nature of reliable knowledge to guide us, again see *Objective Knowledge* by Karl Popper, noted above.

Another and important perspective is the relationship between "art and life" as developed by the arts. Views on this topic that are consistent with the present moral philosophy of economics can be found in: *The Humanist Frame* by Julian Huxley (New York: Harper, 1961); *The Sciences and the Arts: A New Alliance* by Harold G. Cassidy (New York: Harper, 1962); *Art As Experience* by John Dewey (New York: Milton, Balch, 1934); and *The Scandal of Pleasure: Art In An Age Of Fundamentalism* by Wendy Steiner (University of Chicago Press, 1995).

Acknowledgments

I am grateful to the many students who challenged me to refine my thoughts during many years of college teaching. Some have become close friends and contributed immeasurably to the writing of this book. I am awed by the extent of my indebtedness for their individual efforts and collective insights. As there are so many who have given so much I am unable to express here the uniqueness of the contributions of each. However, I am pleased to thank those most crucial to this book: Jim Ganschow, Jinx McCombs, Suzanne Mikel, Peter Morales, Terry Mullins, Rick Ostrov, Rich Thomas, Karen Larson, and David Wellenbrock. I further acknowledge contributions by friends and colleagues: Ted R. Brannen, Eric Ratner, Kathryn Mikel, Herb Reinelt, David Stadtner, and John Tucker.

All these individuals have brought their personal philosophies and unique professional experiences to bear critically and constructively on the content of this philosophy of economics. Further, throughout the book are phrases borrowed from forgotten sources, each of which vivifies an insight. I, of course, accept responsibility for the final content of these pages.

There is a distinguished exception to all of the above. I am grateful beyond my capacity to adequately articulate to the indispensable contributions of a very special scholar and friend. This work is indebted to William C. Frederick, student in the first class I taught and now an intellectual leader in the field of social responsibility of corporations. As a compassionate scientific friend deeply concerned over global economic issues he convinced me that this book should be written. Without Bill's involvement the manuscript would not have been conceived, started, organized, and written. Certainly without his continuous participation it would not have become a completed book.

Subject Index

Name Index

Reference Index
by Title